LANGUAGE
THE SOCIAL MIRROR

Elaine Chaika
Providence College

NEWBURY HOUSE PUBLISHERS, INC.
ROWLEY, MASSACHUSETTS 01969
ROWLEY • LONDON • TOKYO

1982

Library of Congress Cataloging in Publication Data

Chaika, Elaine, 1934–
    Language, the social mirror.

    Summary: Discusses the ways people use language
in society with chapters on kinesics, dialect, and
bilingualism.
        1. Language and languages.   2. Linguistics.
[1. Language and languages.   2. Linguistics]
I. Title.
P106.C49   400   81-9638
ISBN 0-88377-203-5   AACR2

NEWBURY HOUSE PUBLISHERS, INC.

Language Science
Language Teaching
Language Learning

ROWLEY, MASSACHUSETTS 01969
ROWLEY ● LONDON ● TOKYO

First printing: October 1982

Printed in the U.S.A.   5

ACKNOWLEDGMENTS

Special thanks go to Jackie Russom, whose careful reading and excellent suggestions improved the entire; to Robert DiPietro for playing the devil's advocate and for his most kind words of encouragement; to Suzette Elgin and Bruce Fraser who so generously cut into their busy schedules to give me detailed critiques of the first chapter; and to Sandy Giles, whose mighty labors in tracking down references saved me hours. If, despite their help, errors remain, they are my fault.

My family deserves extra special thanks. Bill, ever my kind philosopher, friend, spouse, and greatest fan: without his patience, encouragement and addiction to televised football this book could not have been written.

My younger sons, Daniel and Jeremy, who willingly cooked many a supper and a little less willingly cleaned up when Mom was writing away: without their cooperation this book would have taken years to complete. Daniel gets special thanks for shlepping into the city to deliver pages to the typist and carry out sundry errrands, saving me hours of travel time. Jeremy gets special thanks for helping with the collating of pages.

My mother willingly spent many a hot summer day proofreading and collating rather than basking on the beach in well-deserved retirement. My husband Bill, after his own hard day lawyering, also helped mightily with proofreading. I can only hope that this book justifies the help I have received from scholars and family.

CREDITS AND PERMISSIONS

PREFACE

This text grew out of my conviction that one should not have to be a linguist in order to learn about the ways people use language in society. It has always seemed to me that both linguistics and sociolinguistics are inherently fascinating. Unfortunately, much of the most exciting work in both fields has been written primarily for scholars with specialized training in these fields. The aim of this book is to present that work so that readers without training may understand it.

If only he or she allows, any teacher receives a great deal from students. Certainly my students have taught me a great deal. Their questions and their observations have sharpened my own observations and enriched my knowledge. As a tribute to them, as frequently as possible in this book, I have included data collected by students at Providence College as part of their regular term papers for my course *Sociology of Language*. By including their findings as well as those of professional scholars, I also hoped to show the reader that one needs only eyes to see, ears to hear, and a lively mind in order to increase one's understanding of one's fellow human beings. Given the complexity of human verbal behavior, readers will probably be able to supply more examples of every phenomenon discussed than space has allowed me to treat here.

I sincerely hope that this book raises the consciousness of its readers, making them more sensitive to and appreciative of all people.

A word about words and topics in this book

The real world is what this book is all about. Unfortunately, speech in the real world indulges in words and topics that many in our society find offensive. This includes references to sexual matters, bathroom functions, and racial and ethnic epithets. Because the study of such references helps sociolinguists to understand verbal social behavior, the inclusion in this book of words and topics that many consider taboo has been unavoidable. The very fact that people deliberately use taboo language affords us important insights into underlying social conditions, and the reader may be assured that at no time is taboo material presented here unless it demonstrates the ways that language mirrors society.

To my mother, Rose Mary Ostrach,
who showed me what a woman could be.

CONTENTS

a game of percentages — why variables: why not constants?
— evaluation — subjective reaction tests — the street gangs
— a counterexample — the sociolinguistic survey versus
conventional sociological studies — dialect in popular music
— negative attitudes in dialect copying — hidden attitudes in
a dialect survey — hypercorrection — middle class hypercorrection — lames — the development of an American
standard — implications for education — the origins of
dialect — why /r/? — Creoles — Basil Bernstein and
restricted codes

PHONETIC SYMBOLS
USED IN THIS BOOK

[   ] = phonetic symbol for actually pronounced sound
< > = conventional spelling
/ / = phoneme, sound hearer thinks has been made

Vowels:

[i] = <ee> in *beat, beet*
[ɪ] = <i> in *bit*
[ɨ] = <a>, <i>, <u>   in *band, dinner, jury* (casual speech)
[ɜ] = <o>, <i>, <e>, <u>   in *word, sir, girl, nerd, curd* in r-less dialects
[e] = <e>   in French *été*
[ɛ] = <e>   in *bet*
[ə] = <u>   in *but*
[æ] = <a>   in *bat*
[a] = <o>   in *not*
[u] = <oo>   in *boot*
[ʊ] = <u>   in *put*
[o] = <o>ʾ   in Spanish *loco*
[ɔ] = <ough>, <aw>   in *bought, saw*

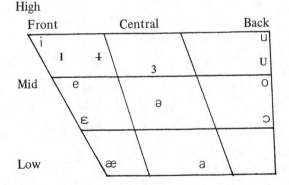

Position of the tongue for vowels

Since dialects of English differ principally in the pronunciation of vowels, it is impossible to give representative words that actually use each sound in each possible dialect. Hence, your own pronunciation of a word might use a different vowel from that given here. For instance [ɨ], is the vowel in *ham* for many Americans, but the vowel in *dinner* for others, and [ɔ] is the vowel in *talk* for some, but [a] is the vowel in *talk* for others.

Diphthongs (two vowels pronounced as one):

[aⁱ] = <i>   in *ride*
[əⁱ] = <i>   in *right*
[eⁱ] = <ai>, <a>   in *raid, made*

[aᵘ] = <ou>   in *lousy*
[əᵘ] = <ou>   in *louse*
[oᵘ] = <oa>, <o>   in *road, rode*

[oⁱ] = <oy>   in *Joyce*
[ɔⁱ] = <oy>   in *joys*

    Some speakers do not use different diphthongs for words in each set above. Depending on dialect, they may use one of each pair for both words.

Consonants:

[p] = <p>   in *soap*
[pʰ] = <p> in *put*
[b] = <b>   in *boot*
[t] = <t>   in *not*
[tʰ] = <t> in *toy*
[d] = <d>   in *dog*
[k] = <c>, <k>   in *Mac, look*
[kʰ] =   <c>, <k> in *cut, kill*
[g] = <g>   in *go*
[m] = <m>   in *me*
[n] = <n>   in *no*
[ŋ] = <ng>   in *sing*
[θ] = <th>   in *thing*
[ð] = <th>   in *they*
[s] = <c>, <s>   in *city, so*
[z] = <s>, <z>   in *lose, zoo*
[š] = <sh>, <ti>   in *wash, nation*
[ž] = <si>, <su>   in *persuasion, pleasure*
[č] = <ch>   in *church*
[ǰ] = <j>, <g>   in *joy, rage*
[r], [ɚ] = <r>   in *read, player*
[l] = <l>   in *lady*
[w] = <w>   in *win*
[y] = <y>   in *yet*

chapter 1

WHAT IS LANGUAGE?

In this chapter, the reader is introduced to the sociology of language and those aspects of behavior with which it is concerned. The reader is asked to stand back from language, and think about how it is constructed. Later chapters will show how speakers use the very structure of language to govern social interactions. The way that children learn their native languages also seems to be related to social uses of language.

1.1   *The subject of sociolinguistics*

Have you ever wanted desperately to voice an opinion but had the words "stick in your throat"? Have you ever had the opposite experience of feeling compelled to speak when you didn't want to? Do you sometimes find yourself forcing small talk with someone you either don't know or don't much care for? Have you noticed how some people can make you do things you don't want to do, even though they've never given an overt command? Do you ever find that you want to flee when someone heaps praise on you to your face and yet you don't get angry at all when someone else insults you, such as calling you "cheap"? Why are some insults taken seriously, while others are just considered teasing?

Has anyone ever accused you of having an accent? Do you notice that other people have accents? Why are there different accents at all, anyway? Why have some immigrant groups lost the languages that their forebears spoke, whereas others have retained those languages? Do you ever feel uncomfortable talking to people from cultures different from your own? Do they seem to stare too much, or, conversely, never to look you in the eye? Have you ever noticed how some people smile too much and others are stony-faced? These are the kinds of questions that interest people who study the sociology of language, the field also known as **sociolinguistics**.

1.2   *Language and society*

Language and society are so intertwined that it is impossible to understand one without the other. There is no human society that does not depend upon, is not shaped by, and does not itself shape language.

1

Every social institution is maintained by language. Law, religion, government, education, the family—all are carried on with language. Individually, we use language to "carry on" love and to "carry out" hate. We use language to reveal or conceal our personal identity, our character, and our background, often wholly unconscious that we are doing so. Almost all of our contact with family and friends, and much of our contact with strangers, involves speaking. And, much of that speaking is strongly governed by rules, rules that dictate not only what we should say, but also how we say it. We manipulate others with language, and they manipulate us, often without either party being at all aware of the manipulation.

Sociolinguistics is the study of the ways people use language in social interaction. The sociolinguist is concerned with the stuff of everyday life: how you talk to your friends, family, and teachers, as well as to storekeepers and strangers—everyone you meet in the course of a day—and why you talk as you do and they talk as they do. Sociolinguistics is concerned with apparently trivial matters, with the talk on streetcorners as well as in the classroom, the things that people do when they want to talk and the ways they signal that they are listening. Even matters like where you choose to sit in a cafeteria or at a meeting, or the amount of space you want between you and someone else when you are talking, concern the sociolinguist.

Such everyday matters are highly revealing, showing how a given society is stratified, that is, what groups make up that society. Examining the speech activities of different social groups casts light on the conditions, values, and beliefs that have helped shape the groups. Conversely, it also shows how social situations determine what kinds of speech will be used and how speech develops to meet social needs. Perhaps most important, sociology of language tells us what messages we are really giving when we speak, messages that are not necessarily put into actual words. It shows how and why we feel uncomfortable, even hostile, to some people, especially those who do not share the rules of speech behavior that we abide by, rules so thoroughly learned that we are not even aware of them.

Most people find that an academic course in the sociology of language is both interesting and exciting, a true consciousness-raising experience. Students become more aware of their own behaviors, how they are responding to other people, and how others behave and respond. What many find most exciting about the sociology of language is the heightening of their sensitivity not only to their own speech behavior, but to the speech of others, and even to song lyrics and TV shows and movies. Above all, students of sociolinguistics gain new respect for all peoples, more than any number of lectures on brotherhood or sisterhood could ever give them. This is because the sociology of language shows the true genius involved in all language activities, even those that do not depend on booklearning or that are carried out in speech considered incorrect or vulgar. Before delving into the fascinating topics of sociolinguistics proper, it is necessary to consider what language itself is.

1.3   *Language is multilayered*

Linguistics is the academic discipline that deals with the structure of human language. Here we will consider only those general properties of language essential to understanding social interaction. Throughout most of this book, dialects rather than language as a whole will concern us. **Dialects** are varieties of a language, usually mutually comprehensible. They are often called **accents**. Strictly speaking, however, accent refers only to differences in the way words are pronounced. The term dialect includes accent, but also differences in grammar and word choice between speakers.

Human language is multilayered. It is composed of a system of meaningless elements that combine by rules into meaningful structures. (These rules are learned automatically, almost instinctively, by children who are learning to speak. Because the rules do not have to be taught, they are considered by many linguists to be governed by an innate language learning faculty of the brain.) Sounds, meaningless in themselves, form meaningful words or parts of words. Technically, these parts of words are called **morphemes**. The word *renewed*, for instance, is composed of three morphemes, *re-, new,* and *-ed*. These are considered morphemes in English because we recognize *re-* as a prefix that is attached to many words to convey the meaning 'again'. *New* is a morpheme that is also a word in itself. That is, it can stand alone with no other morphemes attached. The ending *-ed* is an English morpheme for past tense, required by the grammar of English. The word *renewed* thus illustrates the different kinds of morphemes that appear in languages: those used to add meaning to a given word; words in themselves; and affixes that are required by the grammar of a language. **Affixes** are morphemes that appear at the beginning or end of words. Those, like English *re-*, that appear at the beginning are called **prefixes**. Those that appear at the end, like English *-ed*, are called **suffixes**.

In English and other European languages, typically, morphemes required by grammar are put at the end of words, but other languages have them at the beginning. Although it is rare in the world's languages, some even insert them into the middle of words.

Some languages, such as Russian, which require a great many grammatical affixes, have very few words that can stand alone. Such languages have **roots** to which affixes are added according to the way the word is being used in the sentence. For instance, in the Russian sentence, "Mal'chik videl Marshu," which means 'the boy sees Marsha,' the *-chik* morpheme indicates the one who does the seeing, the *-l* indicates that a third person singular subject did the seeing (as in English *sees*), and the *-u* indicates that Marsha is the one seen.

1.4   *Languages operate by rules*

Each language uses only some of the hundreds of possible sounds that human beings can utter. Then, each language has its own rules for combining these sounds into syllables. Even if two languages use the same sounds, they may not allow them to be combined in the same ways. For instance, both English and Swahili use the sounds [ŋ], [g], [w], and [e]. Swahili allows those three consonants to occur at the start of words, as in ŋgwe ('strings'), but English does not.

There are also rules for combining morphemes into words, so that, for instance, in English, the *re-* meaning 'again' in *renewed* must always come at the start of a word, and the *-ed* meaning 'past' must always come at the end.

Words themselves combine by rules of syntax into sentences. Sentences, in turn, combine into discourse. Although we usually think of sentences as having rules of grammar, we shall see that discourse also has rules. These determine the order in which sentences may be arranged, as well as what can be left out of a sentence and what must be included. Even the forms sentences take are often determined by the rules of discourse.

Human language seems to be the only communication system that combines meaningless elements into meaningful structures. For most speakers, but not all, the meaningless elements are sounds. Languages of the deaf, such as Ameslan (American Sign Language), substitute elements of gesture that are combined into larger units (Bellugi and Fischer 1972).

1.5   *Animal communication systems*

So far as we know, other animal communication systems are not multilayered and use only meaningful elements. That is, every sound, gesture or posture used in a nonhuman communication system means something, in and of itself. Furthermore, the order in which the sounds and movements of nonhuman communication appear does not affect their meaning. If a monkey emits a call for 'food' and one for 'follow me', it will mean 'follow me food' no matter which call comes first. In nonhuman communication systems, the sum of the message always equals its parts.

In contrast, in human language the message does not necessarily equal its parts. *A Venetian blind* is not the same as *a blind Venetian*. Meaning in language can be more than the sum of its parts, as in *Gwen ordered pizza; Fred, chop suey; and Alex, a hot dog*. We know that Fred ordered chop suey and that Alex ordered a hot dog, even though the verb *ordered* is not repeated.

Meaning may as easily be less than the sum of its parts, as in *Max is a good kid*. There is no referential meaning to *is*. Many languages, such as Russian and Chinese, leave the *is* out, saying the equivalent to 'Max a good kid.' Even to an English speaker, 'Max a good kid' has the same meaning as the sentence with an *is*. Indeed, there are some dialects of English that leave out the *is* in this kind of sentence, saying, for instance, "He bad!" Those that require the insertion of *is* do so because of their rules of syntax, not because of its meaning. That is, *is* and its counterparts *am* and *are* do not refer to an actual action or emotion, as do verbs like *run* and *hate*. One cannot define *is* as one can such other verbs. In sentences like *Max is a good kid*, *is* has the major function of filling the slot reserved for verbs in the English sentence. Therefore, the use of *is* belongs to the realm of syntax (Section 1.6).

Some elements of language, notably sounds, have no meaning in and of themselves. Because these can be divorced from meaning, human languages can multiply meanings far beyond those of other communication systems. The essentially meaningless elements of sound and syntax can be combined by rules into a multitude of words, sentences, and discourses. Humans are not confined to a repertoire of inborn messages, as are, for instance, birds, dogs or elephants. Instead, humans can take the elements of their language and use them to create sentences that they have never heard before, sentences that can be understood by others who know the same language (Chomsky 1965).

By contrast, every other creature we know of is limited to messages inextricably tied to meaning, so that meaning for them can never be changed. To a dog, a growl is a growl. True, it can be used for play, but then it is still a growl, as when a dog is pretending to kill by worrying an old rag. The growl, even in play, cannot mean 'I really love you', or 'I want to go with you'. The dog does have ways of "saying" those things, but he cannot make a growl carry those messages. A human, on the other hand, can say *I love you* sarcastically so that it conveys the meaning 'I hate you'. Then, too, the human can use the individual sounds in *I love you* in very different messages. For instance, the /l/ and /v/ in *love* can also be used in *villify*, a word that has quite a different meaning from *love*, as well as in a multitude of other words. Humans can even take sounds of their languages and combine them anew to make up new words, so long as they follow the rules for combination. In English, for instance, one could use the /l/ and /v/ to make up the word *cluvy* if there were a need for a new word to designate a thing, a quality, or an action for which there was no existing word. Alternatively one could take an existing word, say *silly*, and make it mean something new. In fact, English *silly* once meant 'holy'. Apparently, because people used it ironically often enough, it eventually took on its present meaning. Thus old elements, be they sounds, words, or sentences can be used in new ways.

Although there are built-in rules of word and sentence formation in human language, these "rules" are constructed so that an infinite number of new words and sentences can be created in any human language. So far as we know, no other animal, no matter how intelligent, has such versatile options in its communication systems. Therefore, other animals are not able to change their communications to fit new circumstances as humans can and do.

1.6   *Grammar*

The term **syntax** was used to refer to the rules for combining words into sentences. The more commonly used term for putting words together into sentences is **grammar**. Unfortunately, as commonly used, grammar is an evaluative term, so that people think of good or bad grammar. **Syntax** is a neutral term, therefore preferable in a study of social behavior. When discussing different social groups, it is often necessary to speak of differences in rules between their dialects. This is of great importance, both in understanding members of groups other than our own and in teaching. If a syntax rule is not part of a dialect, we say it is **ungrammatical** for that dialect. As of now, there is no word **unsyntactic**, although notice that not only can I make such a word, but you, the reader, understand what it means. Since the world of scholarship already contains enough jargon, the usual term **ungrammatical** will be used in this book, but with a meaning somewhat different from that the reader may be used to. Here it will always mean 'The speakers of a given dialect do not use a particular form or word-order.'

This never implies that using or not using a form or word-order is good or bad. For instance, *I am wanting to know that* is ungrammatical for many Americans, but it is often heard from the British. In dialects of English spoken by urban, educated Americans today, *He don't* is ungrammatical, but it is grammatical for most people who have little formal education. Ironically, *He don't* used to be grammatical for all English speakers, educated or not. This shows how arbitrary judgments are about what is proper in language.

For yet another example of the arbitrariness of grammar rules, consider *I am knowing the answer*. This sentence is not grammatical in English today, although the meaning it conveys is perfectly sensible: 'I know the answer right now (but I might forget it later).'

1.7   *Grammar is separate from meaning*

Often, ungrammatical constructions are readily understandable. Our judgment of whether or not a construction is grammatical is not determined on the basis of comprehensibility alone. The rules of grammar in human languages constitute a system in themselves and do not have a one-to-one correspondence with meaning. One result of this is that we can understand little children and foreign speakers who do not have down pat all the rules of grammar in our language. We can also understand speakers of other dialects who use rules of grammar somewhat different from our own. Poets often make poetry by deliberately changing some grammar rules for artistic purposes. The human ability for poetry rests, then, on our ability to deal with grammars not exactly like our everyday ones.

Another exceedingly important result of our being able to understand those whose grammar differs from our own is that members of different social groups within the same community can understand one another's speech despite dialect differences between them. Therefore dialect can be an important marker of social divisions within a community.

1.8   *Language difference is not language decay*

Above all is the curious fact that using new or different grammar rules does not cause language to decay. Meaning can still be preserved. Only in the speech of victims of severe mental pathologies, such as those occurring from brain damage, is meaning usually lost. In such instances, few or no words may be recognizable or syntax may be so faulty that it is impossible to figure out the relationship of words to each other.

The "grammatical mistakes" that most people call "bad grammar" really are social markers. They do not necessarily reflect poor intelligence or faulty knowledge on the part of the speakers. As much as one might deplore *ain't got none* or *him and me went*, they are regular productions in some dialects of English. It is essential to understand that all human beings, even those with no formal education, speak according to rules. All human language is produced by rules of word formation, sentence formation, and discourse formation. The educated middle class has no monopoly on rule-governed language. For instance, a young 'ghetto' Black male commented to a field worker, "Dey caught de old man 'cause he go roun' tellin' dese stories." The worker asked, "Can't you say 'He went round'?" "No," said the young man, " 'He go' mean he do it all de time. 'He went round mean' he do it jus' once." As uneducated as this young man might sound to college ears, still he spoke according to the grammar rules of his dialect. Most of all, it should be noted that he was capable of very intelligent analysis of the rules of his dialect. Brightness, quickness, and intellectual reasoning are not tied to any dialect, not even the most socially desirable. Indeed, that is what most of this book is about. The differences between dialects are differences between a very few rules. It is not the case that some speakers have rules and others do not. All speak according to rules, but the rules may be different from one dialect to the next.

1.9   *Languages are created equal*

The fact that two dialects or two languages have different rules does not make one inherently better than another. One may be socially preferred, but that is another matter. Today, for instance, using certain kinds of double negatives is considered bad or incorrect in English. Certainly, no one has any trouble understanding that *I didn't do nothin'* means 'I didn't do anything'. No one ever takes it to mean 'I did something' just because, in mathematics, two negatives make a positive. In fact, double negatives still are used by the prissiest of English speakers in sentences like, *I was not unhappy*. Carrie Fisher, the actress who played the heroine of *Star Wars* told a reporter, "I don't do nothing well," meaning that she did not like having nothing to do. Many languages habitually use double negatives. Italian, for instance, allows *Non ho fatto niente* and French, *Je n'ai rien fait*, both of which mean literally 'I haven't done (*or* didn't do) nothing'.

At one time in English, double negatives of the type now frowned upon were considered all right. Shakespeare himself used them frequently, especially for emphasis, as in "No sonne were he never so olde of years might not marry" (Abbott 1870, p. 295). Today the same emphatic use of double and even triple negatives is heard in supposedly nonstandard English, as in "Ain't no cat can't get in no [pigeon] coop" (Labov 1972a). The rule forbidding double negatives is arbitrary. Languages work perfectly well with or without double negation. In English today, however, certain double negatives are socially wrong in certain circumstances. That is, although there is nothing inherently wrong with double negatives, there can be something socially wrong with some of them at this time in history. Throughout this book the difference between the inherent worth of particular kinds of speech and their social implications should always be kept in mind.

Languages are arbitrary in the sounds they use and in their word choice as well. Just because the English say *tree*, the French say *arbre*, and the Germans say *Baum*, one cannot draw any conclusions about their respective national characters. The words themselves and the sounds making them up are arbitrary choices, explicable only in terms of the history of each language. One word does as well as another to designate trees as long as listeners understand what is meant.

Linguists have not been able to find any primitive languages, even among the so-called primitive peoples. All languages spoken in the world as far back as we have any record are equally complex and can potentially do pretty much the same things. For example, every language has some way of indicating whether someone did the action or received it, as in a sentence like *The boy bit the dog*. English does it by word order. Russian does it by endings on each noun. Swahili does it by prefixes on each noun. Each way is as logical and intelligent as the other. The difference between languages or dialects is not what they can do, but how they do it (Gleason 1961, p. 232).

1.10   *Language is not static*

In their vocabulary and discourse rules, languages have developed quite differently, in accordance with the values of their societies. However, no language is fixed at any point. Language is not static. Any language can change in any way its speakers want it to, or need it to, and as soon as they wish. Every language has built into its very structure the mechanisms of change. All normal speakers have the ability to:

- Make up new words;
- Use old words in new ways;
- Compose sentences they have never heard before;
- Combine sentences into wholly new discourses.

Speakers, in short, can make their old language say new things. The corollary is that speakers of a language can understand:

- New words used in a context, often without the speaker's having to define them;
- Old words used in new ways;
- New sentences;
- New discourses.

Noam Chomsky (1959, 1965, 1972) calls the twin abilities of saying and understanding new things *the creative aspect of language*. He believes there is no way to understand the human mind without understanding its ability to handle creativity in language use. This book will show that there is no way to understand human society without considering this creativity. At the very least it means that neither individuals nor their societies are wholly bound by the past. People can encode and convey new ideas because grammar rules enable speakers to combine words, phrases, and sentences in new ways. Then listeners use strategies for decoding, such as matching utterances to the context to figure out what the speakers could possibly have meant (Clark and Lucy 1975; Chaika 1976).

1.11   *Language and thought*

The very fact that language can be made to take on new meanings shows that language and thought are not necessarily one and the same. So far as we know today, there is no one-to-one correspondence between language and thought. Any thought can be expressed in many ways. That is, language is paraphrasable. Furthermore, language also allows ambiguity, so that a word or a sentence can have more than one meaning. *Story* can mean either 'narrative' or 'level of a building'. *Visiting relatives can be boring* can mean 'Relatives who visit can be boring', or 'It can be boring to visit relatives'. Words and sentences can change meaning according to their contexts.

Not only are utterances potentially ambiguous, but the same words or sentences may be perceived to have very different intentions or forces in different contexts. For instance, *It's cold in here* on the surface means 'The temperature in this place is lacking in warmth'. However, given the right context, such as a hot summer's day in an air-conditioned room, it could mean, 'Boy that air conditioner works well'. Under somewhat different social conditions, it could also mean 'I can see I'm not wanted here'.

The same sentence could also have the force of a command. If the person speaking has a right to command the person addressed, either because of social status or just because the person addressed is closer to the switch, then *It's cold in here* could be interpreted as 'Turn the air conditioner off'. If the air conditioner had been reported to be malfunctioning, then the meaning could be construed as 'This thing is working just fine'. So important is context to meaning and force of language that to quote someone out of context can constitute an actual lie. The enraged protests of politicians and other often quoted and misquoted newsworthy folk show us how easy it is to twist someone's meaning just by omitting sufficient context.

Later chapters will demonstrate that the context that determines meaning includes among other things:

- The social status of speakers;
- The speech event and the social conventions governing it;
- The social-cultural and physical environment;
- Previous discourse between the speakers or known to them;
- The intent of the speaker.

Meaning, in other words, has a social base. Words do not just mean. They mean in social interaction in a particular society.

1.12   *Language learning is active*

One very important consequence of the fact that language is always changing is that it cannot be learned solely by mimicking. If people learned language only by mimicking what they heard, they would not be able to use words in new sentences and sentences in new contexts. The fact that utterances may mean very different things in different contexts means that people use active decoding strategies in order to understand. Recent studies of how children learn to use language strongly suggest that no one teaches them how to understand. Even little toddlers extract meaning from what they hear by matching it to the context. Toddlers seem to expect that adults will use such a strategy (Baron 1977). The toddler who says "Mommy sock" will use it to mean 'This is Mommy's sock', 'Mommy, put on my sock', or even, 'I'm putting Mommy's sock on my doll' (Bloom 1970). One wonders how one could explain to fifteen-month-olds that they can utter the same words in the same order to give different meanings in different contexts. Again and again while examining the speech of young children, one finds that they are doing such things with words and sentences, things that no one could have taught them.

A simple, apparently trivial example demonstrates this assertion: Most of us have heard toddlers say "comed" for *came*, "goed" for *went*, and "breaked" for *broke*. Interestingly, babies first use *went* and *came* and other correct forms of irregular verbs as their parents do (Ervin 1964). However, as soon as they perceive that there is a regular past tense ending-*ed*, as in *played*, they apply it to all verbs to indicate 'past time'. Furthermore, babies prove very resistant to correction. They continue in this error for years, despite the fact that the verbs involved are among the most common in the language, and they constantly hear the correct forms from their parents, on television, and in the streets. In fact, one can still hear errors in the participle, such as "tooken" for *taken*, and "blewn" for *blown*, in children of educated parents, even children who read a great deal, when they are as old as ten and eleven.

Paradoxically, this shows how intelligent children are, not how stupid. For a baby to figure out a form like *goed* when all he or she has probably ever heard is *went* means that the baby is actively figuring out how language is working. The baby has somehow categorized words into at least nouns and verbs, without of course calling them that (see, for example, Menyuk 1971; Berko 1958). At least, the baby acts as if he or she has categorized words into different parts of speech, some of which take tense endings and some of which do not. Not surprisingly, at the same age babies are using plural endings on nouns and, again, generalizing them to all nouns, making mistakes like *foots* and *mouses*.

What makes this all the more amazing is that many languages of the world, such as the dialects of Chinese, do not use tense markers on verbs, or any endings on words. Rather, they use words meaning 'before', 'in the future', 'next month' and the like if it is necessary to note the time. Similarly, if the amount of something talked about is relevant, then a quantifying word is used with the noun, without added plural endings. This means that babies are not born expecting grammatical markers of any particular kind, as they have to be able to learn whatever language they will be exposed to in infancy.

1.13   *The baby's task*

Babies must be born knowing how to go about learning language, or else they would not be able to figure out the grammatical rules as they apparently do. English-speaking babies notice that there are tense and plural markers. Russian babies have an even more complicated task in learning word endings, for Russian has far more endings than does English. For instance, Russian has six different endings on nouns to indicate how they are being used in particular sentences, whether as the subject or the object or in some other function. Furthermore there are three different genders of nouns in Russian—masculine, feminine, and neuter—and each uses a different set of endings. Still, before the age of two, Russian babies have begun to use these endings. Typically they are already using at least one to indicate direct objects. Like English-speaking babies the Russian babies start out by generalizing one ending for a function. Just as the English speaker starts out putting -*ed* on a verb like *go,* the Russian baby puts the feminine direct object ending -*u* on all nouns, even masculine or neuter ones. Similar phenomena have been reported for babies who have to learn Turkish, Finnish, or Serbo-Croatian—all languages that use many endings (Slobin 1979).

Babies who are exposed to languages that do not make use of endings, such as the Chinese dialects, have to make different kinds of analyses. For instance, Chinese makes use of an intricate set of noun classifiers, each of which is used with a different set of nouns, such as is marginally seen in English in expressions like *a gaggle of geese* or *a pride of lions.* Although the specifics of the task vary from language to language, apparently the task itself is the same for all babies everywhere. They must figure out for themselves how the language around them works. Babies exposed to more than one language have to do this for each, often concurrently. We do not know how conscious babies are of what they are doing, only that their utterances show the result of analyzing language. To me, this seems to be a wondrous process.

1.14   *Why babies are poor mimics*

Why don't babies just mimic their parents' language? That would seem more efficient than the active analyses just discussed. As mentioned earlier, in order to use language creatively, which is the essence of language use, children cannot just mimic. If that were all they did to learn language, then children would be able to say only what they had already heard. Instead, they have to learn the unspoken rules that will enable them to express new thoughts or describe new situations so that others can understand them. From the start, human beings are not wholly bound by the utterances of others. This, of course, argues for the freedom of the individual, as Noam Chomsky has so often pointed out (Chomsky 1959, 1965, 1972).

There may also be a social reason for active analysis in the language learning process. When they are grown up, children do not necessarily talk like their parents. They talk according to the social conditions facing them, not those facing their parents. Parental speech provides a springboard for children, not a template. From the start, human beings learn language for themselves, so that they can adapt it to whatever situations they find themselves in.

Another reason babies do not just imitate may be that sheer imitation is not a very efficient way to learn. For instance, the irregular verbs in English today are chaotic. They do not form regular classes. There is no rule to tell which should be irregular, or, if irregular, in what way. There really is no way to learn them except to memorize them. For example, there is an alternation of *i, a,* and *u* in a few irregular verbs, as they are changed from present to past and participial forms, such as *sing, ring, sink,* and *drink.* In these, the vowel becomes *a* in the past tense, and *u* in the participle, as in *sing, sang, sung.* However, there are verbs that rhyme with these, such as *bring, sting, cling,* and *think* that do not follow the same pattern. *Bring* and *think* both have only one form for both past and participle, in standard English, *brought* and *thought,* respectively. *Cling* and *sting* also have only one alternant, *clung* and *stung.* Even if there is some discernible pattern in a few of the irregular verbs, there is no single applicable rule that excludes some verbs and includes others. One can only memorize what changes and how. Some of the most common irregular verbs, such as *eat* and *go* have no analogs at all. That is, no other verbs change in the past tense as they do.

In terms of communicative efficiency, saying *eated* and *goed* works as well as *ate* and *went*. By applying the *-ed* on all verbs and ignoring the exceptions, babies lose nothing in communicability, and free themselves for other learning. Language learning is only one of the tasks facing babies, and, in those beginning stages, they also have a great deal of vocabulary and other grammar to learn. When more grammar and basic vocabulary are learned, they can go back and sort out irregular forms.

The actual adult form of many of these verbs var   ) social groups. Often the use of one rather than another marks   member of a particular group. Saying *knew* instead of *knowea,*   nstead of *brang* (and vice versa) gives an essentially social messag.   ⌐ut a person's identity. Such changes in form do not affect the actual meaning of the verb. Therefore, the fine points, so to speak, of verb forms can be deferred until an age when social identity is more important than it is to a toddler.

1.15 Practice drills

Another learning strategy that very young children employ is practice drills, repeating a word over and over, slightly altering the context each time. For example:

1. stoly
   stoly here
   want a stoly
   Dave, stoly
   story, story
   story's de hat
   story's de big hat
   story's a hat

2. turn of de water
   I turn de water
   I turn [th]is water
   I turn off de water
   Here Mommy now
   de bottle

(Weir 1962)

Readers who have studied a foreign language may note the similarity of these drills to oral practice drills.

No one teaches children to create these drills. They do it on their own. They even select the items they choose to practice, here the difference between /l/ and /r/, and /d/ and /ð/ (th). Ruth Weir claimed that this is evidence that children somehow are born knowing how to go about learning language. Certainly, they do a great many things that no one teaches them. It's doubtful, for instance, that parents utter drills like 1 and 2.

Even when a baby can be made to imitate, it does not necessarily affect his or her productions. The literature on first language learning abounds with examples. For instance,

> 3. *Child:*   Want other one spoon, Daddy.
>   . . .
>
>   *Father:*   Can you say "the other spoon"?
>   *Child:*   Other . . . one . . . spoon
>   *Father:*   Say . . . "other"
>   *Child:*   Other
>   *Father:*   Spoon
>   *Child:*   Spoon
>   *Father:*   Other . . .
>   *Child:*   Other . . . spoon. Now give me other one spoon?
>   *(Fromkin and Rodman 1978, p. 251)*

This toddler is not being stubborn or naughty. He shows every sign of trying to cooperate. Although the task clearly makes no sense to him, he dutifully repeats his father's words. The repetition does not make the baby see his error, however. He has made up a rule, one that works for him, and for the time being at least he sticks to it. This is the same sort of behavior as continuing to say *goed* in the face of everyone else's *went*. It has its analog in the child who has been drilled for years in standard English but never learns it.

It is not only words and sentence patterns that children do not imitate well. They may even fail at simple repetition of a sound, even one that they can use under some circumstances. In the following example the child did regularly pronounce /p/ in *party* and *piggy*. However, he had misanalyzed the word *pool* as being *cool*.

> 4. *Mommy:*   Say pool.
>   *Ric:*   Cool.
>   *Mommy:*   No, say pool.
>   *Ric:*   Cool.
>   *Mommy:*   No, listen, puh-ool.
>   *Ric:*   [watching intently, and with great effort]: Cuh-ool
>   *Mommy:*   No! puh- puh- ool.
>   *Ric:*   Oh [relieved], puh-cool.

1.16 *Child language learning and foreign accents: a parallel*

Perhaps such problems have a parallel in those foreign born speakers who, after living in the United States for thirty years, still make grammatical errors in English, such as:

> 5a. I am going to wash mine hairs.
>   b. I am not knowing the answer.
>   c. I am going already to the beach.

Difficulties in mimicking sounds as in example 4 also occur frequently when people try to pronounce words in another language. In southeastern New England, for instance, many Italian-Americans, and even some non-Italians who want to sound "in-the-know," substitute a /g/ for Italian /k/ in the names of food like *ricotta,* a kind of cream cheese, and *manicotti,* a pasta filled with ricotta. In English, the /k/ would be pronounced with a puff of air, but not in Italian. For this reason speakers of English hear the Italian /k/ as a /g/. Also, American English does not use a true /o/. The nearest vowel sound to that in southern New England is [ɔ] 'aw'. Consequently it is not unusual to hear someone speak of 'reegawt' [rigɔt] in their 'maneegawt' [manigɔt], wholly unaware that their attempts at a correct Italian pronunciation are as Americanized as the usual English pronunciations 'ruhkʰahduh' [rəkʰaɒə] and 'manuhkʰahdy' [mɬnikʰaɒ i].

Similarly, my Portuguese sister-in-law corrects my pronunciation of [ž] 'zh' in 'malasadezh', a pastry. She keeps telling me not to say "zh" but, instead, to pronounce it with what sounds to me like the same 'zh' I have just used. Those readers who have studied foreign languages may recall similar episodes when the teacher told you to make a certain sound and you did. But then the teacher said, "No, say it this way," and perhaps feeling a little put out, you thought to yourself, "That's just what I said."

The same phenomenon occurs within a language, as when you are trying to imitate someone else's accent, or someone else tries yours. Such imitation sounds to the native speaker as an exaggeration of his or her pronunciation, which it is. The point is that we do not just hear speech sounds as they are spoken. People hear in terms of the patterns they already know or, in the case of young children, in terms of what they have already figured out on their own.

This does not mean that people are prisoners of their sound systems. They can often learn to discriminate sounds that once sounded alike to them. Although there is still much to learn about speech perception, we already know that such discrimination is strongly influenced by social attitudes and feelings (Labov 1966; Shuy , Wolfram, and Riley 1967). For example, toddlers who speak of their "fums" have not yet distinguished between /f/ and /θ/. Whether or not they ever will is a social matter in the English-speaking world. Those children who belong to the groups that still pronounce both sounds will eventually learn to do so, although it will be a distinction that comes relatively late, developmentally. Other children will grow up hearing the /θ/ in *thumb* as /t/, but the one on *mouth* as /f/; they will go through life saying "tum" and "mouf." Still others will hear both /θ/s as /t/, speaking of their "tums" and their "mouts." These are not individual deficiencies. How these sounds are heard, hence produced in adulthood, can be correlated with social groups (Labov 1966).

Nor are such pronunciations a matter of ignorance. Just about everyone who uses /t/ or /f/ instead of /θ/ has regularly heard the /θ/ on television, in the movies, at school, and even in the streets. As with the baby who says "goed" or "nother one spoon," simple exposure to a form does not in itself change the speaker's behavior. Just as babies often seem to be obeying inner drives when they learn language, so do older speakers when using it. Chapters 8 and 10 will elaborate on these introductory remarks.

EXERCISES

1. Find at least one example in speech or in print (newspapers, magazines) of an old word used in ways that seem new to you. You may include coinages like *Billygate,* which referred to President Carter's brother Billy and was modeled on *Watergate* to indicate corruption that reaches to the highest level of government. (Watergate is a Washington building that was the scene of a scandal involving the Nixon administration.) How were you able to understand these words without the aid of a formal explanation?

2. Pretend that you are instructing a class in spoken English. Try to explain what rules a native speaker of English uses in forming the following sentences:

    a. Has Oscar paid the money to Max for Murgatroyd's ransom?
    b. Into the room ran the frog, followed by my determined cat.

3. Pick out the morphemes in the following English words:

    a. acknowledgement, b. merciful, c. business, d. horrendous

4. If you know an intelligent dog, horse, cat, or chimp tell it that you think it is a disgusting, awful creature, but vary your tone. Try "Let's eat" or "Let's go." Can the animal understand human words, or just tone?

chapter 2

FIELD METHODS

The techniques used to investigate behavior are called *field methods*. Field methods in the sociology of language differ from those in linguistics proper. Theoretical linguists are primarily concerned with investigating the structure of a language, whereas sociolinguists are concerned with interactions between members of a society. However, in both sociolinguistics and linguistics proper, field methods include laboratory experiments as well as observations recorded in the field, in the natural surroundings of the people whose speech is being studied. Even the student who has no intention of being a researcher can benefit from considering what constitutes reliable field methods. Since each year a tremendous amount of tax money is spent for the teaching of language skills and bilingual education in public schools, every taxpayer should understand why the money is allocated as it is. This can be done only by knowing how to evaluate the soundness of the field methods used to arrive at conclusions about language policies.

2.1   *Pitfalls*

The biggest problem with field methods is devising a test or experiment that tells you what you want to know. Often, despite the most careful planning, once a study is completed, the results can be interpreted quite differently from what was originally intended. Experimental subjects may not have reacted as expected; they may have reacted to the wrong cue, or been influenced by a speech feature other than the one being studied.

Having subjects evaluate tape recordings of other speakers is a common methodology used for many purposes. If it is important to know how Americans feel about the pronunciation "uh" [ə] instead of /r/ in words like *other* and *teacher,* a tape of someone who uses the "uh" a great deal would be played and then a tape of a strong /r/ pronouncer. Subjects would be asked to rank each speaker on personal qualities such as intelligence, confidence, sincerity, educational level, and any other traits pertinent to the particular investigation. The investigator could not use just any two speakers, as special care would have to be taken to ensure that the only difference between the two speakers was the use of "uh" instead of /r/. If one speaker pronounced the *th* in *other* as /d/ and a second pronounced it as /ð/, the difference between those sounds, not the /r/s, might determine the evaluations. Or, if one used an "aw" [ɔ] in *talk* and the other used an "ah" [a] those might be the crucial sounds in the evaluations.

Even if the investigator controls carefully for pronunciation, there is still another problem. If one of the taped speakers has a raspy voice and the other a smooth one, or if one is nasal and the other is not, or if there is any other difference in voice quality, then the reaction might be to that difference, not to any particular feature of speech. Even differences in loudness or tempo, one speaking more rapidly than the other, may cause differences in reaction. In other words, there are so many possible qualities of speech to which subjects can react that it might prove difficult to prove exactly what influences ratings. This does not mean that voice evaluations are not good. They are exceedingly valuable sources of information if they are set up correctly (Chapter 8). This is true of most methodology. The importance of good field methods cannot be over-stressed, for what is found depends on how it was sought. The results that get analyzed depend wholly on the field methods used to collect them.

In the social sciences, there is always a temptation to rely on haphazard personal observations. Some scholars do this a great deal, citing their intuitions about various matters. Others criticize insights offered from intuition. Actually everyone uses hunches. It is a hunch that makes one want to investigate some aspect of behavior. Scholars like Shuy (1967), Trudgill (1972) and Labov (1966) who use elaborate field methods still intuitively divine what to test for in each community they investigate. Analysis of data, no matter how those data are garnered, depends to a great extent on a scholar's intuition and insight. Especially when examining broad aspects of human behavior, it is rare that data inexorably lead just to one conclusion. Interpretation is not only important, but, without it, much data are just a random collection of facts. For example, in a brilliant study of Black street gangs in Harlem, a research team headed by Labov (Labov, Robins, Lewis, and Cohen 1968) found that the boys within a gang all spoke somewhat differently. While that was true, it certainly was not interesting in itself. Fortunately the team had first charted the friendship network of their subjects on graphs called "sociograms." When the speech features of the boys were correlated with the sociograms, the variation in speech among the gang appeared to mirror social position within the group. It must have been a hunch that led them to use sociograms in the first place, a hunch based on earlier correlations of speech with social facts. Some of the most interesting and valuable works about human behavior have had their impetus from intuition. The works of scholars like Erving Goffman and Harvey Sacks come immediately to mind. There is nothing wrong with hunches or intuition, so long as a careful attempt is made to verify them.

Because of the richness of language data, triviality in testing is always a problem. It is easy to devise careful experiments that elicit speech because speech can be elicited in so many ways, but still end up with trivial or fragmented data with little, if any, relation to normal functioning. For instance, one can ask subjects to memorize lists of words and recite them backwards. Undoubtedly, people will differ in their ability to perform the task, but the relation of this task to actual speech and memory is obscure. Word association tests, for another example, may tell us a lot about people's associations to given words, but they do not tell us how people select words in a sentence. Normal discourse is not produced by uttering words that are associated with each other. It is produced by selecting words that fit the intended meaning.

Unfortunately it is not always immediately apparent that a given procedure is going to yield trivial results. The best that can be done is to ask questions like the following:

- What aspect of behavior am I testing for?
- Does this task tap the skills needed for that behavior?
- What could my subjects be responding to besides what I want them to?
- What factors could be influencing my results besides those I intended?

If an experiment does not work out as hoped or an investigation yields nothing of interest, that, too, is part of the process of discovery. It happens to everyone or just about everyone at one time or another.

2.2   *Matched guise testing*

Wallace Lambert (e.g., in Lambert, Giles, and Picard 1975) avoided the pitfalls of reactions to taped voices by using the matched guise technique. He found people who could command two languages or two dialects equally well, and had them read passages in each guise. Subjects, not realizing that they were evaluating the same person, rated each. The reaction, then, could be safely taken to be to the given language or dialect, not to other aspects of voice quality. Matched guise testing has proven fruitful in a variety of experimental procedures. For instance, in Great Britain, Bourhis (Giles and Powesland 1975, p. 104) had an announcement made over the loudspeaker in a theater asking patrons to fill out a survey questionnaire. On alternate nights, the same person used a nonstandard dialect and *received pronunciation* (RP), which is the British standard dialect of English learned in school. On the nights that RP was used, more people filled out the forms, and they wrote longer answers. It had already been established that people will write at greater length at the request of someone whose accent they admire (Giles, Baker, and Fielding 1975).

It is not always possible to find a bilingual or bidialectal speaker equally proficient in both varieties under consideration. Actors and actresses can be used, but with extreme caution. Although they fancy that they are giving accurate renditions of dialects or accents, usually they are using stylized stage dialects that do not conform to the genuine. This was recently illustrated for me by a highly experienced professional actor, a member of an internationally known repertory theater, a director of his own company, who also does a good deal of announcing and commercials. He was mocking the eastern New England pronunciation of word final *er* as "uh." When it was pointed out that the upper crust British dialect he professed to admire pronounces that *er* the same way, he protested that they did not. "How do you think they pronounce it?" he was asked. He gave the *ir* [3] sound, as heard in southeastern New England in words like *girl* and *heard*. When his interrogater, to whom that sound is native responded with "Nevir!" ([nɛvɜ]), he backtracked and said, "Well, the British say 'nevuh' and Rhode Islanders say 'nevuh.' Don't you hear the difference?" The difference was that he had changed his voice quality, but the final vowels he used were identical. When asked to give an extended imitation of British *received pronunciation,* he gave a perfect stage version, which differed in several respects from that of, say, Sir Alistair Cooke. It should be noted that this actor is primarily a character actor, often called upon to do "dialect" roles.

This incident illustrates the danger of using actors in studies designed to find reactions to dialects. It also shows how difficult it is to isolate precisely the factor to which a subject has reacted. The actor thought he was reacting to the "uh" pronunciation for *er,* but he was actually reacting to other features of voice quality. This example also shows how arbitrary our judgments are of what is or is not proper. British RP is desirable to this actor; a Rhode Island accent, to him, is not. Despite the fact that the same pronunciation occurs in both and in the same words, he heard them differently and evaluated them differently.

2.3   *Scrambled speakers*

Labov (1966, p. 408) pioneered another way of mitigating the effects of extraneous factors in evaluations of dialects. He taped several speakers reading various passages, each focusing on a different feature of pronunciation (see Chapter 8). Then, when testing subjects' reactions to those features, he selected one taped sentence from each of the passages as read by five different speakers. He played the selected sentences from each passage, mixing up the order of the speakers. When he played back the composite passage to test subjects' reactions to particular features, it was virtually impossible for the subjects to know how they had rated each speaker on previous sentences in such a procedure. Labov's five speakers each pronounced a given feature a different way. A variant of this technique would be to play the voices of at least two who pronounce something the same way. If it is voice quality that is determining a judgment, subjects will react differently to each speaker. If it is the feature itself, then both speakers will receive the same evaluation.

2.4   *An adequate sample*

In order to come to valid conclusions, there must be an adequately representative sampling of the population under consideration. For socio-linguistics, adequacy depends upon distribution as well as numbers. As a rule it is not sufficient simply to have a large enough percentage of a total population. It is also necessary to have representatives of each social group in a given community. Usually, the investigator first groups the population by age, sex, ethnic origin, race, and social class. Investigation may show that some of the groups are not significant, but speakers, today called *consultants,* still have to be chosen from every possible group at the outset of the sampling. Otherwise, significance or lack of it cannot be proven.

One would select representatives, for instance, of both sexes, different age groups, social classes, ethnic groups, even occupations or gang and club memberships if those factors seem potentially important. Strict random sampling, taking every so many persons in a community, every fourth or every twentieth for instance, is rarely of use in a sociolinguistic study since speech behavior correlates with social stratification and attitudes (Chapters 7–10).

This is not to say that random sampling is never of use. It could be, perhaps, in a study of sheer regionalisms not dependent on social class or attitude, if such can be found. Certain kinds of reaction and evaluation testing can also be done by random sampling. These test the reactions of members of a community to various speech forms.

2.5   *The size of a sample and problems in transcribing*

Generally speaking, the larger the sample tested, the more valid the results. However, the analysis of sociolinguistic data is exceptionally time consuming. Tape recordings have to be transcribed in a phonetic alphabet, like the International Phonetic Alphabet (IPA). Such an alphabet differs from normal writing (orthography) in that it utilizes only one symbol for each separate sound, and each sound is represented by only one symbol.

The advent of good tape recorders has certainly made the dialectician's lot simpler than the older method of transcription as the consultant spoke, but tape recorders are not panaceas. For one thing, many recordings prove to be fuzzy when played back. Environmental noises, hissing, and buzzing may intrude. One finds that the consultant's voice fades in and out, or comes out as an indistinct mumble, often in crucial places. Also, even experienced phoneticians may have problems determining exactly which sounds were uttered. Certain sounds come through as almost identical on a tape. For instance, it is sometimes difficult to distinguish between /f/, /s/, and /θ/.

Even with the clearest of recordings on the best of equipment, transcription can be difficult if an investigator has to determine very fine differences in pronunciation. Since fine differences are sometimes socially significant, it is essential that transcription be accurate. There are literally hundreds of potentially important pieces of information in every interview, from fine variations in pronunciation to grammatical choices to the very organization of a narrative. All must be noted, categorized, and correlated with other factors. Giving an interview often takes hours, and it can take days to extract all of the data from each interview. Consequently, sample size must be limited.

The more complex a community, the larger the sample should be because there will be more groups to consider. The purpose of the investigation helps determine sample size as well. If one wishes only to contrast two attitudes in a community, a much smaller sample is needed than if one wishes to delineate general social stratification. Ten to twenty consultants for each social group in the community is generally considered a sufficient number, especially if long and varied interviews are given.

Finding consultants to observe or interview is a problem in itself. Using any given source might skew the distribution of members of the sample so that it is not representative of the population at large. School enrollment lists skew toward the younger population, those with children in school. Voting lists do not give those who are unregistered, often the poorest or lower classes. Telephone books do not give names of people with unlisted numbers; if, as Anshen (1978) thinks, these are the rich, then they will be underrepresented in the sample. Sometimes a skewed population is what is wanted. If the speech of Portuguese bilingual speakers is to be studied, then the investigator deliberately goes to a Portuguese social club or church in search of consultants. Unless such definite groups are the target, consultants usually have to be elicited from more than one source to get a representative population. One good place to start is the sociology department of a nearby college or university to see if a general sociological survey of the area has recently been made. This not only points to the probably significant groupings in the community but is a source of consultants as well.

One skewed population often used, especially in testing reactions to voices, is college students, often students at the same college or university where the researcher is working. Although they are useful as soundingboards, they do not represent the attitudes of older or, usually, of non-middle-class citizens. They are a good population for uncovering changing attitudes of the young to various speech forms, however.

In reporting the results of any investigation, it is essential to state explicitly what population was tested, how it was selected, what methodology and techniques were used, and how the data were extracted and analyzed. This information is all potentially pertinent to the results obtained and their analysis.

2.6   *Form versus content*

A major problem in determining reaction to voice quality or even to dialect features is that the meaning, or semantic content, of what is being said might affect judgment. One obvious way to control for this is to have several speakers read the identical passage. Unfortunately, this bores listeners so much that they may start to tune out the readers. Another is to have each read paraphrases of one passage or successive paragraphs from one article or speech. That way, at least style and topic are limited. Another technique is to mask words by passing recorded speech through an acoustic filter that obliterates the higher frequencies of sound necessary for word recognition but leaves voice qualities like nasality, deepness, tremulousness, or breathiness (Abercrombie

1967; Kramer 1963; Laver 1968). Scherer (1973) has used a Moog synthesizer to approximate certain aspects of voice quality. If such sophisticated equipment is not available, the effect of content on reaction to voice quality or other features of dialect can be lessened by having actors and actresses portray emotions while reciting numbers.

2.7   Interviews

The multifaceted techniques of interviewing are best considered while discussing an actual study (Chapters 7 and 8). Basically, interviews must be conducted so that consultants are put at ease. This means that the investigator must conform to the consultants' culture. If members of the culture are most comfortable talking in competition with peers, then that is how the interview has to be conducted. If they are uncomfortable talking to someone who is wearing a shirt or tie, then no shirt and tie for the interviewer. If they are happiest at the kitchen table, then the kitchen table it is.

I find it best not to use hand-held microphones at all. Many speakers clutch them, face them directly, and earnestly talk into them. Casual, everyday speech is very difficult to elicit and record under such circumstances. The results are equally poor if the interviewer keeps shoving the microphone in the consultant's face, TV newsman style. Even those who are at ease with microphones can cause problems with a hand mike. They forget themselves, start their usual gestures while talking, waving the mike back and forth to the detriment of the recording. A microphone that attaches around the neck is best. Alternatively, a good tape recorder with a built-in microphone can be placed judiciously near the consultant. For some kinds of studies very expensive, supersensitive equipment is essential for picking up fine differences in pronunciation.

2.8   Observation

Observation, both participant and nonparticipant, is vital to the social scientist. A participant observation is one in which the researcher takes part in the action, saying or doing something and then observing the reactions. Nonparticipant observaton is just looking—noting and analyzing what is seen and heard in a situation. Because speech behavior is so complex and so inextricably dependent on context for its meaning, much behavior can be understood only through observation. Researchers like Gumperz, Sacks, Goffman, and Birdwhistell, all concerned with discourse and body motion analysis, rely heavily on nonparticipant observation.

Certainly, there must be some controls. Just going out in the streets and listening randomly is not likely to yield insight. First, the researcher has to define a problem, the object of the investigation. Then, likely spots for observation must be determined. Not only must one choose locales that have the right people doing the right things, but one must consider such ordinary matters as where one is going to sit or stand. Will there be a place for unobtrusive listening and looking? In a participant observation, is there a place to start the interactions naturally so that subjects do not get suspicious? One must also make sure there is not so much noise or movement that confusion could result.

Sometimes the researcher can manipulate a situation that will be observed without actually participating in it. A student who wished to investigate whether the presence of women affected male speech invited friends to his house to watch a football game. While viewing the game they commented loudly with a great deal of profanity, as was usual. The investigator had invited two girls to drop in at the start of the game before there had been too much beer drinking. As the girls walked in, although the viewers did not acknowledge their presence, the comments instantly became devoid of offensive words. The following week, the experiment was repeated, but with the girls showing up after the viewers had drunk a great deal of beer. This time, the profanity did not cease in the presence of the girls. In essence, this was an observation, but one done in which conditions were controlled. The investigator did not actually participate, for he did not interact with the viewers beyond greeting them and saying goodbye. What he demonstrated was that, even in these liberated days, men feel inhibited about swearing in front of women, an inhibition, like so many others, lessened by alcohol.

A classic participant observation is Labov's (1966, pp. 63–89) famous department store survey. Checking on his intuition that /r/-full pronunciation was becoming a sign of middle- and upper-class speech in New York City, Labov visited three department stores: Saks Fifth Avenue, Macy's and Klein's. Saks caters to the wealthy. Macy's is a solid middle-class store, and Klein's, in an unfashionable neighborhood, was a low-price store aimed at the blue collar and lower classes, although, like Macy's, people of all classes shopped there. Starting on the first floor of each store, Labov asked a salesclerk to direct him to a department he knew to be on the fourth floor. He then asked, "Excuse me?" to obtain a more emphatic careful repetition. When he reached the fourth floor, he asked "Excuse me, what floor is this?" On both floors salesclerks had to answer "fourth floor." These words have the /r/ in the two positions that it is not pronounced in so-called /r/-less speech: before a consonant and at the end of a word. As he had predicted, Labov found almost no /r/s in Klein's, somewhat more in Macy's, and the most in Saks. In the exclusive upstairs salons of Saks, there were even more /r/s than on the first floor, which looks more like any other department store and has somewhat less expensive goods. This study yielded a great deal of significant data in a short time. It had the advantage that the speech of the employees being analyzed was wholly unself-conscious and natural.

This survey is an example of an ingenious investigation, but it also illustrates some real dangers of observation. There is no check on what Labov actually heard. We have to take his word for the fact that he heard what he said he did.

Yet, linguists, especially, know all too well that people hear what they expect to hear. There are various degrees of sharpness in pronouncing /r/, as Labov himself noted. Often, listeners fail to hear a lightly constricted /r/ or think that a word pronounced with no /r/ is being pronounced with a very light one. The greatest pitfall in all science is that an investigator finds just what he or she sets out to find. It is not that investigators are necessarily liars. There is simply an all too human tendency not to notice what is not relevant to one's purpose and to think that one has seen or heard what is. Labov himself admits this problem with the department store survey, and he did follow it up with other experiments that studied the same speech feature using careful methodology.

One can lessen the problem of personal bias in two ways. First, get a partner. At least there will be one other pair of ears or set of eyes to verify what is going on. Second, in these days of tiny recorders, tapings are possible if guidelines are observed (see Section 2.10, *Ethics*). Although it is difficult to get the finest quality this way, recordings adequate to the purpose are often possible. Fine discriminations between acoustically similar sounds like *aw* [ɔ] versus *awr* [ɔr] with light /r/ may still be difficult in some instances, but enough clear examples should emerge. There may be doubtful cases with or without a tape, but at least with a recording, one has the opportunity to identify such cases. It is better to verify them later than to depend upon on-the-spot judgments as to the presence or absence of a particular feature.

No matter how such anonymous observation is carried out, there is still one problem with it, as Labov himself noted: there is no way to tell anything about the background of the speakers. Perhaps more /r/s were pronounced in Saks, for instance, because the sales personnel there are less likely to be native New Yorkers than those in Klein's or Macy's. Saks is one of those stores that attract women from all over the country who work there while trying to start careers in modeling, acting, or retailing.

2.9   Other methodology

This brief chapter cannot include all possible field methods. In the following chapters, many others will be presented in the explanations of what has been discovered and what significance the various discoveries hold for greater understanding of social uses of language.

Whether or not one should believe the results of any investigation depends heavily on what field methods were used. If these methods were faulty, then the results are very likely to be correspondingly faulty.

The fact that transcriptions often must be made shows that some background in linguistics proper is necessary for adequate investigations in sociolinguistics. It is also necessary, as will be shown repeatedly in later chapters, for the researcher to understand how language is structured, as well as how people use and process language.

One frequently used method, the imitation test, relies on such knowledge. In such testing, consultants, usually children, are asked to imitate sentences. It has been found that, as in the baby-talk studies in the preceding chapter, the consultant will unconsciously use his or her own grammar rather than the grammar of the given sentence, if there is a difference between the two. This has been found useful, for instance, in determining where children who are speakers of nonstandard dialects are likely to come into conflict with the grammar in their reading books. It is also an aid to teachers of English as a foreign language in discovering where their students need more help in grammar.

Another method relies on questionnaires. Some dialect studies have been conducted by asking people to fill out questionnaires, indicating, for example, what words they use for certain objects. People's reactions to certain kinds of speech—say, Appalachian versus Chicago,—can also be discovered by this means. As we shall see, however, people often have very poor perceptions about how they actually sound and what words and grammar they actually are using, especially in casual situations. They frequently use the very pronunciations, words, or grammar they criticize the most in others. Also, on a questionnaire, there is always the problem of fibbing, of telling the investigator what one thinks he or she wants to know rather than what one actually says.

2.10   *Ethics*

It is not ethical to make people unwitting guinea pigs. If people are to take part in an experiment, no matter how innocuous, their consent must be obtained. The subjects have to be told exactly what is required of them and, as much as possible without wrecking the procedure, the purpose. Under no conditions should someone's performance be ridiculed or criticized in any way. At no time and for no reason should an investigator identify subjects and then report on their individual performances. If a subject tells the investigator something about his or her past or present life, that information cannot be used in any way without consent. Hidden tape recorders and bugging devices should never be used unless subjects are told about them afterwards, and then their contents must not be used unless those who were taped say it is all right. It is far better to inform subjects that they are being investigated, get their consent, and get them accustomed to the presence of a tape recorder. One has to have very strong reasons for any other procedure. If one wishes natural dialogue one can contact a club or gang or other group and ask their consent to record meetings. Students can invite friends to their dormitories or apartments, letting them know that, with their consent, a tape is being made and why. Deborah Tannen (1979) taped friends at Thanksgiving dinner, getting beautiful natural data. There is rarely a need for duplicity.

It does not take much reading in sociolinguistics to come across studies done via hidden tape recorders. This is done only in anonymous studies in which semantic content is not reported in print or orally and then only if the data cannot reasonably be obtained in any other way. Labov's department store survey seems to qualify. The studies on males interrupting females mentioned in Chapter 9 also do. Instances of interruptions could have been gathered at formal meetings as well, but these, by their nature, often involve overt power relationships. A hidden tape recorder in a knapsack recording casual male–female conversations in drugstores and cafeterias gives far more natural situations. Soskin and John (1963) got permission to tape a young married couple all day long every day while they were on vacation. This yielded highly natural data of male–female interaction without resorting to deception, but such a procedure is extremely time-consuming. Few people could be bugged that way. The expense of equipment is too great, and the time needed to transcribe and extract data for each couple is horrendous. Then, too, one would still be missing nonintimate relationships, which would be quite different from that of spouses. For the kinds of general insights into male–female interaction that Zimmerman and West (1975) were studying, the hidden tape recorder was probably justified. It must be emphasized, however, that science is not an excuse for immorality. People are always entitled to privacy. Hidden recording devices are uncomfortably close to eavesdropping. Before moving in close enough to record, the investigator should make sure that the conversation is not private or intimate in any way. No attempt should ever be made to tape a softly spoken interaction obviously not meant for surrounding ears. Only public transactions, such as greetings and chitchat, conversations on buses, on benches at malls, in cafeterias, discussions between clerk and customer or between two customers in a checkout line qualify. If a conversation is loud enough for everyone around to hear easily and no attempt is being made to mask content, it can justifiably be considered public. The same limitations hold for any other method of preserving conversation, such as writing it down as one hears it. Even if one jots down only selected features of a conversation, such as the number of pauses or interruptions, there should be no eavesdropping on private interactions.

EXERCISES

1. Select two groups in your community whose speech you might like to study. How would you go about gathering an adequate sample of speakers from each? Will the same field methods work for both groups? For groups selected by other students in your class?

2. How would you determine the reactions of other students in your class to members of the groups you have selected in Exercise 1?

3. What sorts of tests or observations might you devise to study the normal, casual dialogue of members of the groups you chose to study?

4. With permission, tape some natural dialogue between any two or more people at home, school, or work. Try to transcribe the tape one week later using whatever transcription system you already know. List all the difficulties you experience in transcribing.

chapter 3

STYLE OF SPEECH

We do not always speak in exactly the same way. Speech, like dress, varies with the situation, different situations calling for different styles. Style also controls social interactions. Most interestingly, style gives its own messages, messages that are not supposed to be given via the linguistic system proper. The reasons for this can be understood only in the context of a sociology of language.

3.1   *Style*

Style refers to the selection of linguistic forms to convey social or artistic effects. Style also acts as a set of instructions. The messages it conveys are not normally conveyed in words. Indeed, the idiom "didn't get the message" may refer to a listener's not picking up a speaker's stylistic cues, even though he or she understood just fine the actual words used. We manipulate others with style, even as we are manipulated ourselves, usually unconsciously.

Style forms a communication system in its own right, one that determines how a social interaction will proceed, or if it will proceed at all. If it is to continue, style tells how, whether formally or informally. Style may also tell listeners how to take what is being said: seriously, ironically, humorously, dubiously, or in some other way.

Often when the style of an utterance contradicts the meaning of the words and grammar, the style is believed. Since style tells us how to interpret a message, this is not surprising. For example, if "John is nice" is said sarcastically, the style instructs, 'take these words to mean the opposite of what they actually say'. Thus "John is nice" can mean 'John is not nice'. Similarly, a timid "I'm not afraid" still conveys 'I am afraid'. And, highly formal "I do hope we shall be friends, Miss Tippett" is not likely to yield close confidences. Style forms a mini-communication system that works along with language itself, yet is apart from it.

Many stylistic messages are countered only with other stylistic messages, as illustrated in sentences 9–13, below. Style uses all the resources of language: tone of voice, different ways of pronouncing sounds, even choice of words and grammar themselves. The number of possible variations of style is far more limited, however, than the possible choices of words and their combinations in sentences.

Style overlaps with ritualistic use of language, as in greetings and forms of address. Each language or dialect usually has several of these, each marked for a different style. Considering the function of style as the controller of the interaction, so to speak, this is hardly surprising. Greetings and address start interactions. One expects heavy style-marking on them because they set the tone for what is to follow.

3.2   Co-occurrence restrictions

John Gumperz (1971) once said that one's choice of linguistic alternants "reflects the positions actors [parties in an interaction] wish to assume relative to each other." **Linguistic alternants** in sociolinguistics means sets of words and phrases that share meaning but differ in that one or more members of the set carries a social connotation. This connotation gives information about the speaker's social status and about how he or she wishes to be treated. It also often gives information about what is being talked about.

Gumperz (1964) gives the example of *dine* versus *eat*. Both denote consumption of food, but *dine* connotes more formal surroundings calling for formal manners. It also implies certain kinds of food: *coq au vin* as opposed to fried chicken. Choice of the verb *dine* also carries implications about those who are doing it. Gumperz (1964, p. 139) says, "Not everyone can 'dine'. Certainly not two laborers during a dinner break no matter how well prepared the food . . . and how good their table manners." Few in American society today could seriously say "Dine with me tonight." As much as we hate to admit it in a supposedly egalitarian society, *dine* belongs to upper class speech, and, pretty much, to older people. The refined and aristocratic dine. Everyone else eats.

One way to verify our intuitions about *dine* is to note its **co-occurrence restrictions**. These are restrictions on what words can go together. For instance, in English both people and animals can be *killed*, but only people can be *murdered* or *assassinated*. The latter two verbs imply the victim was a human being. Similar restrictions determine which style goes with certain words. Words that differ in the degree of formality do not usually **co-occur**, to use the linguist's term, nor do words that give conflicting information about social status. Note, for example:

1. Let's dine on fried chicken.
2. Hey, baby, wanna dine tonight?
3. Me and Bob are dinin' out.
4. Wouldja dine with me t'night?
5. Would you dine with me tonight?
6. Mrs. Whitmore wishes you to dine with her.

The first four sentences are humorous. The joke for each lies in the violation of co-occurrence restrictions. No food that is eaten with fingers is an appropriate object of *dine*. "Hey, baby" implies that the speaker is a young male, trying to put forth a macho image. Since, in our society, being macho is not associated with refinement, such speech forms clash with the formal *dine*. In the third, the grammatical variant "me and Bob" is a marker of nonstandard speech. People who use "me and Bob" as the subjects of a sentence are not likely to speak of dining no matter how well they eat. The pronunciation *dinin'* is humorous because the *-in'* replacement for *-ing* is reserved for informal speech, but *dine* is formal. Similarly, *wouldja* is a more casual pronunciation than *would you*. The last two sentences are not humorous because they are entirely formal, hence appropriate for *dine* (although they too could be used facetiously by, say, a person adopting the formal tone for comic effect).

3.3   *The style is the message*

Speakers give a great deal of information about themselves just by the words, grammar, and pronunciation they choose both unconsciously and consciously. This information reveals to the hearer such things as the speaker's social or educational background, and regional affiliation. The style markers of a particular social group or region may be deliberately used for other purposes. For instance, the man who approaches a woman with "Hey, baby—love those threads. How about doin' the town tonight?" may not be a Black street kid. He may be the wealthy scion of as aristocratic a family as America produces. Although his own usual dialect does not normally greet with "Hey, baby—", or use *threads* to mean 'clothes', he still may choose that terminology as a way of asserting his masculinity. But he tempers the assertiveness with a teasing humor conveyed by the slangy speech form and his obvious borrowing of it. "Hey, baby—" lets the woman know that he does not want their encounter to be formal. It is an invitation to intimacy. Of course, she may not be in accord. If she is not, she responds in a style appropriate both to her status and the degree of intimacy she prefers, as in:

7. "I'm busy tonight thank you, Mr. _____"
8. "Were you talking to me, sir?"

She does not need to comment overtly on his style. Rather, by her responding with a formal style, she instructs him to keep his distance. Her style says, "Back off Jack," although her words do not. The message is also conveyed by intonation or inflection. Response 8 uttered with a rising inflection might be interpreted as a coquettish response!

In fact, it would be downright odd if she said something explicit like "I do not want you to be so familiar with me. I do not consider myself a sexually available woman, nor do I wish to be intimate with you." Such messages are given by style. Actual words are used only on the rare occasions that the offending party is too obtuse to "get the message." It must be emphasized that the social message conveyed by style is not coded directly onto actual words that mean what the intended social message is.

This is seen even more in usual greetings. Have you ever answered someone's "Hi! How are you?" with a brisk "Lousy" (or its equivalent), only to get a cheerful response of "That's good" as the greeter traveled on? Conversely, have you ever answered "Fine," but in a glum voice, only to have the greeter stop and ask, "Oh, what's the matter?" In both cases, clearly, the words were ignored, but the style was not (Chaika 1973).

How something is said does take precedence over *what* is said. Yet something more is going on in such situations. In responding to a greeting, it is inappropriate to state one's real feelings in words unless the response is 'fine'. Witness the criticism, "He's the kind of person who, if you ask how he is, tells you." That is, he is a socially inept individual.

Ritual greetings are supposed to convey information about someone's well being, but not in words. Nor are words usual for the messages of status and intimacy. There seem to be three reasons for this: phatic communication, control of interactions, and protection of the ego.

3.4   *Phatic communication*

Greetings have two functions. One is to initiate interaction; the other, which will concern us first, is what cultural anthropologist Bronislaw Malinowski (1923) called **phatic communication**, speech not to convey thoughts, but to create "ties of union ... by mere exchange of words." Phatic communication is speech for the sake of social contact, speech used much the way we pat dogs on the head as a way of letting them know we care.

Greeting, even in passing, is essential to let members of society know that they count. If an acquaintance fails to say "Hi" when we know he or she saw us, we feel hurt. Such a trivial omission, yet we give it a name, a *snub*. We are obliged to greet even when we cannot or do not want to get into a conversation. For this reason, perhaps, the person greeted is supposed just to acknowledge the greeting phatically, not launch into a recital of what's actually "happ'nin'," or the ills of the day. The response "Fine" can properly end the greeting sequence. Whether or not the person is truly fine is immaterial. Phatic communication has been completed with its utterance. If the greeter wants to know more, of course, such as why "Fine" was uttered glumly, he or she can stop and ask for more information. At this juncture it is proper to go into details. Greeting, then, fulfills two functions: first, the requirements of phatic communication, and second, if desired, opening further interaction.

3.5   *Control*

It is amazing how much we can be controlled by the style of a greeting, especially if it is appropriate to the person who uses it. The person with higher rank, if there is one, has the privilege of controlling interaction. This is done simply by choosing the style. Then the lower ranking person is constrained to follow suit.

If one's superior consistently chooses formal greetings, this maintains authority. The underling who must always respond to "How are you today, Mr./Mrs./Miss/Ms. _____" with "Fine, thank you, Mr./Mrs./Miss/Ms. _____" is kept at a distance. Each time the greeting is given, the social distance is reinforced. Casual chitchat and easy confidence are almost impossible with someone who consistently greets and addresses one formally. Most important, it is difficult, sometimes even impossible, to challenge aloof, formal authority. The words metaphorically stick in one's throat. Most of us have had the experience of being at a loss to "speak up to" a teacher, an employer, clergyman, parent, or other dominant person. In earlier, more formal and more authoritarian times it was perhaps a more familiar experience than it is today in our culture.

The person we cannot address by first name is not a peer. The person who forces deference by maintaining formality is the person most difficult to confront. Perhaps this is why respect always takes the form of formality. Respect implies social distance, and social distance defines formality. Being casual implies social intimacy or, at least, equality. One need not obey one's equals nor show them any particular respect beyond the bounds of normal politeness and mutual consideration.

Even if we understand how style controls us, we cannot break its barriers. My immediate superior, a courtly gentleman who outranks me both in position and age, for ten years greeted me, "How do you do, Dr. Chaika." That alternant affirmed his own higher status and announced that he wished to maintain distance. Because he unfailingly greeted me that way, I, of course, was forced into a wholly uncharacteristic "How do you do, Dr. X." Even at parties, it was impossible to say, "Hi, P_____, how's it goin'?" The round of greetings, typically, was, "Hey, Rich! Hi, Jane! How do you do, Dr. X." Recently, Dr. X. announced his impending retirement. The next time I saw him, he greeted me, "Hello, Elaine."

Not all superiors wish to maintain distance, or at least not so overtly as using formal titles plus last names. Nowadays, especially, it is not at all unusual for bosses to first-name their employees and to request first names back. Linguist Robert DiPietro pointed out to me that such first-naming is "at least on the surface, a state which is intended to avoid confrontation." In other words, first-naming allows a pretense of equality even though one outranks the other. We shall see this phenomenon again in commands. Strangely enough, although inferiors cannot bridge social distance by initiating first-naming, they can maintain it by refusing to first-name superiors. Sometimes such refusal is virtually involuntary, as when a person simply cannot bring himself or herself to call an elder or a boss by a first name.

3.6   *Communicating with style*

Style is so integral a part of social functioning that interaction cannot go ahead if one party to it does not speak with the "right" style. Whether or not style is right or appropriate depends partially on the social identity of the speaker. This will be more apparent when we consider greeting and address in more detail. If a style is perceived as correct for a given speaker, then the respondent has to obey that style or, at least, normally does. Style also has to fit the social situation: a funeral does not allow the same range of styles as a backyard barbecue.

Correct use of style is a delicate matter. If the wrong style seems to have been used by one party in a dialogue, **repairs** often will be attempted by the other. These repairs take the form of the respondent's manipulating his or her own style in an effort to get the first speaker to change style. This happens typically when one person speaks too intimately to another. A response in a superformal style is a clue to the first speaker that distance is to be maintained. Style is elevated often far above what is normal in an effort to make someone switch to more formal speech. Responses 7 and 8 in the preceding section are typical, as is a salesclerk's frosty "May I help you sir" to a too-forward customer. These illustrate both the way that style itself is the message and the way we try to control others through style.

It certainly does not seem surprising that we slap someone down for being too intimate. What *is* surprising is that being too polite seems just as bad socially. Politeness, as much as rudeness, calls for stylistic repairs or even anger. Garfinkel (1967) had his students act too politely at home. The results were disastrous. Mothers cried. Fathers became furious. Since politeness indicates formality, therefore social distance, their reaction was perhaps to be expected. One's family interprets intimacy as a sign of affection and belonging. The converse must seem like rejection.

In a near replication of Garfinkel's work, my own students have been instructed to be too polite to their friends. Some results illustrate the social functioning of style.

In the dormitory:

> 9. *Trish:*   Would it be possible for you to wait for me after class?
>   *Ann:*   Yes, of course it's possible. Why are you talking so proper?

In a car on a date:

> 10. *Pat:*   Jacques, could you tell me how far we are from our destination?
>   *Jacques:*   Yes, Patricia. We are about 50 miles from our destination. Are you satisfied? [sarcastic tone]

In the cafeteria:

11. *Robert:*   Hi Dave. Hi Bob.
     Dave: Hello Robert. How are you?
     Robert: Not bad. You take a test or somethin'?
     Dave: Why no. Of course not. Why do you ask?
[Robert gives strange looks as if to say "What are you on?" and leaves without replying.]

12. *Tom:*   Is this seat taken?
     Al: Why no. Won't you join us?
     Tom: [looking puzzled] How was logic today?
     Al: Very instructive.
     Tom: Oh, was it? What did he talk about?
     Al: He talked about fallacies and associated topics.
     Tom: [laughs, looks puzzled, mimics Al and hits him] Would you care to come over for tea?

13. *Ernie:*   Hello. How are you?
     Andy: Tired.
     Ernie: And why is that?
     Andy: [with suspicious glance] Because I haven't gotten any sleep this week.
     Ernie: Oh. That is too bad. I feel sorry for you.
     Andy: [with antagonistic look] Why are you smirking when you say that? Because you are a louse!
[The experimenter and an observer both claim that Ernie was not smirking and his tone was not sarcastic.]

In 9, Ann responded separately to both the linguistic and the stylistic message. She answered the question, then attempted to find out why the style was wrong. Notice though that when Ann answered the question, she matched Trish's formal style (see Giles, Taylor, and Bourhis 1973). "Yes, of course it's possible" is not a usual college girl's response to her roommate. "Yeah, sure" is more likely.

We see style matching as well in 10. The respondent uses the formal variant of his girlfriend's name: Patricia. Even the "yes" is a formal answer. He continues in a superformal style, to the point of actually mimicking Pat's words. His sarcastic tone throughout indicates that this is more than mere style matching. Normally, it is very rude to mimic someone whom you perceive as not having spoken correctly. It would be unthinkable to do that to a foreigner or someone with a speech impediment, for instance. If someone uses the wrong style to you, however, apparently the social conventions can be dismissed.

We see another social convention dismissed in 11. Usually it is the height of rudeness to leave a conversation without saying "goodbye" or one of its equivalents. It is doubly rude simply not to answer a question. Robert, like the respondents in the preceding examples, immediately perceives the inappropriate formality. His repair takes the form of asking why they are "talking so proper." His "You take a test or somethin'?" is another way of asking that. In fact, unless one considers style, Robert's question would seem bizarre. It has no relevance to anything that has been said in actual words. Clearly it means 'Is something wrong?' He wonders whether something unsettling happened to his friend to cause him to seem remote or cold. Naturally, the receiver of too formal a style, especially if normally intimate (as is a buddy like Robert or a family member, roommate, or lover), wants to know what is wrong. If the first speaker does not use an appropriate style in responding that nothing is wrong, then the other party, far from being reassured that the world is all right, is getting the wrong cues. He or she cannot behave normally. This in itself bars interaction, hence the anger and the termination of conversations.

3.7   Why style is the message

Why do people respond to style with style? Why don't they just say, "Your style is inappropriate!" The most overt comments on style are of the variety "Why are you talkin' so proper? You take a test or somethin'?" These are attempts at repair, at finding out why the style is off, so that the hearer can deal with the situation but, as with style, the message is often not overt.

It has already been demonstrated that style gives messages about the social status and mood of the speaker. It would be very odd to say, "I am a middle-class educated female from Rhode Island. Today I am feeling tired and irritable, and I do not wish intimate conversation with you, although I consider you my peer and acknowledge your existence." Yet, a greeting, in both the form chosen and the tone of voice of its delivery, conveys that information. Also, the style selected during the entire conversation either reinforces or contradicts that information. Using style carried along with a greeting and conversational message is more efficient than having to encode that information at the outset or continually during a conversation.

Having such information given via style has another advantage. It allows status and mood to be known, without ever bringing them to the fore. It saves face. The lower status person does not have his or her social inferiority rubbed in, so to speak. Constant assaults to the ego are spared by placing messages of rank in the background, by having style carry them.

Then, too, people can behave in accordance with style without any arguments about it. If stylistic messages were overtly encoded, they could as overtly be commented on. The person who said, "I am of higher status than you. Treat me with respect"—or even, "I am your equal"—would be inviting comment. Wrangling about status, intimacy, and mood is kept to a minimum if they are signaled only by style. By keeping such information backgrounded, it can be acted on virtually automatically.

Style, then serves social interaction three ways: it saves time and egos, as well as cuts down on friction. Finally, if the style given is perceived as wrong, as we have seen, style rather than overt comment is used to effect change. This can be viewed as an extension of using style to control social interaction.

3.8   *Features of style*

Just as the language itself can be broken down into elements that combine in various ways, so can style. There are three important differences, however. Whereas the elements of language proper can be combined and recombined into an infinite number of sentences, the system of style appears to be finite. Whereas language can be used to say anything, style is confined to messages about social status, moods, and desired degree of intimacy between speakers. Whereas language must be broken down into elements if it is to be understood, style is virtually **isomorphic** with the message. That is, there is a one-to-one correspondence between the message given by style and its meaning.

Style is akin to the signal system of animals. It is not as inherently ambiguous as language itself. Any word or sound in the linguistic system proper can be used to mean many, many different things, and their meanings can change in new situations. Since style is processed separately from the meaning of words and grammar, it is not surprising that its messages are unambiguous. To have two sets of messages coming at once and to have both potentially ambiguous would probably make the decoding of speech too complex a task. Also, as noted previously, style is often used to tell hearers how to take the message given by words: seriously, as sarcasm, as something the speaker is happy or sad about, or in some other way. Style is an instruction to hearers superimposed upon the content of the communication. The less ambiguous the instruction, the more likely it will be understood.

3.9   *Voice control*

The messages given by style depend heavily on features like tempo, pitch, loudness, intonation, and timbre. This last refers to voice character or quality—whether it is resonant, harsh, thin, nasal, breathy, creaky, mellow, musical, twangy, or the like (Abercrombie 1967).

The voice we use is not entirely the one we are born with. To be more accurate, each person is born with a possible range of voices, one of which we adopt as the base or normal voice. Most of us could talk either on a lower or higher pitch than we do, and we can vary our timbre, making it more or less resonant, twangy, mellow, or harsh, for instance. Sometimes we do change our voices, making them sexier or kinder or sweeter. When we mimic others, we may change our voices so radically that we do not even sound like us any more.

The linguist Edward Sapir noted in 1927: "On the basis of his voice, one might decide many things about a man . . . that he is sentimental . . . sympathetic . . . cruel . . . [or] . . . kind-hearted." Experimenters like Allport and Cantril (1934), Kramer (1963), and Laver (1968) have all found that people indeed judge personality and even physical appearance on the basis of voice alone. To some degree the voice quality we adopt is that of our social group or dialect. Eastern prep school "lockjaw," Black "resonance," and Midwestern "twang" are all examples. This does not mean that all Eastern preppies or all Blacks or all Midwesterners adopt the same voices but, rather, that certain voices are associated with those groups, as with others. Individuals who fit those categories may not choose to sound that way, however. They may adopt a voice quite different from that of the group to which they ostensibly belong. Alternatively they may switch into and out of particular voices at different times.

3.10   *Style, dialect, language, register*

Just as a particular voice quality is associated with a particular style, such as being tough or formal or intimate, so may a voice quality be associated with a particular dialect or language. There is no hard and fast division between style, dialect, and language. One melds into the other. Style is relatively minor variation in usage. Dialect indicates rather more difference, and language the most. It is virtually impossible to pinpoint exactly when a style switch graduates into a dialect change. A working rule is that dialect signals regional variety of speech or one associated with a social group (either class or ethnic group) whereas style signals only a change in mood or intimacy.

Also, a style may be associated with a particular social occasion. Then it is called **register** or **functional variety** of speech. One uses a different style at a funeral than at a barbecue; there is a register appropriate for each. Sometimes, an occasion calls for switching into a second dialect for bidialectal speakers or even into another language for bilingual speakers; the dialect switch or language switch is associated with occasion or even mood. We cannot make neat categories for style, dialect, and language. There is a continuum from style to register to dialect to language. This may disconcert the reader who wishes nice, tidy labels and definitions. The typical fuzzy borders of language categories are what ultimately make language flexible. To put it another way, human beings can handle variation. The thing to remember is that the elements of speech that get varied are the same in style, dialect, and language. Styles differ from one another just as dialects and languages do. Since dialect and language differences will occupy the rest of this book, here only style will be discussed.

3.11   *How features of style work*

There does seem to be one difference between stylistic variation and that of dialect. For each feature such as tempo, pitch, loudness, timbre, or intonation there seems to be a base that indicates that everything is fine. The base is not a fixed point or line but a range within which no special message seems to be given. Moving out of that range indicates that something is wrong or out of the ordinary.

For example, each dialect or language seems to be spoken at a characteristic rate. Speeding up indicates excitement. Slowing down may indicate exhaustion, boredom, or uncertainty. Raising the normal pitch may indicate a number of emotions: anger, surprise, fear, or excitement. Lowering it can be either threatening or confidential. Speaking more loudly than normal can be a sign of happy excitement or even rage. If loudness and slow tempo are combined, it can be a signal that the speaker's patience is wearing thin. One's normal voice can be made more honeyed when an attempt is being made to ingratiate oneself with another. That one wants unquestioning obedience may be evinced by making one's voice harsh and raspy. One's normal intonation (rise and fall of the voice) changes to show surprise or sarcasm or exasperation. In combination, especially, these features give many different emotional messages. Then, too, different languages may use them differently to signal somewhat different messages.

Using a Moog synthesizer, Klaus Scherer (1973) created tone sequences by varying tempo, pitch, loudness, and intonation. He found that to each sequence judges could assign meanings of pleasantness, activity, potency, interest, sadness, fear, happiness, disgust, anger, surprise, elation, or boredom. There was good interjudge reliability in the task. That means that a significant number of people had the same opinion about each sequence.

In general, Scherer found that moderate pitch variation in intonation indicates generally unpleasant emotions, such as sadness, disgust, and boredom. Extreme pitch variation produces ratings of pleasant, active, and potent emotions, such as happiness, interest, and surprise. Fast tempo is more active and potent than slow, with the former indicating interest, fear, surprise, or anger, and the latter indicating boredom, sadness, or disgust. Both fear and anger can be indicated in diametrically opposed ways, either by low, slow sounds with moderate intonation or high, fast sounds with extreme intonation. The difference seems to be that of potency with the slower, lower, flatter variation indicating cool anger and fear without activity. The faster, higher, more extreme tone sequences indicate hot anger and a more potent, excited fear.

Other experiments confirm that people assign meaning to voice quality, intonation, and tempo apart from the linguistic message per se. People from the same social groups tend to assign meaning the same way. Different languages and different dialects use the features of style somewhat differently, leading to cross-cultural misunderstanding. The normal tempo of some dialects of the

American South seems slow to Northerners. Consequently, they may label Southerners as lazy or stupid. Speakers from Midwestern cities like Detroit sound overpositive and bossy to many New Englanders. The slightly "too rapid" tempo and the pitch higher than "normal"—to New Englanders—create that illusion.

An almost classic example of a similar misanalysis is mentioned in the book *There's a Rhino in the Rose Bed, Mother* (Leslie-Melville 1973). The American author, a transplant to Africa, justifies the expulsion of Indians from Uganda because, she says, they could often be seen haranguing the Black Ugandans in a most arrogant manner. She apparently was unaware that natives of India typically speak English on a much higher pitch and at a more rapid rate than do many Americans. It is just the style of Indian speech and does not necessarily indicate arrogance, although it may be interpreted that way.

Interestingly, people differ in their judgments of tempo. Although New Englanders may judge urban Midwestern speech as being rapid, there are Midwesterners who find New England speech fast. The less familiar a dialect or language, the more rapid it may sound. A Southern-bred friend has a great deal of difficulty talking to Northerners because not only is Northern speech too rapid for her, but it does not require pauses long enough at the end of an utterance for her to break in. The tempo and pauses she considers normal seem slow, even hesitant to many Northerners.

Dialects may also differ in their normal degree of loudness. In England the voices of American tourists seem to be booming out in pubs or on the streets. Apparently many American dialects are spoken more loudly than many British ones. Ethnic groups also may differ in their normal degree of loudness. One second generation Italian consultant commented to me about her Weight Watchers lecturer, "I knew she was one of my kind. She talked so loud." The friendly, happy unself-conscious talk of Americans of Italian and Eastern European Jewish background, those who still identify with their ethnic groups, often seems to be somewhat louder than, for instance, speech of descendants of the English settlers.

As with tempo, however, the loudness perceived by listeners of another culture may not be actual loudness at all. Many factors may lead to a judgment of loudness when, in fact, a speaker is not talking especially loudly. If the rules of conversation of one group of speakers do not usually allow one person to break into another's speech, dialogue with a member of a group that *does* allow such interruptions may be uncomfortable. The member of the former group gets the feeling that the interrupter is speaking too loudly. The same perception can occur if someone breaks into speech after a shorter pause than another person's rules for conversation allow. Perhaps this is because one speaks loudly when one wishes to override another who is speaking, as when one is outraged by what someone is saying. Speaking loudly is a way of impinging on conversational space. Therefore, if someone breaks into someone else's speech in violation of that person's conversational practices, the behavior is perceived as speaking loudly.

Whether differences in loudness are real or imagined, misunderstandings result if people feel someone speaks too loudly or too softly. People accustomed to what they consider to be soft voices may misinterpret as being strident, overbearing or vulgar those voices they perceive as louder. However, people accustomed to louder voices often judge speakers they consider soft-voiced as being cold, distant, unfeeling, unfriendly, or mousy. Generally, adolescents often adopt louder voices than their elders. The elders find them rude and loud, and they, in turn, find their elders stiff and cold. Such judgments are easily gathered by playing tapes of people speaking with different degrees of loudness, then asking consultants to rate them on a questionnaire.

Pitch also yields different messages in different cultures. The late comedian and actor Freddy Prinz in one of his most memorable monologues commented on the high pitch used by New York City Black youths when signaling anger, as opposed to the super-low pitch used for love talk. Prinz played the part of a Black male simultaneously arguing with someone and reassuring his girlfriend. The humor lay in the abrupt changes in pitch from super-high during the argument to super-low in the asides to the girl. This high pitch is not always understood by Whites. Even if a Black youth has clearly signaled extreme anger by such a pitch rise, a White adversary may complain, "He attacked without warning!"

Upper class British males and females often use a much higher pitch than Americans do. As a result, the males are likely to be pegged as being somewhat effeminate and the females as imperious. Americans apparently equate masculinity with deep voices, but this is not a universal evaluation. Depth of voice is not universally considered a masculine characteristic. For instance, part of the stereotype of Black males in the United States is that they have deep-pitched, resonant, loud voices. However, such tones are never heard from the Nigerian Black male Yoruba speakers of my acquaintance. By American standards their voices are very high and thin.

3.12   Stereotypes

The dangers of stereotyping on the basis of voice quality should be apparent from the foregoing example. If not all cultures signal masculinity by deep voices, then masculinity and deep voices obviously are not necessarily related. Furthermore, there can be no such thing as a "Black" voice if Blacks from different cultures utilize very different voice qualities. Such matters are learned.

Within a culture, people assign what Laver (1968) terms indexical meaning to voice quality, intonation, pitch, and other features of style. Laver means that these features serve as indexes or markers indicating social status, age, and personality characteristics. This is hardly surprising. It would be of little use to signal that I am angry if others in my culture do not understand my cues for anger. Laver notes: "Listeners, if they are from the same culture, tend to reach the same indexical conclusions from the same evidence, but the conclusions themselves may on occasion bear no reliable relation to the real characteristics of the speaker." In other words, we judge voice quality according to our stereotypes of the people who, we believe, use a particular voice or style.

A person can adopt a particular style to project a false image. Laver mentions that a harsh voice "is correlated with more aggressive, dominant, authoritative characteristics," so it is likely to be adopted by, say, a drill sergeant. A breathy voice projects an image "more self-effacing, submissive, meek." That description aptly describes the sex kitten voice, such as the late Marilyn Monroe's.

Perhaps the hardest lesson for students to learn is that voice quality is not completely inborn. For instance, the "Black voice" is not a biological inheritance. It has already been noted that the voice associated with Blacks in the United States is not heard from Blacks who come from other regions. Even in the United States not all Blacks are identifiable as Black by their voices (Labov 1964, pp. 491–93). Those Blacks who do adopt the American Black voice often can and do speak in a "White voice" as well. Furthermore, non-Blacks can and do imitate supposedly Black voices quite convincingly. As tasteless and racist as it was, the old *Amos and Andy* radio show proved that; Caucasians played the lead roles so convincingly that many listeners never realized that they were not Black. Many Blacks are bidialectal, changing their voice quality from "White" to "Black" and vice versa, depending on the situation they are in. Similarly, blue-collar males of Italian ethnic background in southern New England speak in a raspy, harsh, loud voice when talking about fights or other street concerns but adopt a smooth, mellow one for recounting personal memories of a less hostile nature. Voice switching can yield voices so different that students evaluating speakers on tape consistently fail to recognize two segments as belonging to the same speaker. Furthermore, they consistently rate the supposedly different speakers in very different ways, according to the voice used.

3.13   *Isolating features*

Matched guise testing and subjective reaction testing of the kind used to determine reactions to dialects can be adapted to determine reactions to features of style. This can be very important in the training of teachers and social workers who need to realize that they may unconsciously evaluate pupils and clients unfavorably just because of their pitch, loudness, tempo, timbre, or intonation. One of the complaints that people make when they have to deal with members of other cultures is "You never can tell what they are thinking." Actually, one never knows what anyone is thinking, but we automatically respond to the cues of style (and body motion; see Chapter 4). If those cues differ from the ones we have internalized, then we do not quite know how to react. We are put into the position of the students whose friends tested them by speaking in a too formal style. Perhaps this explains the preference of some people to be "with their own kind."

3.14　*Linguistic features of style: sounds*

The features of style so far delineated are nonlinguistic. They do not involve the system of sounds, words, and grammar that make up language proper. Some other aspects of style do, however. These are **phonetic variants,** different ways of pronouncing the same sounds; **lexical variants,** different words for the same thing; and **syntactic variants,** different grammatical constructions for the same meaning. These variants are stylistic when choice of one or the other does not change the content of the message but does signal a different social or emotional message or belongs to a different register.

For instance, it is normal and usual in American English to convert a word final /t/ into *ch* [č] if the next word starts with /y/. A word final /d/ turns into *j* [ǰ] under the same condition. Thus, *won't you* becomes "woncha" and *did you* becomes "dija." The technical term for this process is **palatalization.** That this is in the realm of style, not language proper, is shown in two ways. First, one variant is normal and usual, and a departure from it signals that the circumstances of the utterance are not ordinary. Second, the words are perceived as remaining the same, whichever pronunciation is adopted. In contrast, *tin* and *chin,* and *dale* and *jail,* are perceived as being different words because of the difference between /t/ and /č/, and /d/ and /ǰ/, respectively. The meanings and possible contexts of usage are changed because of the presence of one or the other sounds. There is no such difference between "won't you" and "woncha", "did you" and "dija," despite the fact that the same sounds are alternating in each pair. We perceive the change from /t/ to [č] and /d/ to [ǰ] as linguistic in *tin* vs. *chin, dale* vs. *jail,* but as stylistic in "woncha" vs. "wont you," "dija" vs. "did you." "Would you please eat your lunch?" with no palatalization, each /t/ and /d/ clearly articulated separately from the /y/s, signifies that the speaker outranks the person spoken to or is angry or wishes to keep distance between them or all three. A nurse might rebuff a difficult patient that way, for instance. "Wouldja eatcha lunch?" carries the same linguistic message but connotes normal peer relations. In the encounters described in examples 9–13, a prime signal of superformality was, in each, the lack of palatalization, "could you" rather than "couldja" in 10, for instance, and "won't you" rather than "woncha" in 12.

3.15　*Linguistic features of style: words*

Words, more technically termed *lexical items,* may also show stylistic variation. In 9–13 we saw several lexical variants: "destination," "very instructive," "associated topics," even phrases like "Would it be possible. . . ?" and "And why is that?" The choice of one word or phrase rather than another gives a stylistic message although the linguistic meaning remains the same. In all of these instances, the message given by style indicates that the speaker outranks the hearer and wishes formality, hence distance.

Lexical variants can also give quite the opposite stylistic message. For example, choosing "Let's split" over "Let's go" shows one's identity with youth and establishes an informal, casual mood. Referring to a man as a "dude" shows one's hipness. Saying "dichotomy" instead of "split," "division," or even "two sides to the question" shows that one is educated. The person who speaks of "shooting the breeze" instead of "chatting" is referring to a very casual conversation and is more likely to be a male than one who "chats."

3.16   *Linguistic features of style: syntax*

Syntactic variants involve the choice of one rather than another grammatical construction for the purpose of giving a different social message. Saying "Have I not?" instead of "Haven't I?" is one example. Although the use of double negatives and *ain't,* as in "I ain't got nobody," is often a difference between educated and uneducated dialects, in actual fact many educated speakers, especially younger ones, will on occasion use such forms stylistically. At casual parties, rock concerts, and sports events, educated middle-class speakers can be heard to say such things, as, "Ain't no way that's goin' to happen" and "He never brings no beer." Use of such forms heightens camaraderie and the general informality of the occasion.

There seem to be relatively few syntactic markers for style in American English. Perhaps this is because usage of certain "correct" grammar forms is so important for one to be pegged as a member of the educated middle class. Not to use these forms, even in jest, leads to the risk of one's being misidentified as ignorant. Consequently, Americans may be somewhat more prone to rely upon phonological and lexical variants than on syntactic ones to effect stylistic messages.

3.17   *The linguistic versus the stylistic*

Linguistic meaning can only be extracted from speech by an active decoding process during which the hearer has to figure out:

- What sounds have been used;
- Which meanings should be extracted from the words used;
- How to fit the meaning of the words into the syntax used;
- Which way to interpret a syntactic construction if it is ambiguous.

In contrast to these complex decoding strategies, to decode style the hearer must only determine which variant was used. There is little, if any, segmenting out of features and fitting them to the context. This is true even in those instances in which style is carried by phonological, lexical, or syntactic variants. All the hearer has to do is note which variant has been used in order to get the stylistic message.

Language itself is open-ended. There is no limit on the number of different utterances a person can make. Although there are limits on the possible meanings of a given sentence or word, both can change meaning somewhat in different contexts. Style, on the other hand, is virtually a closed system. There are a limited number of pitches, speeds, timbres, and intonation contours available. There are bounds on softness and loudness. There are a relatively few sounds involved in phonetic variation, and only a few syntactic constructions for stylistic manipulation, compared to the language as a whole, that is.

Perhaps the most open-ended feature of style is the lexical variants, which bear the brunt of adapting rapidly to new situations. Even so, the number of lexical items available for purely stylistic choices is very limited in contrast to those in one's entire vocabulary. Furthermore, far from the changeability of meaning that characterizes language, the elements of style are quite fixed, with the element given and the message it gives being virtually one and the same. This makes it possible for style to function as it does, as a set of instructions telling the speaker how to take whatever is being said. A hearer need only note the markers of style as he or she decodes the sentence proper.

3.18   *Summons, greetings, address*

It is not surprising that style is especially heavily marked at the outset of conversations. Lexical variation is prominent here. The other features of style certainly are also used, but the outset of conversations—summons, greetings, and address—have separate words for different social messages. These may also be modified by varying timbre, loudness, and the like, but the prime marking usually is by the form itself. This seems to be a reflection of the importance of this initial style-marking. Perhaps word variation is more perceptible, especially in the flurry of greeting, than general tone of voice.

The form of address in itself is a powerful controller. Susan Ervin-Tripp (1972) recounts a sad example. Dr. Alvin Poussaint, a well-known Black psychiatrist and author, was riding in his native Mississippi in 1967. A White policeman stopped him.

> What's your name, boy? [the policeman asked]
> Dr. Poussaint. I'm a physician.
> What's your first name, boy?
> Alvin.

In a *New York Times* article, Dr. Poussaint admits, "As my heart palpitated, I muttered in profound humiliation . . ." Ervin-Tripp explains that the source of Dr. Poussaint's extreme emotion was that he was forced to insult himself publicly and that this was done through widely recognized American rules of address. The policeman did not say overtly, 'You're a nigra and, therefore, not worthy of adult status or earned respect.' His use of address form alone conveyed that message.

Ervin-Tripp calls *boy* "a social selector for race." That is partly true. To call a male of any race "boy" in American society indicates that he is a servant. Not a personal servant who has an identity, but an anonymous servant to anyone. Note, for instance, the terms *busboy, bellboy,* or *messenger boy*. All of these are called "boy" regardless of age or color. Dogs are also called "boy," faithful servants that they are. The word *boy* refers to a faceless person who is there to carry out a function, but whom one otherwise barely notices. By extension, *boy* can be used as a wholly impersonal form of address to any male inferior, as in "Hey, boy! get off my car." This last was observed spoken to a White teenager in front of a theater.

When the policeman called Dr. Poussaint "boy," he immediately degraded him. The doctor first responded by giving his appropriate address form: [title + last name]. Then, he provided a justification ("I'm a physician") for that title. What makes this all the more poignant is that, in our society, anyone who claims the title "Dr." is automatically accorded the highest respect. Physicians are first-named only by close family, friends, and colleagues in the United States. "Dr. + Last Name" is the usual response of a physician to "What's your name?" The policeman's "What's your first name, boy?" is a way of saying, 'I don't care what titles you claim. To me, you're a nigra, and nigras are nothing, entitled to no respect.' By using the address *Boy* the policeman asserted the facelessness of Blacks in Mississippi in those days. In his view, they were menials, with no identity beyond being every White person's servant, or boy.

3.19   *Greeting versus address*

Address is often part of greeting. When it is, it must match the greeting in style. Together they can signal the same message of what Brown and Gilman (1960) called "power and solidarity". The policeman who humiliated Dr. Poussaint asserted power both by his use of *boy* and his failure to issue any greeting at all. My superior discouraged solidarity both by his "How do you do" and the address form "Dr. _____ ."

Address differs stylistically from greeting in two ways. First, address is used almost solely for power and solidarity. Between two people, then, it remains constant throughout a relationship unless that relationship changes. An example is an older person's saying, "Oh, call me Marge" when previously she was called "Mrs. Doohickey." She is signaling that she wishes more solidarity in the relationship. My superior's eventual "Hello, Elaine" was a clear signal of shift away from power.

Greetings may vary between two people depending on their mood. Two people who address each other the same way each time they meet may vary their greetings, "Hi!," "Wha's happ'nin'?," "How's it goin'?" "How are you today?" Second, address can be repeated constantly throughout a conversation to reinforce the relative intimacy and power between people. Greeting, on the other hand, only sets the stage.

3.20 Rules of addressing

The actual rules of address in a society are as complex as society itself. Most studies of address concentrate on whether or not first name is used, or titles like *Mr., Mrs., Dr., Father, Reverend,* and *Professor* + last name. Address also involves nicknaming, use of *sir* or *ma'am, man,* and *boy,* as well as *your honor, your eminence,* even *aunt* and *uncle.* Some cultures, such as Japan, use honorifics as well, endings on names that carry the meaning of 'honorable', for instance. These, too, are address forms. So is the variation between the singular *you* to indicate intimacy and the plural *you* indicating formality in European languages (French *tu* vs. *vous*). These, like other address forms, may be manipulated to regulate intimacy and power. The ways that they are used also reflect social conditions and attitudes.

3.21 The United States, a case in point

Some address rules seem to be pretty uniform throughout the United States. [Title + last name], for instance, generally indicates social distance. That address is given to one's superiors and to relative strangers. It may also be used by superiors to those they outrank but who are, nevertheless, of relatively high status. What constitutes superior versus inferior in this country is itself quite a complex business. For instance, age is one clear determinant of use of the form [title + last name]. An older person usually commands *Mr., Mrs.,* or *Miss,* especially from younger people. What happens, however, when a younger person is the boss of an older one? Age often wins out, so that the boss calls his or her employee by [title + last name], unless, of course, the older one says, "Call me by my first name."

First-naming has extended itself to one group who formerly were sacrosanct: teachers and professors. In some colleges students call all or some of their mentors by their first names. It is usually younger teachers, those who prefer a great deal of discussion in their classes, who encourage this. In many universities undergraduates call professors by their [title + last name], but graduate students call them by their first names. At some colleges and universities, professors are called *Dr.* if they hold the Ph.D. At others, in a sort of reverse snobbism, *Dr.* is never used, and those with the degree are called *Mr., Mrs., Miss,* or *Ms.* Sometimes, in the unkindest cut of all, males with Ph.D.s are regularly called *Dr.,* while their female counterparts are chagrined to hear themselves addressed as *Mrs., Miss* or *Ms.* or even by their first names. Some college teachers wish to be called only *Professor*. In some schools the particular address most used varies from department to department.

There is no such ambivalence for medical doctors in the United States. They are almost always and everywhere called *Doctor*. Even if a physician is younger than the patient, *Doctor* is the usual address. Occasionally, one hears someone consistently refer to his or her physician by first name, as in "I told Dave just before he put me under . . ." Since it is, indeed, a privileged patient who first-names his or her physician, one cannot help feeling, in many such instances, that this is a way of affirming special status.

There are two reasons for the consistency in addressing medical doctors. One is the high respect they have in our country. Their position is virtually exalted. Despite backbiting at the profession in recent years, medicine is still a highly respected endeavor. The second reason for always calling a doctor *Doctor* may be for control. Doctors have to be, or feel they have to be, obeyed. They are in authority, in charge. Those whom we first-name, with whom we have casual relationships, are our peers. We do not obey them, as a rule. They may suggest, not order. We may argue back. However, it is difficult to argue much with those who are always above us, always at a distance, by virtue of the title *Doctor*.

Interestingly, the address *Doctor* can be used alone without a last name, and still be respectful. This is not so true of *Mr.* or *Miss*. If those titles are used without last names, they become very impersonal as in

14. Hey, Miss, your lights are on.
15. Hey, Mister, you dropped your wallet.

or even rude, as in

16. Where do you think you're going, Mister?

But the title *Doctor* retains its respectability with or without a last name. Oddly enough, doctors who do not have M.D.s are properly addressed only by [*Dr.* + last name]. The exalted *Doctor* alone is denied them. Whenever he goes out, one Ph.D. of my acquaintance tapes a notice on his office door that says "The Doctor is not in." The humor lies in the fact that *doctor* without a last name refers to a medical doctor, not a Ph.D.

Other titles that can or must be used without last names are *Father, Sister, Rabbi, Reverend, Your Eminence,* and *Your Honor*. These denote the religious or judges, who by definition in our society are morally better and certainly above the rest of us. The most respectful terms, *Your Eminence* and *Your Honor* cannot be used with last names at all. It is as if their position takes precedence over their individuality. We barely dare to breathe their names. In monarchies *Your Highness* is used this way. In line with our own country's political base, our leader is called *Mr. President,* a title that combines the everyman's *Mr.* with the respected *President,* and, like *Your Honor* or *Your Highness* is not used with a last name.

One good way to keep someone in an inferior position is to insist on being addressed with a title, but to address him or her by first name alone. This is the typical situation that children find themselves in both at home and school. This sort of inequality of address was a major complaint of Blacks in many areas of the South in the past. One ex-resident of Louisiana commented to me, "She called me Mamie, and I had to call her 'Mrs. Whitmore'."

In some schools or businesses, inferiority is underscored by last-naming alone. Superiors receive [title + last name], but inferiors are called by their last names alone. If novels and mystery stories are to be believed, in England servants were often last-named without titles, as were students. As late as the 1950s, in the staid New England high school I went to, boys were last-named alone, but girls were [*Miss* + last name]. In some schools or social circles today, mutual last-naming by peers is a sign of intimacy or affection.

It is quite usual in many societies to find the same address forms being used both to keep inferiors in their place and as a sign of intimacy. Those who have studied European languages may recall that the intimate form of *you* is also the one used to definite inferiors. In French, for instance, one says "I love you" using the *tu* form for *you,* as in "je t'aime," but to *tutoyer* someone (use *tu* to him or her) without permission is an insult. The same situation used to occur in English before the old *thou* form died out. In Shakespeare, one notices an alternation between *thou/thee* and *you* often to the same person and from the same person, with the *thou/thee* co-occurring with insults and the *you* with more ordinary speech. Of course, as today, *thou* was also used for special intimacy, as to God. Formality implies social distance. Both intimacy and insulting imply little social distance.

Some address practices are confined to certain regions or social classes. Southerners and Midwesterners who carefully append "Ma'am" or "Sir" at the end of statements are likely to be considered "smart alecs" in the Northeast. These forms are often used sarcastically there, as when someone has been too familiar. If another wishes to hold him or her at bay, the forms "Excuse me, Sir" or "Look, Ma'am", will be chosen. There is no honor at all in such a *Sir* or *Ma'am.*

[Title + first name] seems to be localized to the South, as in "Miss Lillian." It has the interesting effect of showing respect by the title, but intimacy by the first name.

Special nicknames are often used among close friends or members of teams. Nicknames are signs of intimacy. On athletic teams, where special bonds have to be forged between players, nicknaming seems to help. One is reminded of the German and French mountain climbers who, after they reach a certain height start to use the intimate *du* and *tu,* respectively, but, on their way down, revert to the usual *Sie* or *vous* (polite words for *you* in German and French).

Many names have recognized nicknames that are used as a matter of course, with the given name virtually never being used. If it is, something is unusual. It is the rare William who is not *Bill* or *Will(ie). Robert* is about always *Bob(by). Charles,* willing or not, turns into *Charlie,* and *James* becomes *Jim. Daniel,* of course, must be *Dan(ny)*, and *Patrick, Pat*. There seem to be fewer such names for females, names that are automatically nicknamed, but still, *Patricias* turn into *Pats, Katherines* by any spelling become *Kathy*. To be sure, an occasional recipient of such a name insists on the full form, and, even more occasionally, manages to get it. A *Deborah* may valiantly fight being called *Debbie,* and a *Charles* can wage a lifelong battle against *Charlie*. Still, for the most part, with such names, the long form is reserved for signatures, reprimands from parents, and, perhaps, address from rather old-fashioned teachers. The social conventions for such names clearly win out over individual preference.

One exception among some college students occurs when females call their boyfriends "William," "Robert," "James," or the like. This is considered a sign of special intimacy, almost as good as an engagement ring.

3.22   *First-naming*

Recently in America there has been a strong trend toward first-naming as many people as possible as soon as possible. People who never would have dreamed of calling each other by their given names twenty-five years ago regularly do so today. Certainly in most parts of the country, neighbors, if they speak at all, use first names, unless perhaps there is a great age difference or one is a medical doctor. One practice that disconcerts many East Coast over-thirties is to have physicians' receptionists call out patients' first names, rather than using [title + last name]. The trend toward students' addressing teachers with first names is another facet of this general lessening of social distance.

Use of address mirrors social reality. This was illustrated in Dr. Poussaint's experience with the Southern policeman. It is seen in the special titles our society accords those who perform honored functions. The trend toward first-naming also reflects the social scene today, with its general aura of casualness. To some degree, the casualness in social relations and social behavior can be seen as an extension of the youth culture. The young are traditionally less stiff and formal than their elders, and even old people try to act young nowadays. First-naming, casual attire, casual dining, and casual entertaining are all of a piece.

It seems to me that there is another possible reason for the trend toward easy first-naming: the fact that we have become a mobile population. In the old days when people lived in the same neighborhoods for most of their lives, as did their neighbors, the progression from formal to casual, if it occurred at all, often did so slowly. After all, casual address goes with friendship. If neighbors are likely to be stuck with each other for life, they have to be careful to whom they extend the privileges of friendship. Also, in the days when people were occupied with large families, unto distant cousins, and work weeks were far longer than today, many did not have much time for a large circle of friends. In modern transient neighborhoods, if people waited a long time to become friendly, many would never make any friends at all. With the breakdown of the extended family, that would leave many mighty lonely. Easy first-naming seems to me to be a response to the need to replace the family with other networks of relationships. It is apparently furthered by the circumstance that the ways of youth are the reference point for much of society. Tradition, with its respect for old ways, formality, and titles, belongs to the aged, and they no longer set the pace for society.

Who uses certain address forms is as revealing as which ones are used. For instance, Black street youth address each other as "man," with or without greetings like "Wha's happ'nin'?" In recent years, White youths from middle class to street kids have adopted this address form. In the 1930s and 1940s, Black speech was not often adopted by Whites. Indeed, speech considered characteristic of Blacks was not even adopted by all Northern Blacks; three Black female consultants remarked to me that the young Blacks in Rhode Island have sounded like "Southerners" only since the late 1960s. These consultants, like many Black Rhode Islanders forty and over, speak indistinguishably from White Rhode Islanders. Thus, it is not only the White youth who are sounding more Black; so are the Black. William Labov (1964) claims that Blacks have become the point of reference for young white males, epitomizing sexuality, athletic prowess, and toughness, all aspects of the "naturalness" that is in favor today.

3.23 *Summons*

Every interaction has to have a formal beginning. This is an indication that the hearer is supposed to start decoding a linguistic message. At large gatherings or in public places we hear talking all around us, but it is only a jumble of sound. Then suddenly amid the babble a name or key word penetrates our consciousness, and we find ourselves hearing what one voice out of the many is saying. People usually tune out conversation not relevant to them, even when conditions are fine for hearing. One of the reasons that Robert Altman films like the original *M.A.S.H., McCabe and Mrs. Miller,* and *Nashville* are so confusing at the first viewing is that, in an attempt to simulate actual social situations, he has several people talking at once, often carrying on several conversations. In many scenes, for the first few seconds, the viewer is given no clue as to which conversation to focus on. In actual social situations, we typically zero in on one and ignore the rest.

One sure way for a conversation to become relevant is for someone to give a summons or greeting. The summons grabs one's attention. This need not include names. A simple "Uh" or "Excuse me" can function as a summons. A summons is the verbal equivalent of catching someone's eye. No conversation can proceed without one or the other.

Summons typically is followed by a conversation: a request or imparting of information. Catching someone's eye may be followed only by a greeting with no other conversation. The fact of summoning, but not of greeting, implies that more is to come.

A summons may take many forms: *Uh, Excuse me, Waiter,* Joe, Dr. Dreidel. The last two are also address forms. If these precede a greeting, they function as summons, although there is overlap. A few greetings may also function as summons, notably the shorter, more informal ones, such as Hi! or Hey!. Pitch and intonation distinguish between the summons *Hi* and *Hey* and the greeting version. In English, pitch and intonation distinguish between meanings of a word only in such stylistic variants, more proof that style is a communication system in itself, subject to its own rules.

3.24   *Encounters with strangers*

If a stranger is summoned, polite forms, those that signal that social distance is to be kept, are used. An example is the common, "Excuse me, Sir. Could you please tell me the time?"

If a person approaches a stranger and asks "What time is it?" without at least an "Uh" or "Excuse me" to act as summons, the person spoken to usually ignores the question. If the asker persists, the stranger may turn, saying, "Were you talking to me?" or its equivalent. This occurs even if the two involved are the only two present, as at a bus stop or waiting for an elevator. "Were you talking to me?" is not a request for information. It is really a repair meaning 'You are not using the correct form to start a conversation.' This is generally invoked for any inappropriate approach, as when males come on too strong to females. A "Sir" attached to the question has the added effect of 'Keep your distance.'

The use of formal distancing style to strangers is an indication that, although a request must be made, there is no intention of intruding on the person's privacy. The request is not to be construed as a bid for friendship. If, being bored or whatever, one of the parties does wish to continue a conversation, polite forms are still used until it is evident that both wish to talk further. If the person approached does not want to converse, he or she need only answer briefly and turn away. Notice that this option is open only after the original summons and request are answered.

People feel compelled to answer a summons. If someone does not, we assume that something is wrong. Moreover, despite the fact that it is a stranger ignoring a summons, the one who gives it feels hurt and even angry, as if receiving a slight. Indeed, one has, considering the social rules that decree that people are supposed to answer appropriate summonses for appropriate purposes. In our society queries to strangers about time or location are proper if preceded by a summons using polite forms. Their obligatory nature can be seen by the declaration, "I wouldn't give him/her the time of day." Since we are obliged to give that much to anyone who asks for it, provided that they have used the correct style, the declaration is tantamount to saying 'He/she is beneath my notice as a human being.'

If a casual, informal style, normal between persons who are acquainted, is used as a summons to a stranger, the recipient is under no obligation to answer. "Hi, there. Know the time?" can sound fresh and rude. If a male says that to a female and she answers, he may well assume that she is willing to give more than the time. If a female uses a casual, informal style to summon a male, he is likely to assume that it is a sexual invitation. Even if a same sex stranger asks it, the other party need not answer. Not allowing the casual style at the outset of interactions with strangers protects our privacy. It ensures that we need not spend our emotions and time with every stranger who comes down the pike. At the same time it ensures that strangers can get necessary information such as time or directions. This is another example of how crucial style is to social interaction. It also illustrates the rigid conventions that govern even trivial interactions, as well as the social reasons for those conventions.

EXERCISES

1. Find two examples of stylistic variants in any social situation(s) of your choice. Write each down, along with the context that elicited it, the status of both speaker and listeners, and the message conveyed. Explain why you think these are stylistic variants, not part of the linguistic system itself.

2. Jot down the address forms that you give and receive in any locale of your choice: work, school, home, party, or the like. Do not work from memory. From these forms can you make any judgments about the social structure of the community or locale you observed?

3. If you know someone who seems to speak more loudly or softly than others, observe that person closely. Is your sense of loudness or softness caused by an actual difference in amplitude or by differences in the number of times the person interrupts or the rapidity with which the person responds to slight pauses in another's speech?

4. Try to violate co-occurrence restrictions in greetings and address with people you know well. How do they respond? Do they attempt repairs, and, if so, how?

5. Find one example of the use of a particular register in your speech. Correlate it with the social situations that require its use.

chapter 4

KINESICS

Facial expressions, posture, and gesture, all part of body motion, more formally known as *kinesics*, form yet another component to the human communication system. Style and kinesics together are called *paralanguage*. Some kinesic messages seem to be much the same for all human beings. Others vary from culture to culture. Along with style, kinesics, which includes the way we space ourselves or direct our eyes, controls social interactions. Moreover, how we are perceived by others is strongly influenced by the way we handle our paralinguistic system.

4.1 The silent messages

Communication is not by voice alone. It is by posture, gesture, and facial expression, even how we space ourselves relative to others. As with the vocal cues such as pitch and timbre that give purely social and emotional information, body movement is difficult to describe and analyze because we respond to it subconsciously. We are often not even aware of what we are responding to (Hall 1959). Frequently, if we are miscued or feel something is wrong, we simply feel uncomfortable without quite knowing why. As with style, this can be a basis for discomfort when interacting with people from cultures different from our own. It may also cause us, in all innocence, to ascribe the wrong characteristics to those whose "silent language," to use Hall's term, differs from ours.

Kinesics refers to matters of body movement, posture, gesture, facial expression, eye gaze and physical placement between parties in an interaction. Along with those elements of style like pitch, timbre, and loudness, it constitutes the **paralinguistic system** that operates with the linguistic system proper (*linguistic* referring to phonemes, morphemes, words, and syntax, as discussed in Chapter 1).

4.2 Nature or nurture

Like language itself, kinesics seems to be both inborn and culturally determined. There seem to be certain facial expressions, gestures, and body motions that generally mean the same thing in all cultures. There are other kinesic messages, perhaps most, that have specific meanings to particular cultures. Even if they are seen in more than one culture, they will mean different things in each.

Charles Darwin (1965) felt that human expressive movements are the vestige of biologically useful movements that later became innately linked to emotional experience. A pushing away movement of the hand accompanying a negative response, for example, may be viewed as the vestige of actually pushing away a danger.

Darwin and later ethologists like Lorenz and Goodall noted the similarities of expression between man and other animals. One example is the brief raising of the eyebrows to indicate recognition. This has been observed in wolves and apes as well as man. In many human cultures, this has extended its meaning to indicate sexual desire or invitation. Old movie buffs will recall that male and female movie stars in the 1920s and 1930s had the entire area from eyebrow to eyelid painted to emphasize looks of sexual invitation. Groucho Marx's exaggerated eyebrow lifts were a parody of this sexual message. With or without paint, raising of the eyebrows is used for flirting in many cultures. It also commonly occurs to indicate surprise or agreement with ideas. The Polynesians carry it one step further, using an eyebrow lift alone to mean 'yes' (Eibl-Eiblesfeldt 1972). Universally, all eyebrow liftings mean 'yes' to social contact, sexual or not.

Raised eyebrows signal to another person that he or she is being looked at. In our own culture, the idiom "looking at him/her/them with raised eyebrows" means that someone disapproves of a particular behavior. *Raised eyebrows*, in this instance, refers to staring, as the idiom implies that the eyebrows remain raised for more than the split second necessary to signal recognition or invitation. Like so many other idioms, this one reflects our virtually subconscious knowledge of what is going on in ordinary interactions. Although raised eyebrows universally signal that someone is being looked at, still the degree of raising, the duration of raising, whether it is with or without eye widening may all be manipulated to give different messages within cultures and cross culturally.

4.3   *Two cases in point*

Ekman and Frisen (1976), comparing the Fore tribesmen in New Guinea with American college students, found great similarity in signaling specific emotions by facial expression. Their result argues that nature more than nurture governs facial expressions.

The Fore selected for the study had had virtually no contact with Europeans or Americans. The experimental protocol was simple yet ingenious. The Fore were told simple narratives, such as "His/her friends have come, and he/she is happy." The subjects had to point to a photograph of a face that illustrated this emotion. Experimenters were careful to avert their faces from the subjects' view so that they would not inadvertently influence the results by making the appropriate face themselves. Later, the investigators showed pictures of the Fore tribesmen to American college students, and asked them to identify the facial expressions as happy, sad, disgusted, surprised or fearful. The two groups, the Fore and the Americans, agreed in their judgments. Because people could identify emotions on the faces of people from other cultures, Ekman and Frisen concluded that specific facial expressions are associated with particular emotions for all human beings.

Eibl-Eiblesfeldt (1972) offers even more conclusive evidence for the same position. He noted that three deaf and blind children with no hands smiled, sulked, laughed, and showed surprise and anger with expressions like those of children who can see. He also observed blind children with hands, but critics were quick to point out that such children could have learned normal facial expressions by touching faces making different expressions.

4.4   There are smiles, and then there are smiles

Although the basic human repertoire for facial expression may be the same, there is plenty of evidence showing that each culture modifies that repertoire. Smiles provide us with a good example. All human beings smile, but there are many kinds of smiles. Each culture smiles in somewhat different ways for somewhat different purposes. Even within a culture, there are many smiles. In the United States, for instance, there are friendly smiles, wide grins, sly smiles, skeptical smiles, derisive, threatening, and sick ones. Some cultures demand a wide smile, teeth showing, upon greeting. Others find this too forward, greeting people with close-mouthed or only narrowly open-lipped smiles. Others greet each other deadpan. Some smile when scolded or asking a favor. Others do not.

The situations that call for smiles and for each type of smile seem to be culturally determined. In a multicultural society this can cause misunderstanding. Persons who do not smile enough for one group are pegged as cold and unfeeling. Frequent smilers, or those whose smiles are broader than other groups, strike nonsmilers as being phony or stupid. One of the most often quoted examples of cultural misunderstanding because of differences in smiling habits is that of Japanese–American children. In Japanese culture, children smile when they are being scolded as a sign of respect to their elders. If their teachers are not aware of this, they assume that the children are being rude. LaBarre (1947) mentions the Japanese custom of smiling even at the death of a beloved. This is not because of any hardheartedness. Rather, the bereaved smiles so as not to inflict his or her sorrow upon others.

Birdwhistell (1970) counted the frequency of smiling in different regions of the United States. He found that people in Ohio, Indiana, and Illinois smiled more often than those in Massachusetts, New Hampshire, and Maine. Western New Yorkers smiled less than New Englanders. People smiled the most in Atlanta, Georgia, and both Memphis and Nashville, Tennessee. Those from the Appalachian areas of those states smiled much less.

4.5   *Kinesics and culture*

Studies of kinesics and culture usually confine themselves to culture specific gestures. That is, they are concerned with the way a given message is expressed in the kinesics of a given culture. Many, if not all, human groups often express 'yes' and 'no' kinesically, although not necessarily with the nodding and head-shaking that we associate with positive and negative. Examining the signs for 'yes' and 'no' is a study in how varied kinesics can be in different cultures, although there are some widespread similarities. For instance, we have already seen that eyebrow raising is universally a 'yes' to social interaction. The Dyaks of Borneo raise their eyebrows to mean 'yes' and contract them—frown—to mean 'no'. Actually, so do Americans under certain circumstances, as when surreptitiously trying to 'throw' a message to someone. The contracting eyebrows, or frown, is often accompanied by a slight shaking of the head to mean 'no'. This head shake is very common among both humans and animals. Darwin related it to the baby's refusal to nurse when it is full. Eibl-Eiblesfeldt found it in deaf-blind children. He feels it stems from the way animals and birds shake themselves.

Still, there are many culture-specific ways to say 'no'. The Abyssinians jerk their heads to the right shoulder, in a sort of modified head shake. They indicate 'yes' by throwing the head back and raising the eyebrows. This is a neat combination of a culture-specific motion with the apparently universal eyebrow lifting motion. Just how different cultures may be can be seen in the Maori 'yes' and the Sicilian 'no'. The two cultures use the identical motion, but for the opposite meaning: they raise their chins, tilting the head back (LaBarre 1947).

Even a transparent gesture such as pointing with the finger to indicate location is not universal. The Kiowa Indians point with the lips. Sherzer (1973) found that the Cuna Indians of San Blas, Panama use lip pointing to indicate direction, to acknowledge a joke, especially one mocking one party to the interaction, or as a greeting between people who have a joking relation. Interestingly, Americans, although pointing with fingers, not lips, can also use a pointing gesture in the same ways that the Cuna do.

4.6   *Kinesics caused by culture*

Efron (1972) attempted to relate differences between kinesic systems to cultural facts. He studied Jews and Italians in New York City in the 1920s at the end of the great waves of immigration. On the one hand, he found that Eastern European Jews who had been persecuted for centuries had confined gestures with elbows close to their sides. They walked with a shuffle and stood hunched with rounded shoulders. Their entire appearance was apologetic, timid, depressed.

Italians, on the other hand, moved the whole arm widely, expansively. Efron felt that the Italians' feelings of personal freedom are expressed in their arm movements, as the Jewish feelings of repression and inhibition are in theirs. Studying first generation Americans as well as immigrants, Efron found that persons who retained ethnic loyalty retained their group's gestures, but the assimilated adopted more American gestures.

Birdwhistell (1970) found that the body motions of a bi- or trilingual speaker change according to the particular language being spoken. He claimed that if the sound is turned off in movies of the late Fiorello LaGuardia, the famous mayor of New York City, one can tell if he was speaking Italian, Yiddish, or English just by his gestures.

4.7   *Signaling sickness*

Birdwhistell (1970) offers a neat description of the complexity of kinesic signaling. It also demonstrates that certain behavior one might assume to be inborn is actually learned. Birdwhistell compared cues for signaling that one is sick in two Tennessee communities situated only fifteen miles apart.

Dry Ridge is an example of Tennessee hill culture, and Green Valley, of Tennessee bluegrass culture. In neither community is it permissible for someone to announce in words that he or she is sick until someone else brings up the matter. This seems to be a common American ban. Giving in to illness seems to be construed as weakness of character in our culture. Discussing one's ill health unless first asked about it, other than in initial greeting, is taken as complaining. This is not necessarily true in all cultures. People in some cultures actively enjoy their aches and pains as part of regular social interaction (Frake, 1961). For them illness is an acceptable and enjoyable topic of conversation.

In Dry Ridge the stiff-upper-lip syndrome is practiced. Ideally one is forced to go to a doctor, go to bed, or take medicine. Although it would be considered weak of Dry Ridgers to say they were sick, their kinesics say so very well. Illness is shown by the following actions:

- The scalp is retracted.
- The forehead is tightened.
- Stance is hypererect.
- Hand and arm movements are slowed.
- Motions become overprecise.
- Both feet are placed on the floor while standing or sitting

If none of this is noticed, it is permissible to sag for two to five seconds, followed by pulling together. Men may sag and pull together no more than once in fifteen minutes, but women can do it every five, as can the very old. Birdwhistell, who observed this community for over one year, also noted that the ill health movements are very like those for anger in Dry Ridge, differing mainly in eye focus. Anger calls for avoiding another's eyes altogether, but sickness calls for looking at someone, then looking away.

In Green Valley, ill health is enjoyed more. Residents love to discuss their symptoms, and compare them. Even here, however—after all it is still in America—someone else first has to notice illness before the sick person is permitted to mention it. In Green Valley, to show illness:

- The eyebrows are squeezed together.
- Lids sag, as do upper cheeks.
- Lips fill.
- Lower lip falls slightly away from teeth.
- Neck is lax and forward.
- Upper torso sags back, as do shoulders.
- Belly is forward.
- Arms and hands hang.
- Feet drag while walking.

As soon as someone notices, the ill person's body becomes erect, and he or she presents a verbal recital of symptoms accompanied by pointing and touching the involved body parts. Birdwhistell says that in this culture even persons who are apparently quite ill according to a doctor's diagnosis become quite animated during such conversations. Such animation, however, is interrupted intermittently by sagging and recovery like that the Dry Ridger uses for first announcement of illness. One wonders what happens when a Dry Ridger marries a Green Valleyite!

4.8   *Eye contact*

Very rarely can interaction begin until eye contact is made. When a person is summoned by another, it is not sufficient to answer verbally. One must turn his or her head toward the summoner. Then the interaction can begin. Once eye contact is made, one is compelled to respond. This is why waitresses as they rush about simply will not look at patrons. That way, they are not compelled to take any more orders. Once they allow eye contact, they might feel that they have to stop and listen, even at another waitress's table.

Anger is frequently signaled by refusal to make eye contact. Such refusal means 'no' to social interaction. We have all known the discomfort of waiting for elevators with strangers. Where to put one's eyes? If we inadvertently make eye contact with strangers, either we quickly look away, embarrassed, or we are compelled to engage in chitchat. That is how strong a signal eye contact is for beginning social interaction.

During a conversation, eye contact is never steady. Steady gaze is staring. In most if not all cultures, staring is impolite. Perhaps this is because, even in other species, in creatures as lowly as chickens and turkeys (Sommer 1965), staring is both threatening and cowing. If dominant birds, for instance, stare at lower ranking ones, the latter look away submissively. Staring in human beings can also be a sign of dominance and may be taken to mean haughtiness. Only a dominant person can "stare another down." Many a teacher knows how often a class can be quelled simply by staring. Staring also implies that the one stared at is outside the pale of society. One deserves staring if one's behavior is out of normal bounds or if one is some sort of freak to society. That is another reason that staring is rude: it implies that the one stared at deserves it, and only outcasts are believed to deserve it.

During conversation regular fluctuations of eye contact are followed by looking away. The length of time eye contact is held and the number of times it is made during a conversation depends partly on the topic of conversation. Within cultures there may be differences in eye gaze between the sexes, different age groups, and those whose status differs on other parameters.

Culture determines both the frequency and length of eye contact. This can cause severe cross-cultural discomfort. Those who are used to little eye contact feel that those who habitually engage in more eye contact are staring. This is a common complaint about "Anglos" by members of some American Indian tribes. Conversely those who are used to more eye contact feel that those who give less are not paying attention.

As with the features of style, deviation from the conversational norm connotes a special message. For example, in American culture, sexual attraction is signaled by two people looking into each other's eyes. Flirting in this culture is carried out by prolonging eye contact.

4.9   *Proxemics*

In order to carry on ordinary conversation, people have to learn the correct patterns for their society. They also have to learn how near or far to stand from those with whom they are conversing. Normal distance between speakers varies from culture to culture and between subcultures of the same society (Hall 1959).

In the United States, speakers normally stand eighteen to twenty inches apart. This is the closest distance for comfort. However, Latin Americans and Middle Easterners stand closer. If someone stands too far away for a given culture, it is virtually impossible for others in the culture to continue a conversation with that person. In fact, one good way to signal the end of a conversation is to walk backward slowly, even while maintaining eye contact. As one crosses the invisible line, the boundary of conversational distance, the speaker will suddenly stop, even in midsentence, saying the equivalent of "Oh— see ya."

Cross culturally, since the distance considered normal varies, those who are used to a closer distance will keep moving closer if they are conversing with one used to a greater gap. The latter will keep stepping backward, and so it goes. Once, entangled in just such an uncomfortable conversation, I realized that I was dancing around my office, with my co-conversationalist in hot pursuit. What made it even more uncomfortable was that I am only four feet eleven and the student is over six feet tall. To minimize the distance between us, as he was explaining his problem, he also kept leaning down toward me. The effect must have been that of a question mark chasing its dot. In any event, there seemed no way for him to talk over my normal distance. As he kept violating it, my feeling of being closed in was almost palpable.

The extreme discomfort caused by someone's moving in too close was well illustrated when one of my students did so experimentally. She placed her tray adjacent to a casual acquaintance's in the cafeteria. Returning from getting some drinks, she found her tray had been pushed across the table. She pushed it back, and sat next to the hapless acquaintance. The victim sat fiddling with her napkin, not contributing much to the conversation. When the experimenter moved even closer, the subject moved away, and finally asked, "What's your problem?"

Repeating this procedure in a student lounge, the experimenter kept moving in too close to a boy eating a grinder (hero or submarine sandwich). He abruptly picked himself up, leaving about three-quarters of it. Before his hasty departure he signaled discomfort by looking tense, speaking abnormally little, and nervously jabbing at the ice in his glass.

Yet a third subject, approached while sitting in a library carrel, finally laid her head down and said, "I really can't help you anymore. I'm so tired from studying." By hiding her eyes, she effectively closed off all interaction.

Perhaps the most original repair tactic was displayed by a girl chewing bubblegum. When the experimenter started walking out of class far too closely by her side, the gum chewer proceeded to blow a huge bubble. This forced the experimenter to move aside before the bubble burst in her face. As with style, it is rare for violations of proximity to be commented on overtly. Rather, people try other adjustments to force a proper distance to be maintained.

The delicacy with which we must observe the "rules" of distance in conversations should underscore for the reader how intricate our socialization into a society actually is. It is not surprising that an occasional person might not get all the "rules" down pat so that he or she frequently seems to "crowd" others. What is surprising is that so few ever move in too close or stand too far away.

4.10   *Eye gaze, kinesics, and conversation*

Scheflen (1964) presented an excellent example of the way in which eye gaze and posture work together in an interaction. His particular example came from psychiatric interviews. Scheflen found that in such interviews posture changes in predictable ways every few sentences. The position of the head and eyes especially corresponds with the points being made. Scheflen observed three to five posture changes in each session. While listening to the patient, the doctor's head would be slightly down, cocked to the right, the eyes averted. This position coincided with Point 1, the first point being made in the interview. At the termination of Point 1, the doctor's head would go up. Interpretation of what the patient had said, Point 2, was signaled by an erect head, looking directly at the patient. It is interesting to note that in the psychiatric situation, rules for eye gaze seem to differ from those in normal interaction, in which speakers gaze away when they have a lot to say, looking back only near the end of their speeches. This difference may be related to the power structure of psychiatric discussion. The dominant person has the right to look at the submissive one. In the interviews Scheflen describes, the doctor is in charge, telling the patients how to interpret their own words. The psychiatrist has the right to speak without interruption, whereas in normal interaction between peers, each has the same right to speak. Teachers and parents who are also in authority often look directly at those to whom they are explaining something or whom they are reprimanding.

Head position and eye gaze serve both to regulate interaction and to underscore the purpose of actual words. The interpreting posture and direct eye contact in the psychiatric interview alone give the message 'These words are interpretive or explanatory of what you just said.' In teaching or punishing situations, the direct eye gaze at the recipient says, in effect, 'Pay attention. I am the dominant party in this interaction.' Most of us at some time or other in our childhoood have had an adult reprimand "Look at me when I talk to you" as the start of a complaint about our actions.

Like style, eye gaze and head position must be correct for interaction to continue smoothly. We are all familiar with the discomfort caused by the person who persists in looking down or away as we attempt to talk with him or her. As parents know, young children have to be taught to look at someone who is talking to them or to whom they themselves are talking. Two-year-olds, for instance, often look down at their toys while talking to parents or when they are spoken to.

4.11   *Controlling turns*

In order for social interaction to proceed, there is some kind of speech exchange system in all societies. The rule may simply be that the person who has the floor has it until he or she wishes to give it up. Other societies regulate turn-taking more overtly. For instance, in American and much European society, there are signals that one person wishes to talk or to continue to talk. There are also signals that others should be listening, or be getting ready to talk themselves.

Kinesics plays a large part in controlling turns. There are speaker-distinctive movements, such as head bobbing in rhythm with speech and gesturing to punctuate speech. By stopping such movements, a person signals that he or she is giving up the floor.

In general, listeners look at speakers more than speakers look at listeners. When a speaker gets ready to let another take over, he or she will look at that person. Before long utterances speakers look away until nearing the end. Looking away prevents the listener from breaking in. Looking at the other person invites that person to speak. If someone actually stops talking, someone else rushes in to fill the silence.

Conversations are regulated differently from culture to culture, so much so that, often, outsiders do not catch the cues. The Warm Springs Indians in Oregon (Philips 1976), for example, use much less body motion, shifting of body, and moving of head than most other Americans to indicate the course of an utterance. Rather, they rely more on movement of the eyes and eyebrows: widening, lifting, and narrowing. They themselves refer to the eyes most when describing emotions. For instance, "They were snapping eyes" means 'They were very angry.'

Lips are not moved much in this culture, at least by non-Indian American standards. Arm and hand movements are also more confined than for most Anglo groups. These Indians make much less eye contact, and complain that Anglos stare too much, even when Anglo observers verify that the Anglos were just glancing. One man's glance is another man's stare.

In an Anglo group, those addressed behave differently from others in the group. This does not seem to be so among the Warm Springs Indians, however. Speakers do not align their bodies toward anyone in particular. Non-Indian observers get the feeling that speakers are talking in general to the entire group because no one in particular aligns himself or herself with the speaker. In the interactions between other Americans, aligning motions are prime determinants in who will take the next turn. In classrooms, for instance, often the student who aligns his or her body motions to the teacher is the one who gets called on.

The Anglo kinesics that control conversation have a counterpart in utterance pairs (Chapter 5). For instance, if a question is asked, it must receive an answer, even if that answer is "I don't know." The Warm Springs Indian does not have such rigid rules for responding. One asks a question but may not receive an answer for hours or even days. Similarly, in much American culture, if one receives an oral invitation, one must give some sort of answer right away. If a Warm Springs Indian gets one, he or she need not respond at all.

Susan Philips (1976) who sat in on meetings at the reservation, shows that Warm Springs Indian interactions seem vague and unstructured to outsiders, so much so that they get the feeling that nothing is being responded to at all. At the reservation, if an issue is raised, or an accusation made, the next speakers do not necessarily even mention it. If someone does bother to comment, he or she may do so almost as an afterthought.

Philips gives the example of a woman who complained, "[A tribal member] goes to Washington too often." After eight others spoke, the apparent accused got up, read a fifteen-minute report, then entered into a discussion on the report. During this discussion the accused said, "I can account for all of my trips to Washington." During the entire meeting, Philips notes, no one spoke directly to anyone, and no one ever asked for any response to any statement. Nobody interrupted, and there were no visible kinesic clues that someone was no longer listening or wanted to talk as there are in Anglo conversations. Philips feels that the Indians control when they speak. They are not "forced" into it as Anglos are by having to respond in utterance pairs. Also, since nobody interrupts, the Indians control the length of their own turns. Actually, Anglos exercise a good deal of control over when they speak and for how long. They just do it differently. The Indians' control over their turns is not necessarily greater than other Americans'. If someone is not free to interrupt or to give kinesic signals that he or she wishes to speak, then that is a very great restriction. One is not controlling when and for how long one may speak if one has no way to make the other guy give up the floor. Besides, Anglos have some measure of control over giving up the floor. They just do not look at their hearers until they are ready to.

4.12   *When to speak*

It is not only kinesic cues and utterance pairs that determine whether or not someone will speak. The occasion itself is just as important in determining who will speak. There are times when it is all right to speak and times when it is not. In a great cathedral if a worshipper disagrees, or even agrees, with the homily, he or she does not stand up and comment to the preacher. In an English chapel, a fundamentalist Baptist, or a Black American congregation, one might call out asssent, but never criticism. In an Orthodox Jewish congregation, however, if one of the men reading from the Bible in Hebrew makes an error, the congregation may call out the correction. This is in line with the fact that, in Judaism, the rabbi has no special powers and members of the congregation can and do participate in every aspect of the service. The congregation is not in a subservient position, and every man in it has a thorough enough religious background to officiate at services.

Philips (1970) showed that Warms Springs Indians do not feel free to speak up in school because they are not socialized into the kinds of responses that other Americans are. The Warms Springs Indians feel that to make mistakes publicly is very humiliating. When tribespeople have to learn something, they observe it until they think they know it. When they are ready, they ask others to come watch a demonstration. The idea of learning by humiliation, as in European based societies, is repugnant to these Indians. The Bureau of Indian Affairs (BIA) Schools are run by those imbued with general American culture. Often, these administrators think the only conceivable way to learn is to ask public questions, demand answers, and, in essence, insist that pupils display their knowledge or their ignorance. Warm Springs Indian children are not socialized into answering any questions at all on demand, much less those that might reveal their ignorance. Rather, these children are used to practicing skills in private, then inviting others to see them display those skills when and only when they feel ready.

Steven Boggs (1972) found that Hawaiian children would not answer questions put to them directly by a teacher. They perceive such questions as threats. If the teacher asks questions of the group at large, however, pupils answer readily.

Similarly, non-middle-class Black children have not been socialized to tell adults what they, the children, know the adults already know. One researcher asked such a child where he lived. Since she had given him a ride from his house to the park where they were picnicing, he vaguely pointed 'over there'. Then her husband who had not been in the car asked the child. The boy answered with specific directions, complete with the requisite lefts and rights and numbers of streets to cross.

Researchers like Deutsch (1967) and Bereiter and Engelmann (1966) claimed that Black children were deficient in language skills. Labov (1969) showed that the methodology these researchers used to test Black language skills was guaranteed to produce defective language. Taking a Black child into a room with an adult tester, a White tester at that, then asking the child to identify something obvious like a toy car elicited silence or a scared "I don't know." The child knew that the tester knew that the toy was a car. Since any normal child of two knows what a car is, the child suspected some kind of trap. Why else would this strange adult in this strange environment be asking such a stupid question? In Black ethnic culture, children interact with peers, not one-on-one with adults. Such children are used to questioning from adults only if the child has to supply some genuine information, or, most usually, if the child has done something wrong. Adult questions are threatening, especially if the adult patently must know the answer.

Labov showed that one gets very skillful language from these same children by interviewing them in groups and setting up competition with each other. The same kind of children who mumbled and stumbled over Deutsch and Bereiter and Englemann's testing showed exceptional facility under Labov's testing situations. Oral competition is a skill these children start learning in earliest childhood.

Middle-class Black and White children are taught to tell adults all sorts of trivia, things that adults certainly know, such as "And what does the doggie say?" or "Where's your hand? And your tootsies?" This is first rate training for middle-class school teaching. But not all children receive this kind of training. In essence, many, such as the Warm Springs Indians, the ghetto Blacks, and Hawaiians do not learn the proper situations to speak in for success in dominant culture schools.

This may also explain the frequency of low scores on IQ tests by such minorities. It may not be the particular questions that are asked that are culturally biased but the testing situation itself. Ghetto Blacks, for instance, are socialized into showing off their intellectual skills in oral competition (Chapter 8) but not by sitting and marking answers with a pencil. Anthropologists testing for cognitive skills in exotic cultures among primitive tribes often fail because they do not know how to elicit information from the culture's members (Scribner 1977; Cole 1977).

4.13   *Small groups*

Bales (1955) found that people in small group interactions who speak more than average and give more than the average rate of suggestions and opinions will be judged as "having the best ideas." This is true regardless of the worth of the ideas expressed. In getting others to think one is bright, one's ideas themselves are not as important as their frequency. Furthermore, the member ranked the highest by a group addresses considerably more remarks to the group as a whole than to individuals. Lower ranking members address individuals more than the group.

Riecken (1958) went one step further than Bales. Riecken provided both high ranking and low ranking members of groups with a solution to a human relations problem that the groups were considering. Using thirty-two four-man groups, he verified Bales' finding that those who talk the most are ranked the highest. He also found that those who are ranked highest by the group got their ideas accepted. Lower ranking members who advanced the same ideas did not get them adopted. Moreover, Riecken found that the high-ranking members influenced others because of their ability to win support by talking the right way and using the right techniques of kinesics and eye contact. Neither measured IQ nor fluency in speaking seemed to be important factors in determining who could persuade.

4.14   *In sum: styling*

It can be seen that even the simplest of conversations requires a good deal of learned behavior, all fine-tuned. Whether or not one may speak at all depends upon the situation and whether one's culture allows speech in it. Not only does the content of a message have to be appropriate for the context, but the speaker has to encode his or her meaning with words and grammar that hearers can understand. Even that is not enough. The style used must be appropriate for the occasion. Then, too, the speaker must stand just the right distance away, make the right amount of eye contact, holding it just the right length of time, looking away the culturally correct amount of time. Eye contact has to be finely tuned to the requirements of turn-taking as well as topic of conversation. Heads must move to signal points as well as to signal turn-taking. Gestures must correlate with meaning and, again, with turn-taking. Although so far as we know today, all cultures have such restrictions on speaking and how it may be done, the exact rules for interaction vary from society to society.

Roger Abrahams (1974) provides a neat description of the interplay between eye contact, proxemics, and kinesics for different kinds of conversation among non-middle-class Black urban youths. As with the middle-class groups that Bales and Riecken studied, such a speaker's skill in this interplay plays a large part in how he will be evaluated by others in the group. Abrahams calls this complex of behaviors **styling.** In his description, he uses the terms from Black street talk that appear in italics in the next paragraph.

In a Black inner city neighborhood, two or more males engaged in close talk face each other maintaining eye contact. This indicates that something *deep* is going on. One is *running something down* to the other, passing on valid information, on which he is supposed to act. It might also mean that one is passing on false information, *running a game, hyping,* or *shucking.* If two are arguing or engaging in *talking smart,* they will face each other, but be farther apart and more mobile than when getting the *rundown* on something.

Casual talk is signified by looking outward. This is true even when two friends meet on the street. They will gaze away even while still shaking hands. The more other-centered the talk becomes, of the "Have you heard about so-and-so" variety, the closer the two come, and the more their bodies face each other.

Ghetto Black youths to whom casual speaking is especially important call their kinesics "walking dat walk," just as they call good talking itself "talking dat talk" (Chapter 6). A Black inner city male's *rep* ('reputation') for being hip and cool depends a great deal on correct styling, the right kinesics.

The works of Bales and Riecken show that other groups are also evaluated on the basis of what they do and how they do it as much as on what they say. Whether or not participants in an interaction are aware of the fine adjustments they are making while talking, still they have to be made. As Harumi Befu (1975) has shown, this can occur even when participants cannot see each other, as in Japanese bowing. Both the depth and timing of each bow vary with the status and degree of intimacy of participants. Furthermore, one's bows have to be synchronized with the other party's. Once a bow has begun, however, one cannot see the other. "Bowing occurs in a flash of a second, before you have time to think. And both parties must know precisely when to start bowing, how deep, how long to stay in a bowed position and when to bring their heads back up." (Goody 1978) Although American culture does not include such bowing, like all cultures its body motion, eye contact, and distance must all be exact in order for interactions to take place successfully.

EXERCISES

1. Observe kinesics of people watching television shows or movies. Include both males and females of at least two generations, such as grandparents, parents, and children of one family. Adolescents and

young children may be considered as separate groups as well. List as accurately as you can the differences in body motion, facial expressions, and eye gaze between the sexes and between age groups. Try to make your observations as unobtrusive as possible. Certainly, do not announce that you are observing, or stare overtly at anyone.

2. Describe your family's meal preparation and eating practices at one meal as if you were a sociologist describing the customs of a strange people.

3. Analyze the postures and kinesics of a student in one of your classes. Also analyze the teacher's. What kinds of interactions are going on? Who gets called on? Are their kinesics different from those who do not?

4. We usually know who is the "good guy" and who the "bad" in a movie or TV show. Examine the kinesics of two actors in very different roles in one show, to determine how they reveal or deliberately conceal the personalities of the characters they are portraying.

chapter 5

DISCOURSE ROUTINES

We control others and they control us by shared discourse routines. By saying certain things, the other party in a dialogue forces certain responses in us. Questions demand answers, and compliments elicit thanks, for instance. In order to understand these routines, one must understand the society in which they occur. Simply knowing the language is not sufficient, for the true meaning often lies not in the actual words uttered but in a complex of social knowledge. Examining such routines can help us understand the unspoken assumptions on which a society is based.

5.1   *A paradox*

Language makes us free as individuals but chains us socially. It has already been demonstrated that we are not mere creatures of conditioning when it comes to language. We can say things we never heard before, as well as understand what we have not previously heard.

When we consider discourse rules, however, we find a strange paradox. The social rules of language often force us into responding in certain ways. We are far from free in forming sentences in actual social situations. Frequently we must respond whether we want to or not. Furthermore, we must respond in certain ways (see Givon 1979; Schenkein 1979; Labov and Fanshel 1977).

5.2   *Meaning and the social situation*

The actual meaning of an utterance depends partially on the social context in which it occurs.

Rommetveit (1971) gives a classic example of this. He tells a story about a man running for political office who is scheduled to give a talk in a school auditorium. When he arrives, he sees that there are not enough chairs. He calls his wife at home. Then he goes to see the janitor. To each, the candidate says, "There aren't enough chairs." To the wife, this means 'Wow! am I popular,' but to the janitor it means 'Go get some more chairs.' The full meaning evoked by the statement "There aren't enough chairs" is largely a product of the context in which it is said, including the relative social statuses, privileges and duties of the speaker and listener. The remainder of this chapter is concerned with the obligations society places upon us in discourse, as well as the real meaning of utterances in a social context.

5.3   *Speech events, genres, and performances*

A **speech event** is the situation calling forth particular ways of speaking (Gordon and Lakoff 1975). **Genre** refers to the form of speaking. Usually, it has a label, such as *joke, narrative, promise, riddle, prayer,* even *greeting* or *farewell.*

Members of a speech community recognize genres as having beginnings, middles, and ends, and as being patterned. "Did you hear the one about . . .", for instance, is a recognized opener for the genre *joke* in our society. "Once upon a time . . ." is a recognized opener for the genre *child's story,* and the ending is "They lived happily ever after." The end of *joke* is the *punch line,* often a pun, an unusual or unexpected response to a situation or utterance, or a stupid response by one of the characters in the joke. Typically the stupid response to a situation is one that reveals that the character is lacking in some basic social knowledge or one in which the social meaning of an utterance is ignored and its literal meaning is taken instead. For instance, an old Beetle Bailey cartoon shows Sarge saying to Zero "The wastebasket is full." Instead of emptying the basket, Zero responds "Even I can see that." The joke is that Zero took the words at their face value rather than interpreting them as a command, which was their actual social force.

Sometimes the genre is the entire speech event but not always. Church services are speech events, for instance. *Sermons* are a genre belonging to church, but sermons do not cover the entire speech event. Prayers, responsive readings, hymn singing, and announcements also constitute the speech events of church services.

The way that participants carry out the demands of a genre is their **performance.** In some communities, this is more important than others. Also, performance is more important in some speech events than others. A professor's performance, for instance, is far more important than that of the students in the classroom. The exception would be those classes in which students have been assigned special speaking tasks.

Perhaps *important* is not quite the right word. The professor's performance will be judged more overtly than a student's and judged according to different criteria. These are the criteria judged in public performance, such as clarity of diction, voice quality, logic of lecture, and coherence. Correct performance in less formal speech events is just as important, but in those judgment is often confined to how appropriate the speech was to the situation. Everyday discourse routines are as much performances as are preaching, joke-telling, and lecturing.

Linguists often use the word **performance** in a more general sense than here. They use it to refer to one's actual speech, which may contain errors, such as slips of the tongue. Since people often realize that they have made speech mistakes, linguists say that there is a difference between **competence** and performance. In this chapter, performance will refer specifically to one's ability to carry out the requirements of a speech event in a given social situation. This, too, may differ from one's competence in that one can be aware of errors in one's performance of a genre. A professor may realize with a sickening thud, for example, that a prepared lecture is boring a class to sleep, or a partygoer may be unable to think of any of the small talk or repartee called for at a party.

Performances in discourse routines are strongly controlled by turn-taking rules that determine who speaks when. Co-occurrence restrictions (Chapter 3) operate stringently on genres. Often the speech event itself determines them. The genre of sermons occurs in the speech event of church services. Therefore, only features that go with formal style are usually used in sermons. Jokes, in contrast, occur in informal, play situations or as a means of helping someone relax and become more informal. Therefore, formal style features are inappropriate in jokes, so that they are included usually only in the reported conversation of a character in the joke.

5.4   Intention

In all interaction, the parties assume that each person means what he or she says and is speaking with a purpose. Esther Goody (1978) points out that people impute intentions to others. In fact, she notes, they "positively seek out intentions in what others say and do." What people assume is another's intention colors the meaning they get from messages. How often has someone suspiciously said to a perfectly innocent comment of yours, "Now what did you mean by that?" The question is not asking for literal meaning but for your intention in saying what you did. Presequences rely heavily on our perceiving a speaker's intentions or thinking we do. The child who hears an adult's "Who spilled this milk?" may rightly perceive the question as the precursor to a command "Wipe it up!"

Often, intentions are not perceived correctly, causing misunderstandings as harmless as hearing an honest question as a command or as serious as hearing an innocent comment as an insult. To illustrate the last, consider a man who, in front of his slightly plump wife, looks admiringly at a model, "Wow! what a body on that one!" The wife immediately bridles (or dissolves in tears, depending on her personal style) with a "I know I'm too fat. You don't have to rub it in."

The only time that we are freed from the obligation to carry out the socially prescribed roles in speech events is when the other party is incapable of acting with a purpose, as when drunk, stoned, or insane (Frake 1964). Perhaps one of the reasons that we get so angry when someone does not act or speak appropriately for the situation is that we can not figure out his or her goals. Without knowing someone's goals, we do not know how to act ourselves when dealing with another person.

5.5   Speech acts

People usually think of speech as a way of stating propositions and conveying information. Austin (1962) also stressed the functions of speech as a way of "doing things with words." Sociolinguists and anthropologists have been very concerned with how people use language to manage social interactions. Threatening, complimenting ("buttering someone up"), commanding, even questioning can all be manipulative. Another person's behavior may be affected quite differently from what one might expect from the actual words used. "See that belt?" may be sufficient to restrain a child from wrongdoing. The words themselves are an action. The child, of course, imputes intention to the words. They are heard as a threat of a spanking with the belt.

5.6   *A case in point: the telephone*

The ritual nature of conversation as well as the role of social convention in determining meaning is easily seen in rules for the telephone (Schegloff 1968). The telephone has been common in American homes only for the past fifty or so years. Yet very definite rules surround its usage. Exactly how such rules arose and became widespread throughout society is not precisely known, any more than we know exactly how a new dialect feature suddenly spreads through a population. All we know is that whenever a social need arises, language forms evolve to meet the need.

The first rule of telephone conversation in the United States is that the answerer speaks first. It does not have to be so. The rule could as easily be that the caller speaks first. That makes perfectly good sense, as it means that the one who calls is identified at once. Of course, the American way makes equally good sense in that callers are ensured that the receiver is at someone's ear before they start to speak. There are often several equally logical possibilities in conversation rituals, but any one group may adopt just one of the possible alternatives. In other words, if we come across ways different from our own, we should not assume that "theirs" are any better or worse than "ours."

In any event, in the United States, the convention is that the answerer speaks first. If the call could conceivably be for the answerer because he or she is answering the phone in his or her home, the usual first utterance is "Hello."

In places of business or in a doctor's or lawyer's office, wherever secretaries or operators answer the phone, "Hello" is not proper. Rather, the name of the business or office is given, as in "E. B. Marshall Company," "Smith and Carlson," "Dr. Sloan's office" or "George West Junior High." Giving the name in itself means 'This is a business, institution, or professional office.' At one time it was appropriate for servants in a household or even neighbors or friends who happened to pick up the phone to answer "Jones' residence" rather than "Hello," unless the call might conceivably be for the answerer. Increasingly, however, it appears that people answer "Hello" to a residential phone even if the call might not be for them. This situation can lead to complications, especially since the callers still seem to assume that whoever answers "Hello" belongs to that phone.

The British custom of answering with one's name, as "Carl Jones here" seems to be a very efficient solution. Many American callers get thrown off by such a greeting, however. Being impressed with the British rule, I have repeatedly tried to answer my own home phone with "Elaine Chaika here." The result is usually a moment of silence followed by responses like "Uh . . . uh. Elaine?" or "Uh . . . uh. Is Danny there?" The "Uh . . . uh" probably signifies momentary confusion or embarrassment, somewhat different from the "Uh" hesitation that precedes a request to a stranger for directions or the time, as in "Uh, excuse me . . ." Predictably, answering my office phone the same way does not elicit the "Uh . . . uh," although the moment of silence still often occurs.

Godard (1977) recounts the confusion on both her part and callers' in the United States because her native French routine requires that callers verify that the number called is the one reached. Violation of discourse routines, like violations of rules of style, hinders social interaction at least a little even when the violations otherwise fit the situation just fine.

After the answerer says "Hello" or another appropriate greeting, the caller asks, "Is X there?" unless he or she recognizes the answerer's voice as being the one wanted. If the caller recognizes the answerer's voice but wishes to speak to someone else, he or she might say, "Hi, X. Is Y there?" Some do not bother to greet the answerer first. Whether or not hurt feelings result seems to depend on the degree of intimacy involved. Students in my classes report that their mothers often feel hurt if a frequent caller does not say the equivalent of "Hi, Mrs. Jones. Is Darryl there?" Sometimes callers wish to acknowledge the existence of the answerer (phatic communication), but do not wish to be involved in a lengthy conversation so they say the equivalent of "Hi, Mrs. Jones. It's Mary. I'm sorry but I'm in a hurry. Is Darryl there?" On the surface, "I'm sorry but I'm in a hurry" seems to have no relevance. It does, though, because it is an acknowledgment that the caller recognizes acquaintance with the answerer and therefore, the social appropriateness of conversing with her or him.

5.7　Compulsion in discourse routines

In terms of social rules, perhaps what is most interesting is that the person who answers the phone feels compelled to go get the one the caller wants. This compulsion may be so great that answerers find themselves running all over the house, shouting out the windows if necessary to get the one called.

One student of mine, John Reilly, reported an amusing anecdote illustrating the strength of this obligation. He called a friend to go bowling, and the friend's sister answered the phone. She informed John that her brother was cutting logs but that she would go to fetch him. John, knowing that the woodpile was 100 yards away, assured her it was not necessary. All she had to do was to relay the message. Three times she insisted on going. Three times John told her not to. Finally, she said, confusedly, "Don't you want to talk to him?" John repeated that she could extend his invitation without calling the friend to the phone.

Suddenly, she just left the phone without responding to John's last remarks and fetched her brother.

As extreme as this may sound, it is actually no more so than the person who leaps out of the tub to answer the phone and, still dripping wet with only a towel for protection, proceeds to run to another part of the house to summon the person for whom the caller asked. It is the rare person who can say, "Yes, X is here, but I don't see her. Call back later." Indeed, there are those who would consider such a response quite rude. It seems as if the person who picks up the phone has tacitly consented to go get whomever is called, regardless of inconvenience, unless the called one is not at home. The sense of obligation, of having to respond in a certain way, is at the core of all social routines, including discourse.

5.8   *Meaning in discourse routines*

Actually, if the one called on the phone is not at home or does not live there any more or never lived there at all, the semantically appropriate response to "Is X there?" should be "No." In fact, however, "No," is appropriate only if X does live there but is not now at home. For example:

If X once lived there, but does not now, an appropriate answer is

> 1. X doesn't live here any more.
> 2. X has moved.

or even

> 3. X lives at _____ now.

Although "no" has the correct meaning, it cannot be used if X no longer lives there.

If X has never lived there, one may answer

> 4. There is no X here.
> 5. What number are you calling?
> 6. You must have the wrong number.

Again, "no" would seem to be a fitting response, but it cannot be used. "No" to "Is X there?" always means that X does belong there but is not there now. Notice that 4 semantically fits for a meaning of 'X no longer lives here', but it never would be used for that meaning by someone socialized into American society.

In discourse routines, frequently an apparently suitable response cannot be used in certain social situations or the response will have a greater meaning than the words used. For instance, one apparently proper response to:

7. Where are the tomatoes? (in a store)

is

8. I don't know.

Most people would find such an honest answer rude, even odd. More likely is

9. I'm sorry, but I don't work here.

or

10. I'm sorry, I'll ask the manager.

If the one asked is an employee, then 10 is appropriate. As with the telephone, the answerer feels obligated. In this instance, the obligation is to supply the answer if he or she is an employee.

5.9   *Preconditions*

The response 9 would be bizarre except that we all know it is not actually the answer to "Where are the tomatoes?" Rather, it is a response to the preconditions for asking a question of anyone (Labov and Fanshel 1977). These are:

I. The questioner has the right or the duty to ask the question.
II. The one asked has the responsibility or obligation to know the answer.

Preconditions for speech acts are as much a part of their meaning as actual words are. If one asks someone in a store where something is, one probably has categorized that person as an employee, and employees have an obligation to know where things are in their place of work. Hence 9 really means 'You have categorized me erroneously. I don't work here, so I am not obligated to know the answer.'

Sometimes people answer

11. "I don't work here, but the tomatoes are in the next aisle."

The giveaway here is the *but*. It makes no sense in 11 unless it is seen as a response to precondition II. When *but* joins two sentences, it often means 'although,' as in 11, which means 'Although I don't work here, I happen to know that the tomatoes are in the next aisle.' That is, 'Although I am not responsible

for knowing or obligated to tell you, since I do not work here, I will anyhow.'
Note that the statement "I don't work here" really adds nothing to the pertinent
information. It is frequently said anyhow as a way of letting the asker know that
he or she miscategorized by assuming that the answerer was an employee.

5.10   *Presupposition*

Some meaning in discourse is also achieved by presupposition. This
refers to meaning that is never overtly stated but is always presupposed if certain
phrases are used. If one says "Even Oscar is going," the use of *even* is possible
only if one presupposes that Oscar usually does not go, so that the fact of his
going means that everyone is going. Both preconditions and presuppositions are
part of the meaning of utterance pairs to be discussed shortly, and both may help
constrain the kinds of responses people make to utterances.

5.11   *Utterance pairs*

The phenomenon of responsibility which we have already seen as part
of telephone routines and answering questions is part of a larger responsibility
that adheres to the discourse rules that Harvey Sacks called **utterance pairs**
(1968–72, 1970). These are conversational sequences in which one utterance
elicits another of a specific kind. For instance,

- Greeting–greeting
- Question–answer
- Complaint–excuse, apology, or denial
- Request/command–acceptance or rejection
- Compliment–acknowledgment
- Farewell–farewell

Whomever is given the first half of an utterance pair is responsible for giving the
second half. The first half, in our society, commands the person addressed to
give one of the socially recognized appropriate responses. As with the
telephone, these responses often have a meaning different from, less than, or
greater than the sum of the words used.

Furthermore, the first half of the pair does not necessarily have to sound like
what it really is. That is, a question does not have to be in question form nor a
command in command form. All that is necessary for a statement to be
construed as a question or a command is for the social situation to be right for
questioning or commanding. The very fact that a speech event is appropriate for
a question or a command may cause an utterance to be perceived as such, even if
it is not in question or command form. As with proper style, situation includes

roles and relative status of participants in a conversation. Situation, roles, and social status are an inextricable part of meaning, often as much as, if not more so, than the surface form of an utterance.

5.12   *Questions and answers*

Let us consider questions and answers. Goody (1978) points out that questions, being incomplete, are powerful in forcing responses, at least in our society but not, recall, in others such as the Warm Springs Indian society. We have already seen that certain preconditions exist for questioning and that an answer may be to the precondition rather than to the question itself. In the following discussion, it is always assumed that the preconditions for questioning are fulfilled. We will then be able to gain some insights into how people understand and even manipulate others on the basis of social rules.

There are two kinds of overt questions in English, *yes–no* questions and *wh*-questions. The first, as the name implies, requires an answer of yes or nor. In essence, if the *yes–no* question forms are used, one is forced to answer "yes," "no," or "I don't know." There is no way not to answer, except to pretend not to hear. If that occurs, the asker usually repeats the question, perhaps more loudly, or even precedes the repetition with a tap on the would-be answerer's shoulder (or the equivalent). Alternatively, the asker could precede the repeated question with a summons, like "Hey, Bill, I said . . ." or any combination of the three.

It is because members of our society all recognize that they must answer a question and that they must respond "yes" or "no" to a *yes–no* question that the following question is a recognized joke:

12. Have you stopped beating your wife?/your husband?

Since you must know what you do to your spouse, "I don't know" cannot be answered. Only a "yes" or a "no" will do. Either answer condemns. Either way you admit to spouse-beating.

Yes–no questions can also be asked by tags:

13. You're going, *aren't you*?
14. It's five dollars, *right*?

If the preconditions for questioning are present, however, as Labov and Fanshel (1977) point out, a plain declarative statement will be construed as a *yes–no* question, as in

15. Q: You live on 114th Street.
     A: No, I live on 115th.

The *wh-* questions demand an answer that substitutes for the question word. An "I don't know" can also be given. The *wh-* words are *what, when, why, who, where,* and *how* appearing at the start of a question. These words are, in essence, blanks to be filled in.

What has to be answered with the name of a thing or event; *when* with a time; *where* with a location; *why,* a reason; *who,* a person; and *how,* a manner or way something was done. There is actually yet another *wh-* question, "Huh?" which asks in effect, 'Would you repeat the entire sentence you just said?' That is, the "Huh" asks that a whole utterance be filled in, not just a word or phrase.

The answer to any question can be deferred by asking another, creating **insertion sequences** (Schegloff 1971, p. 76). For instance,

16.　A:　Wanna come to a party?
　　　B:　Can I bring a friend?
　　　A:　Male or female?
　　　B:　Female.
　　　A:　Sure.
　　　B:　O.K.

Note that these questions are answered in reverse order, but all are answered. Occasionally, insertion sequences can lead conversationalists "off the track." When this happens participants may feel a compulsion to get a question answered even if they have forgotten what it was. Hence, comments like:

17. Oh, as you were saying . . .
18. Oh, I forget, what were we talking about?

Note that the "oh" serves as indicator that the speaker is not responding to the last statement, but to a prior one. Such seemingly innocuous syllables frequently serve as markers in conversation.

5.13　*Using the rules to manipulate*

It is easy to manipulate people subtly by plugging them into the presuppositions and preconditions behind statements (Elgin 1980; Labov and Fanshel 1977). For example, a wife might try to get her husband to go to a dance by saying "Even Oscar is going" (Section 5.10). The presupposition is that if Oscar is going, then everyone is. There is a further presupposition that if everyone else is doing something, then so should the person being spoken to. If Oscar is going then everyone is going, ergo, so should the husband. Readers may recognize in this rather common ploy the childhood "Everyone else has one" or "Everyone else is going."

Elgin (1980) also discusses manipulations of the "If you really loved me . . ." variety. These are actually subtle accusations. What they mean is 'You should love me, but you don't. The guilt you feel for not loving me can easily be erased, though, by doing whatever I want.'

Another manipulation is the "Even *you* should be able to do that" type. Here we have *even* again, the word that tells someone that he or she is alone in whatever failing is being mentioned. Its use with *should* is especially clever because it implies that the hearer is stupid or some sort of gross misfit, but it backgrounds that message so that it is not likely to be discussed. Rather, the hearer is made to feel stupid and wrong, so that he or she will be likely to capitulate to the speaker's demands in an effort to prove that if all others can do it, so can the hearer.

One can achieve both manipulation and insult by preceding a comment with "Don't tell me you're going to _____" or "Don't tell me that you believe _____!" Notice that these are questions in the form of a command. They are actually asking, "Are you really going to _____?" or "Do you really believe . . . ?" However, the presuppositions behind these questions in command form are (a) 'You are going to do _____' (or 'You believe _____') and (b) '[your action or belief] _____ is stupid.' For instance,

19. X: Don't tell me that you are going to vote for Murgatroyd!
    Z: Well, I thought I would, but now I'm not so sure.

The really clever manipulation is that Z is instantly made to feel foolish because of presupposition b. However, since X has not overtly accused Z of stupidity, argument is difficult. Z is not even allowed the luxury of anger at the insult, because the insult has not been stated. It is contained only in the presupposition. Z might become immediately defensive but still feel quite stupid because of the implied insult. Not only does X get Z to capitulate, but also X establishes that Z is the stupider of the two. As a manipulatory device, this one is a "double whammy."

Labov and Fanshel (1977) show that some people manipulate in even more subtle ways by utilizing common understanding of social and discourse rules. Using patient-therapist sessions which they received permission to tape, they describe the struggle of a woman named Rhoda for independence from a domineering mother. The mother finally leaves Rhoda at home and goes to visit Rhoda's sister Phyllis. Rhoda cannot cope, but neither can she ask her mother to come home, because that would be an admission that the mother is right in not giving Rhoda more freedom. Rather, Labov and Fanshel say that Rhoda employs an indirect request both to mitigate her asking her mother for help and to disguise her challenge to the power relationship between them. Rhoda calls her mother on the phone and asks,

20. When do you plan to come home?

Since this is not a direct request for help, Rhoda's mother forces an admission by not answering Rhoda's question. Instead, she creates an insertion sequence:

21. Oh, why?

This means 'Why are you asking me when I plan to come home?' In order to answer, Rhoda must admit that she cannot be independent, that the mother has been right all along. Furthermore, as a daughter, Rhoda must answer her mother's question. Her mother has the right to question by virtue of her status, and Rhoda has the duty to answer for the same reason. So, Rhoda responds with

22. Things are getting just a little too much . . . it's getting too hard.

To which the mother replies:

23. Why don't you ask Phyllis [when I'll be home]?

Since, in our society, it is really up to the mother when she will come home, and also, since she has a prior obligation to her own household, "It is clear that Rhoda has been outmaneuvered," according to Labov and Fanshel. The mother has forced Rhoda into admitting that she is not capable, and she has, in effect, refused Rhoda's request for help.

It seems to me that this mother also has conveyed very cleverly to Rhoda that Phyllis is the preferred daughter and has said it so covertly that the topic cannot be discussed openly. Clearly it is the mother's right and duty to come home as she wishes. By palming that decision off on Phyllis, she is actually saying to Rhoda 'No matter what your claim on me is, Phyllis comes first.' That is, for Phyllis's sake, she will suppress her rights as a mother and allow Phyllis to make the decision. Notice that all of this works only because at some level both Rhoda and her mother know the rights and obligations of questioners and answerers.

5.14   *Indirect requests and conflict with social values*

All indirect requests do not arise from such hostile situations, although most are used when individual desires conflict with other social rules or values. Classic examples, spoken with an expectant lift to the voice, are:

24. Oh, chocolates.
25. What are those, cigars?

(Sacks, 1968–72)

Assuming that 24 and 25 are spoken by adults who have long known what *chocolate* denotes and are familiar with cigars, these observations are perceived as requests. This is shown by the usual responses to either:

26. Would you like one?
27. I'm sorry, but they aren't mine. (*or,* I have to save them for X.)

Young toddlers just learning to speak do practice by going about pointing at objects and naming them. Once that stage is past, people do not name items in the immediate environment unless there is an intent, a reason for singling out the item. All properly-socialized Americans know that one should never directly ask for food in another's household or for any possibly expensive goods such as cigars. That would be begging. Therefore, one names the items in another's home or hands so that the naming is construed as an indirect request. There is rarely another reason for an adult to name a common object or food. The responses to 24 and 25 make sense only if the hearer construes those as really meaning 'I want you to offer me some of those chocolates/cigars.'

5.15   *Commands*

Requests for food are not the only discourse routines arising from conflicts between general social rules and the will of the individual. Both commands and compliments, albeit in different ways, run afoul of cultural attitudes.

Commands share virtually the same preconditions as questions.

I. The speaker who commands has the right and/or duty to command.
II. The recipient of the command has the responsibility and/or obligation to carry out the command.

The problem is that, even more than with questioning, the one who has the right to command is usually clearly of higher status than the one who must obey. The United States supposedly is an egalitarian society, but having the right or duty to command implies that some are superior to others. This runs counter to our stated ideals. Therefore, in most actual situations in American speech, commands are disguised as questions. The substitution of forms is possible because both speech acts share the same preconditions. Moreover, phrasing commands as questions maintains the fiction that the one commanded has the right to refuse, even when he or she does not. Consider:

28. Would you mind closing the door?

Even though it is uttered as a *yes–no* question, merely to answer "No" without the accompanying action or "Yes" without an accompanying excuse would either be bizarre or a joke. In the movie *The Return of the Pink Panther,* Peter

Sellers asks a passerby if he knows where the Palace Hotel is. The passerby responds "Yes" and keeps on going. The joke is that "Do you know where X is?" is not really a *yes–no* question but a polite command meaning 'Tell me where X is.'

Direct commanding is allowed and usual in certain circumstances. For instance, parents normally command young children directly. For example,

> 29. Pick those toys up right away.

Intimates such as spouses or roommates often casually command each other about trivial matters, such as

> 30. Pick some bread up on your way home.

Often these are softened by "please," "will ya," "honey," or the like.

Direct commanding in command form occurs in the military from those of superior rank to those of inferior. During actual battle it is necessary for combatants to obey their officers without question, unthinkingly, and unhesitatingly. Direct commands yield this kind of obedience so long as those commanded recognize the social rightness of the command or the need. It is no surprise that direct commands are regularly heard in emergency situations, as during firefighting:

> 31. Get the hose! Put up the ladders!

A great deal of direct commanding is also heard in hospital emergency rooms:

> 32. Get me some bandages.
>   Suture that wound immediately.

In situations that allow direct commands, the full command form need not always be invoked. Just enough has to be said so that the underling knows what to do, as in

> 33. Time for lunch. (meaning 'Come in for lunch.')
> 34. Scalpel! Sutures! Dressings!

Note that such commands are contextually bound. They are interpretable as commands only if the participants are actually in a commanding situation. Similarly, Susan Ervin-Tripp's (1972) comment that

> 35. It's cold in here.

can be interpreted as a command works only in a specific commanding context. The speaker uttering 35 must somehow have the right to ask another to close a window, if that is the cause of the cold, or to ask another to lend his or her coat. In this situation, the fact that one person is closer to an open window may be sufficient reason for him or her to be responsible for closing it. The duty or obligation to carry out a command need not proceed only from actual status but may proceed from the physical circumstances in which the command has been uttered. That is why in the right circumstances ordinary statements or questions may be construed as commands, as in:

> 36. A: Any more coffee?
>   B: I'll make some right away.
>   A: No, I wanted to know if I had to buy any.

If is is possible to do something about whatever is mentioned, an utterance may be construed as a command. In 36, it was possible for B to make some coffee, and B must have been responsible for making it at least some of the time. Hence the question about coffee was misinterpreted as a command to make some. The same possibility of misinterpretation can occur in the question

> 37. Can you swim?

Said by a poolside, it may be interpreted as a command 'Jump in,' but away from a body of water, it will be heard merely as a request for information.

Although questions are often used as polite substitutes for commands, the question command can sometimes be especially imperious:

> 38. Would you mind being quiet?

Similarly, a command like the following may seem particularly haughty:

> 39. If you would wait, please.

I suspect that both 38 and 39 carry special force because the high formality signaled by "Would you mind" and "If you would . . . please" contrasts so sharply with the banality of keeping quiet and waiting that the effect of sarcasm is achieved.

5.16   *Compliments*

Compliments are another utterance pair type that create conflict. This is because of general social convention and the rule that the first part of an utterance pair must evoke a response. Compliments call for an acknowledgment. The acknowledgment can properly be acceptance of the compliment, as in "Thank you." The problem is that to accept the compliment is very close to bragging, and bragging is frowned upon in middle-class America. Hence, one typical response to a compliment is a disclaimer, like

> 40. This old rag?
> 41. I got it on sale.
> 42. My mother got it for me.

An exception is special occasions when compliments are expected, as when everyone is decked out to go to a prom or a wedding. Then, not only are compliments easily received with "Thank you," but not to compliment can cause offense or disappointment.

Except for such situations, complimenting can lead to social embarrassment. If one persists in complimenting another, the other person often becomes hostile, even though nice things are being said. At the very least the recipient of excessive praise becomes uncomfortable and tries to change the subject. Often he or she becomes suspicious and angry or tries to avoid the person who is heaping praise. The suspicion is either that the complimenter is being patronizing or is trying to get something, to "butter the person up."

Once, I ordered a class to persistently compliment their parents, spouses, or siblings. The most common response was "OK. What do you want this time?" One of the students received a new suit from a friend who owned a men's clothing store, with the friend practically shouting, "OK. If I give you a new suit will that shut you up?"

Many of those complimented became overtly angry. Others quickly found an excuse to leave, and several students found that those on whom they heaped praise shunned them the next time they met. I suspect that the anger results from the social precariousness of being complimented. As with style, when a person is put at a social disadvantage so that he or she does not know how to respond, anger results. It is very uncomfortable to receive too much praise. It is tantamount to continually being asked to tread the line between gracious acceptance and boasting. Most people prefer to ignore anyone who puts them in that situation.

5.17   *Presequences and saving face*

An interesting class of discourse rules is what Harvey Sacks called *presequences* (lecture, November 2, 1967), particularly preinvitations. Typically, someone wishing to issue an oral invitation, first asks something like

> 43. What are you doing Saturday night?

If the response includes words like *only* or *just*, as in

44. I'm just washing my hair.
45. I'm only studying.

the inviter can then issue an invitation for Saturday night. If, however, the response is

46. I'm washing my hair.
47. I'm studying.

the potential inviter knows not to issue the invitation. Following a response like 46 or 47, the inviter signals a change in conversation by saying "Uh— — —" and then speaks of something other than Saturday night (or whatever date was mentioned). Issuing of preinvitations is an ego saver like the use of style to signal social class. Having been spared overt refusal, the inviter is able to save face (Goffman 1955).

5.18   *Collapsing sequences*

Sometimes utterance pairs are collapsed (Sacks, November 2, 1967) as in the following exchange at an ice cream counter:

48. A: What's chocolate filbert?
    B: We don't have any.

B's response is to what B knows is likely to come next. If B had explained what chocolate filbert is, then A very likely would have asked for some. Indeed, by explaining what it is, B would be tacitly saying that he or she had some to sell. In a selling situation in our society, explaining what goods or foods are is always an admission that they are available. Imagine your reaction, for instance, if you asked a waiter or waitress what some food was like, and he or she went into detail telling you about it. Then, if you said, "Sounds good. I'll have that," and the response were, "We don't have any," you would think you were being made a fool of.

Another common collapsing sequence is typified by the exchange:

49. A: Do you smoke?
    B: I left them in my other jacket.

Such collapsing sequences speed up social interaction by forestalling unnecessary explanations. They are used for other purposes as well, as when a newcomer joins a discussion in progress:

50. Hi, John. We were just talking about nursery schools.

This either warns John not to join the group or, if he is interested in nursery schools, gives him orientation so that he can understand what is going on.

5.19   *Repairs*

If a person uses the wrong style for an occasion, the other party(ies) to the interaction try to repair the error (Chapter 3). Schegloff, Jefferson, and Sacks (1977) collected interesting samples of self-correction in discourse, people repairing their own errors. Sometimes this takes the form of obvious correction to a slip of the tongue, as in

>   51. What're you so *ha*—er un—un*ha*ppy about?

Sometimes speakers make a repair when they have made no overt error, as in

>   52. Sure enough ten minutes later the bell r—the doorbell rang.

Because such repairs do not show a one-to-one correspondence with actual spoken errors, Schegloff et al. preferred the term **repair** over **correction**. In both 51 and 52, for instance, neither repair was preceded by an error that actually occurred in speech.

Schegloff et al. found an orderly pattern in speech repair. Repairs did not occur just anywhere in an utterance. They occurred in one of three positions: immediately after the error, as in 51 and 52, or at the end of the sentence where another person would normally take the floor:

>   53. An 'en bud all of the doors 'n things were taped up—I mean y'know they put up y'know that kinda paper stuff, the brown paper.

or right after the other person speaks:

>   54. *Hannah:*   And he's going to make his own paintings.
>   *Bea:*   Mm hm.
>   *Hannah:*   And—or I mean his own frames.

If the speaker does not repair an obvious error, the hearer will. Usually this is done by asking a question that will lead the speaker to repair his or her own error. Some examples:

>   55. A: It wasn't snowing all day.
>   B: It *wasn't*?
>   A: Oh, I mean it was.
>
>   56. A: Yeah, he's got a lot of smarts.
>   B: *Huh*?
>   A: He hasn't got a lot of smarts.

57. A: Hey, the first time they stopped me from selling cigarettes was this morning.
    B: From *selling* cigarettes?
    A: From buying cigarettes.

Often, the hearer will say "you mean" as in

58. A: We went Saturday afternoon.
    B: You mean Sunday.
    C: Yeah, uhnnn we saw Max . . .

In most of the repairs by hearers, it seems that the hearer knows all along what the intended word was. Still, it is rare, although not impossible, for the hearer actually to supply the word. This seems to be a face saver for the person who made the error. The hearer often offers the correction or the question leading to correction tentatively, as if he or she is not sure. That way, the speaker is not humiliated as he or she might be if the hearer in positive tones asserted that an error was made. Another reason that hearers offer corrections tentatively may be that in doing so, the hearer is in the position of telling someone else what must be going on in his or her mind.

Schegloff et al. (1977, p. 38) state that "the organization of repair is the self-righting mechanisms for the organization of language use in social interaction." In other words, it maintains normal social interaction. We have already seen this in attempted repair of inappropriate style.

The importance of the self-righting mechanism is shown in the following almost bizarre interactions. These involve repairs in greetings and farewells collected as part of a participant observation by a student, Sheila Kennedy. While on guard duty at the door of a dormitory, she deliberately confounded greetings and farewells, with fascinating results.

    To a stranger:
59. *Sheila:*   Hi. [pause] Good night.
    Stranger: Hello. [pause] Take it easy.

Note that the stranger also gave both a greeting and a farewell, even matching the pause that Sheila used between them. This is highly reminiscent of the exchanges in which subjects so frequently matched the experimenter's style, even when they questioned or objected to it (Chapter 3).

    To a female friend:
60. *Friend:*   Bye, Sheila.
    Sheila: Hello.
    Friend: Why did you say hello? I said goodbye. [pause] Hi.

Even though the friend questioned the inappropriateness of Sheila's response, she still felt constrained to answer the greeting with a greeting.

To a male friend:
61. *Friend:*   Hi!
    Sheila: So long.
             [Both spoke at the same time, so Sheila starts again.]
    Sheila: Hi!
    Friend: Bye. [laughs] Wait a minute. Let's try that again. Hi!
    Sheila: Hello.
    Friend: Bye.
    Sheila: So long.
    Friend: That's better. [laughs and leaves]

What is interesting here is the lengths the subject went to in order that the appropriate pairs were given. Note that he had to get both greeting and farewell matched up before he would leave. The degree to which we are bound by the social rules of discourse is well illustrated in 59–61. The very fact that people go to so much trouble to repair others' responses is highly significant. It shows the importance of discourse routines to social interaction, that one cannot be divorced from the other. Not only must style and kinesics be appropriate for social functioning but so must the discourse itself. Even when people know what the other must mean, as in 55–58, they ask that the discourse be righted. And, even when it makes no difference in a fleeting social contact, as in 59–61, they demand that the right forms be chosen.

5.20   *New rules of discourse*

New situations may involve learning new discourse rules. Anthony Wooton (1975, p. 70) gives an example from psychotherapy. Psychiatrists typically do not tell patients what to do. Rather, by asking questions, they try to lead the patient into understanding. The problem is that the questions asked and the answers they are supposed to evoke are different from those already learned as part of normal routines. As an example, Wooton gives:

62. *Patient:*   I'm a nurse, but my husband won't let me work.
    Therapist: How old are you?
    Patient: Thirty-one this December.
    Therapist: What do you mean, he won't let you work?

Here, the patient answers the psychiatrist's first question as if it were bona fide, a real world question. The psychiatrist was not really asking her age, however, as we can see by his next question. What he meant by that question was 'You are old enough to decide whether or not you wish to work.' His question was aimed at leading her to that conclusion.

The patient in therapy has to learn new discourse routines in order to benefit from the therapeutic situation. The therapist uses modes of questioning different from everyday discourse. This is not surprising, since the aim of psychotherapy is for the psychiatrist to lead the patient into self-discovery. Some patients become very annoyed by the questioning, feeling that the therapist is refusing to tell them anything. In traditional psychoanalysis it was accepted that there had to be a period during which the patient 'fought' the analyst by refusing to dredge up the answers from the murky subconscious. It has occurred to me that this period may actually represent a time during which the patient must learn to respond to the new question and answer routines demanded by analysis.

It is very hard to gain insights into oneself by sustained self-questioning, perhaps because questioning is rarely used that way outside the therapeutic situation. Furthermore, repeated questioning in itself is threatening. In many societies, including our own, it is associated with accusation of wrongdoing and ferreting out the truth of one's guilt. It is used as a technique for teaching, to be sure, but even then it is often a way of ferreting out the pupil's lapses in learning.

5.21   *Topic in normal and psychotic speech*

The first half of an utterance pair strongly limits what can come next. It limits both form and subject matter. These are intertwined virtually inseparably: a greeting is both a form and a subject matter. The response to a *wh-* question must use the same words as the question, filling in the missing word signaled by whichever *wh-* word was used. The answer to "Where did you go?" is "I went to [place X]." The answer to "Whom did you see?" is "I saw [person X]."

The larger conversation, beyond utterance pairs, is not so strongly constrained as to form. The entire syntax of the language can be drawn upon to encode new ideas, not just the syntax of greetings or compliments or invitation. The first sentence or so of an answer is predetermined by the question just asked, but the speaker becomes free as soon as an answer is given that fills in the *wh-* word or supplies the *Yes, No,* or *I don't know.* The constraints upon topic, however, remain very strong.

In normal conversation, everything has to be subordinated to topic, whatever is being talked about (see VanDijk 1977). Schegloff (1971) likens this to co-occurrence restrictions such as we saw in style. Once a topic is introduced, it must be adhered to unless some formal indication of change is made. Paradoxically, in American English, this often is "Not to change the subject, but . . ." This disclaimer always changes the topic. Other signals that change topic are "Oooh, that reminds me . . ." or "Oooh, I meant to tell you . . ." The "Oooh" in itself, uttered rapidly on a high pitch with a tense throat, is a warning that an announcement about topic change is coming.

Adherence to a topic is so important that failure to do so is evidence of mental incapacity. A person's mind is said to wander if his or her words wander off topics with no warning. Many observers of patients diagnosed as schizophrenic have noticed peculiarities in their speech, peculiarities traditionally called *thought disorder* (TD). Since not all schizophrenics show these speech disorders, some are termed *non–thought disordered* (NTD). As a result of my own extensive analyses of speech termed TD, I think that such speech differs from normal or NTD speech mainly in that it does not stick to a topic. For instance,

> 63. My mother's name was Bill and coo. St. Valentine's Day was the start of the breedin' season of the birds.
>
>> *(Chaika 1974, 1977)*

> 64. Looks like clay. Sounds like gray. Take you for a roll in the hay. Hay day. May day. Help! I just can't. Need help. May day.
>
>> *(Cohen 1978)*

> 65. I had a little goldfish like a clown. Happy Hallowe'en down.
>
>> *(Chaika 1974, 1977)*

The greatest abnormality in such speech is that the patient is not sticking to a topic. Other than that, each part of the utterance is normal; grammar, word choice, and sounds are correctly used.

The words and phrases chosen do have a connection with one another in each of the samples just given. They are related on the basis of similarity of sound, especially rhyme, and on the basis of shared meaning. "Bill and coo" is an old metaphor for 'love' based upon an image of lovebirds or doves, which bill and coo. Love is also associated with St. Valentine's Day. "Roll in the hay" means '(sexual) fun'. "Hay day" not only rhymes with "hay," but if, as seems likely, the patient meant 'heyday', it also refers to good times. "Hay day" rhymes with "May day," which is another way of saying "SOS" or 'Help!' "Happy Hallowe'en" seems to be an association with "clown," with which "down" is a chance rhyme.

No matter how tightly such associations can be woven into the utterance, still 63–65 are obviously pathological speech. It is topic that determines normal speech, not other kinds of associations between words. Some people have suggested that schizophrenic speech is poetic, because, like poetry, it often rhymes. One major objection to this view is the high interjudge reliability when people are asked to distinguish schizophrenic utterances from others (Maher, McKeon and McLaughlin 1966; Rochester, Martin and Thurston 1977).

The schizophrenic rhyming and figurative speech occurs only because of chance association. Poetic rhyme and artistic language in general seem to be as constrained by a topic as any other kind of normal speech. Rhyming and other features of poetry, such as unusual associations and figurative language, are poetic when they are subordinated to a topic. Comparison of 63–65 with the extensive rhymes and metaphors in Black toasts (Chapter 6) shows the difference.

In the twentieth century certain authors have deliberately set out to recreate stream of consciousness in their fiction, and some poetry is deliberately formless. Dr. Nancy Andreasen (1973) claims that James Joyce's *Finnegan's Wake* would appear to be schizophrenic to most psychiatrists. Even in such modern literature, however, form is usually subordinated to general topic.

5.22   *What to mention*

Besides adhering to a topic, a speaker is constrained to follow another related rule: 'Say only what needs saying.' Personal and cultural knowledge that speakers share is not mentioned but is assumed. This is why the speech between two intimates is often obscure to outsiders. For instance:

> 66. A: Saw Mary today.
>   B: She better?
>   A: Yeah, she went to Bob's last night.
>   B: When's the date?

This works if both know the one Mary, that she has just been sick, that she is engaged to Bob, but the wedding has been postponed because of her illness. To reiterate what each of the speakers knows would be boring or insulting or both.

One kind of bore is the person who insists on telling you more than you have to be told about something. Also, if someone insists on being overdetailed in an explanation, it implies that the hearer does not know those details. This is why people feel insulted if someone tells them obvious facts.

A difficulty that grown children have in dealing with their parents is that the parents persist in 'treating them as if they were children'—that is, telling them things they already know. It is hard for the children not to feel insulted and defensive. Often repairmen are guilty of insulting by mentioning the obvious. For instance, when taking my computer in to be repaired, I felt very put out when the technician said "It's probably your diskette. They're very fragile." Since the first thing one learns about such equipment is that the diskettes are fragile, the effect was insultingly condescending.

In conversation it is assumed that all parties are cooperating (Gordon and Lakoff 1975). It is also assumed that they mean what they say. If something is mentioned that is known, therefore, unless it is taken as a putdown it will be construed to be newly important. Searle (1975) says that mentioning of extraneous matters leads listeners down false trails, as they try to figure out how those matters fit the topic at hand. It seems to me that this is why our courts of law have such strong rules against introducing irrelevant matters. To do so clouds the issue for the jury.

Mentioning too much, even if it is related to the topic, can be as distracting as actual departures from the topic itself. People assume that anything known to all parties in a given conversation will not be overtly stated unless there is some special reason for so doing.

EXERCISES

1. In the course of a day, find at least one example of each of the
following. Note the exact words used and the response to them.

   a. A question not in question form
   b. A command not in command form
   c. A collapsing sequence
   d. Language used for manipulation

2. For each of the above, answer the following questions in writing:

   a. Was the response a response to the overt statement?
   b. Was the response to a precondition that had to exist before
   such a statement could be made?
   c. Was the response made to a presupposition rather than the
   actual statement?

3. Try to compliment three people. What were their responses?

chapter 6

VERBAL SKILL,
THE SOCIAL UNIVERSAL

Some people with formal education imagine that their education confers special mental powers. Unbiased examination of the discourse of people with little schooling, however, reveals that they too reason logically, argue cogently, and manipulate language intelligently and effectively. The everyday speech activities of a social group reveal underlying attitudes and some of the conditions under which they are living. Finally, discourse activities play an important role in ego-boosting.

6.1   *Discourse activities*

Almost every social group grants high status to members with good verbal skills, but different social groups value different skills. In middle class American culture, the skills most respected are those associated with formal schooling: reading books designated as texts and reproducing part or all of their contents on paper. This is known as passing tests. A good deal of adult rank depends upon the skill with which this was done in childhood and how long into adulthood test passing was carried on. But there are more kinds of verbal activity than book learning. So much do we forget this fact that when we come into contact with people to whom book learning is not important, we assume that they are nonverbal.

6.2   *The training of the man of words in talking sweet*

Roger Abrahams (1972) shows how fallacious such middle-class attitudes are. He studied Afro-Americans on St. Vincent's Island, a population that traditionally has had little opportunity for formal education. As is common in the Caribbean, daily interaction is carried out in an English–African Creole. Creole means that two languages have melded together into one new one. The Afro-Americans call this Creole "talking bad" or "talking broken," and they call Standard English "talking sweet" or "talking sensible." There is nothing intrinsically broken or bad about Creole, but people everywhere seem to evaluate their own speech in the way the most prestigious members of society do. As Labov (1966) showed, all members of a community have pretty much the same norms, no matter how they actually speak (Chapter 8).

It is the duty of the head of each household in St. Vincent's to ensure that the children learn to talk sweet. They send children to learn from members of the community known for speech-making ability. Talking sweet is displayed at occasions calling for speeches. A gifted speech-maker is known as "a man of words." Everyone is expected to make a speech at weddings, baptisms, and send-offs, but only the best speak at big fetes like Christmas. Then, during serenading, songs alternate with orations of praise.

Although the custom was already dying out by the time of his writing, Abrahams explained that, traditionally, speech skills are sharpened at a "tea meeting." Here, an orator or oratress has to get up and speak while "pit boys" in the audience bang sticks. This is called "rapping." The pit boys "rag" the speaker, usually by shouting mocking rhymes. The orator not only has to keep cool and finish the speech but, by use of facts and by being sensible, confuse the mockers. All this must be done while adhering to a speech that was memorized.

The man who teaches such consummate oral skill is called a "professor." The pupil is a "scholar," and the speech the scholar learns is called a "lesson." The professor not only writes the speeches and teaches elocution but stresses mental and verbal agility: being quick on the uptake, being original, and clever. The entire contest is a battle of wits as well as a demonstration of the ability to talk sweet. One must remember that these are the poor, the unlettered, those relegated to menial labor. Yet they engage in activities worthy of those with Ph.D.s. In fact most Ph.D.'s would be hard put to compete orally with the quick cleverness of the St. Vincent's scholar and his or her professor. Just because people do not engage in formal booklearning, it does not mean they do not have verbal skills comparable to those who do.

6.3   *Logic and nonstandard speakers*

Labov, Cohen, Robins, and Lewis (1968) give a very good example of logical argumentation in a nonstandard speaker. At the time of their investigation, the Harlem street gangs were heavily involved in the Muslim religion. The same boys who were virtually illiterate in regular school were studying history, science, and reading in the Muslim schools. They often took oral tests, which was called "being put on the square" or displaying "heavy knowledge", although that terminology may not have been used in other Black communities.

That the tests were oral is significant. Unlike the dominant middle-class culture, ghetto Blacks have an oral culture. It is speaking skill that gives one prestige, not writing. The ability to win arguments by quickness, facts, and logic is at a premium.

Labov et al. often took gang members on trips. Since one tenet of the Muslim religion is vegetarianism, this posed a problem in providing lunches. Once, unthinkingly, Labov and his team prepared tomato sandwiches with mayonnaise. Since mayonnaise has eggs in it several boys objected, saying, in effect, eggs are from chickens, chickens are meat, so eggs are meat. To this, one boy, Quahab, responded, using the dramatic intonation of Black preaching style.

> 1. No, bro', we din't eat no meat. You might as well say we drunk it because it was in a liquid fo-orm.
>
> *(Labov et al. 1968, p. 143)*

The preaching style includes a chanting, as well as an elongating of the final word of a sentence, often one crucial to the argument. Quahab continued:

> 2. Dig it, it ain't even in existence yet, dig that. It ain't even in existence yet. It didn't come to be a chicken yet. You can detect it with a physical eye, you can detect that.
>
> *(p. 143)*

Both the logic of the argument against eating mayonnaise and Quahab's hairsplitting are worthy of theologians and the argumentation is not hampered by the nonstandard speech forms like *ain't*.

It often comes as a surprise to the college educated that the uneducated who speak what is considered incorrect English are capable of sophisticated intellectual argumentation. Deep discussions about human nature, theology, and politics are far from rare in the bars, on the streetcorners, and in the clubs where non-middle-class men and boys gather. This is not to say that women do not also indulge in such considerations. It is just that we do not know. So far, working and lower class women, Black or White, have rarely been investigated, and most studies of Black speech have been of the speech of males.

In what has come to be called the ghetto, the discussions of the males often take on a competitive aura, much like that of scholars. Each participant seeks to gain supremacy by his brilliant argumentation. Quahab's glib reasoning suggests a skill born of practice. This is not only because of his preoccupation with the Muslim religion. Larry, a fifteen-year-old nonbeliever, was asked if he knew what happens to people after death. His response is the heart of William Labov's *The Logic of Nonstandard English* (1969). Larry argued that it is not true that one goes to heaven if one is good, and hell if one is not. He noted that · everybody has a different idea of god:

> 3. I have seen black gods, pink gods, white gods, all color gods.

therefore, nobody knows if there is a god, and

> 4. Your spirit goin' to hell anyway, good or bad . . . You ain't goin' to no heaven 'cause it ain't no heaven for you to go to.

When he was asked how there can be a hell if there is no heaven, Larry recovered quickly, saying that hell is right here on earth. Later he argued that if there is a god, He is White. His reasoning was impeccable, although his facts arguable. Larry said that the "average Whitey" has everything, and Blacks have nothing. In his own words, in order for that to happen there couldn't be a Black god. Larry handled cause and effect very well. Beside his liberal sprinkling of obscenities and grammar forms horrible to the middle-class ear, such as double negatives and *ain't*, were the words marking logical connection. He used *if*, *'cause*, and *in order to* the same way his educated counterparts would. This must be emphasized considering the view of Bereiter and Engelmann (1966), Deutsch (1967), and Bernstein (1971) that the uneducated have restricted codes that limit their ability to think, especially their ability to make use of the very logical connectors that Larry used.

Abrahams (1972, 1974) and Labov (1969), among others, have shown that logical argumentation is part of everyday verbal gaming in Harlem and other Black ghettoes. Throughout his works, Labov supposes that such gaming is unique to Blacks. Indeed, he implies that lower class Whites are verbally dull compared to Blacks (Labov et al. 1968, p. 90). But this is not so, for lower class Whites as well as Blacks engage in verbal competition of all sorts. The specific forms some of the activities take may be somewhat different, but the activity itself is essentially the same, demanding the same abilities.

Both Whites and Blacks with little formal education argue about weighty matters like politics, religion, and life in general, as well as engage in verbal play. Different ethnic groups may play somewhat differently, but verbal jousting exists for them in one form or another. Verbal play may consist of any or all of the following:

- Being quick on the uptake;
- Verbal thrusting such as joking insults;
- Making a joke out of something another has just said;
- Conning others by telling outrageous lies with a straight face;
- Dueling verbally in boasting contests, riddles (Dundes, Leach, and Ozkok 1972), song writing, telling jokes, or making up rhymes of various kinds.

Certainly educated Blacks and Whites do the same things, but among them such activities appear to be more a matter of individual taste than of social obligation. Perhaps people lacking formal education and formal high status use such oral displays as a way of gaining status. Wit, repartee, and drollness are all admired by the formally educated, but for them a person's ultimate status is determined less by oral performance than by bookish or business skills.

Much of the literature on Blacks reads as if only Blacks indulge in feats of oral skill. Very little research has been done on such skills among Whites, and the little that has been done (e.g., Schatzman and Strauss 1972) has compared lower and working class Whites to the middle class. Since such research has measured middle class skills in middle class settings, Whites with little formal education have fared poorly. In contrast, Black oral activities have been studied for their own sake, without measuring them against the yardstick of middle-class skills.

Yet one need not go very far to get clever repartee from non-middle-class Whites that rivals that of Blacks. The following dialogues show a punning game very prevalent among working class White males in Rhode Island. Jean Shields, a student, collected the samples in 5 from Len, a man in his sixties without a high school education, working as an unskilled kitchen worker in a cafeteria. The samples in 6 were collected from three men with education ranging from the eighth grade to a high school diploma. Their occupations were carpenter, carpenter's assistant, and delivery truck driver. Len, in 5, an urban dweller, is of Irish ethnic background. Those in 6, from rural New England villages, were all descendants of English settlers.

5. *Jean:*   I have a date tonight.
   Len: Last night I had a date with a fig.

A day later:
   Jean: I used your line about having a date with a fig on a linguistics test.
   Len: Oh, lines. I've got a lot of 'em (points to his face).

During inconsequential chatting about Len's family:
   Jean: What's the difference between your coat and his?
   Len: Oh, well, the blue jacket means he has big hours, and the tan ones mean we got little hours.
   Jean: What are little and big hours?
   Len: Little hours are four hours a day, and bigger ones are eight hours.
   Jean: I gotta go—You're a real peach.
   Len: I may be a peach on the outside, but I'm a nut on the inside.

6. *Pete:*   [to me] You still studying schizophrenia?
   Charley: Schizophrenia? That's in the genes isn't it?
   Ed: I got something in my jeans once.
   Pete: Pig ripped my jeans last night.
   Dave: The pig in the field or the pig you was out with last night?
        [Continues for two hours nonstop]

Len is so intent on making his every utterance colorful that he uses *big* and *little* to describe the number of hours men work rather than *more* and *less*. This works because in some contexts *big* and *little* are synonymous with *more* and *less,* as in "give me more cake," when it means 'give me a bigger piece of cake.' Such unusual usages, so long as they fit the topic at hand, are the heart of creative language use.

The game in 5 and 6 consists of making a pun out of another person's statement. Among peers, if one can also include an insult to the conversationalist whose words are being punned, that is even better. The resulting conversations are like those familiar to viewers of the television show *M.A.S.H.* The difference is that these speakers do not have anyone writing their material. The speakers in 6 are old friends who hunt, snowmobile, and play pool together regularly. During their weekly pool games, the bantering never ceases, and no one is immune. There is never apology or hurt feelings. The activity is understood for the game it is. Unlike the verbal sparring of Blacks described in the next section, there is never overt judgment on any statement, beyond general laughter, although some members of the group are acknowledged to be more skillful talkers than others. Among Rhode Island teenagers of Italian background, however, if one succeeds in insulting another, especially by turning his own words back on him as an insult, others in the group might say, 'He used your face.''

In rural Maine, at least through the 1950s, one favorite activity of males was to see who could tell the most outrageous stories to an outsider, a city slicker, and still be believed. A variation was for men to boast about the stories they had caused said slicker to believe. Yet another variation was to recount quick repartee that had bested an outsider, preferably also humiliating him. The entire genre of city slicker jokes attests to this sort of activity in other rural areas as well.

In the Appalachian mountains there is a tradition of song-making among descendants of the original Scots-Irish and English settlers. Any devotee of American folk music is familiar with one version of this song-making, the talking blues. Songs may be written about any topic: love, death, hard times. If asked about an event such as a mining disaster or strike, an Appalachian is likely to say, "I've written a little song about that." and proceed to sing it. (One can see such a sequence in the movie *Harlan County, U.S.A.*) Those not "into" that kind of music often find it almost tuneless at first, more of a chant than a song. The talking blues are actually spoken, with no attempt to modify the voice toward singing but with a strong repetitive rhythm. The talking is always accompanied by a guitar or banjo. Both the Appalachian song-making and talking blues have always reminded me of the epic poetry sung or chanted by the minstrels of early Europe. Often accompanied by music, this poetry told of the history of the people, its hard times and good times.

In different parts of the country and in different ethnic groups, undoubtedly many other kinds of verbal activities can be found. The situations that call them forth may well differ from group to group.

6.4   *Rapping*

Although it has largely been ignored in Whites, the gaming aspect of speech and the concern with rhetoric has been well studied in Blacks. Claudia

Mitchell-Kernan (1972) gives an example of a young man *rapping* to her. Sitting on a park bench, she was approached by three young men, one of whom started a conversation:

7. *M:* Mama you sho is fine.

  M-K: That ain' no way to talk to your mother.

The conversation continued. Mitchell-Kernan told the man what she was doing. He immediately adjusted his style:

  M: Baby, you a real scholar. I can tell you want to learn. Now if you'll just cooperate a li'l bit, I'll show you what a good teacher I am. But first, we got to get into my area of expertise.

  M-K: I may be wrong, but seems to me we already in your area of expertise.

  [General laughter]

  M: You ain' so bad yourself, girl. I ain't heard you stutter yet. You a li'l fixated on your subject though. I want to help a sweet thang like you all I can. I figure all that book learnin' you got must mean you been neglecting other areas of your education.

  2nd man: Talk dat talk (gloss: olé)

  M-K: Why don't you let me point out where I can best use your help.

  M: Are you sure you in the best position to know?

  [Laughter]

  I'm'a leave you alone, girl. Ask me what you want to know. Tempus fugit, baby.

  [More laughter]

This man used the grammar and words of what is often termed NNE, Nonstandard Negro English. Furthermore, his rap to Mitchell-Kernan is a typical ghetto activity between men and women. Even though he probably has not received much formal education, he uses the jargon of scholarship: *expertise, fixated,* and the Latin *tempus fugit.* Mitchell-Kernan herself did not present M's credentials. However, having been raised in a mixed Black and White working and lower class neighborhood and having taught such students both in public school and an Upward Bound program, I can vouch that even virtual illiterates often have amazingly erudite vocabularies, as well as a facility with words that puts many a scholar to shame. Typically those in the lower classes are more familiar with upper class speech than the upper classes are with theirs. Whether or not M is educated makes little difference, however. Mitchell-Kernan's aim was to show the characteristic Black skill with language. It is not likely that M realized that he was going to meet a female scholar while strolling through the park that day. His innuendos based upon scholarly speech had to be made up on the spot. Mitchell-Kernan comments "By his code selection . . . the speaker indicates that he is parodying a tête à tête and not attempting to engage the speaker in anything other than conversation." She apparently means that despite the sexual double meanings, M's display is actually a verbal one not necessarily intended as a real invitation. Notice that once the young man has demonstrated his virtuosity, it is he who ends it.

Rapping is a display of verbal skill, often but not always entailing the use of ordinary language in such a way that it takes on a sexual double meaning. The term may also be used for rapid witty exchanges of other kinds. In the encounter just presented, once the young man finds out that Mitchell-Kernan is a scholar, he adjusts his rap toward scholarly language. The adjustment is significant. For successful rapping, it is not enough merely to make innuendos; they must be made in language appropriate to the person being spoken to. Like the dialogue in 5 and 6 above, the rapper as much as possible takes what Mitchell-Kernan says and builds on it.

M does this, for instance, by offering to be her teacher. The "other areas of your education" imply sexual ones, especially since she is "a sweet thang." When the man says "I ain't heard you stutter yet," he is complimenting Mitchell-Kernan's quick comebacks. The "talk [that] talk" from M's friend is a Black congratulatory comment when a speaker uses language both colorful and appropriate to the social context. That the juxtaposition of scholarly and street language is deliberate and intended for humor is shown by both that comment and the laughter at "Tempus fugit, baby."

More recently, rapping has been taken up by Whites. Each of the following had one White and one Black participant. A White male initiated 8 to a Black female, and a Black male initiated 9 to a White female.

8. *Terry:*   Hey, wha's happenin'?
   Jean: What's it to you?
   Terry: Hey, no need to get nasty.
   Jean: S– –t, man, I ain't gettin' nasty.
   Terry: That's a good thing, 'cause we we should be makin' beautiful music together.
   Jean: Sucker, the only music I'll make with you is if we play the same tape.
   [Both laugh, and male walks away]

9. *Arthur:*   Hey, baby, wha's happenin'?
   Linda: Not much, what about you?
   Arthur: I can sure make somethin' happen.
   Linda: Sure you know how?
   Arthur: Just let me show you.
  Onlooker, male: Rap City, baby!
   Linda: I don't think it'd be worth my time.

Arthur:	Honey, you'd be dreamin' of me for sure afterwards.
Linda:	Honey, I can do without the nightmares.
[Both laugh]	

In both of these encounters, once the female has successfully bested the male by humorously, but finally, rejecting his invitation, the rap session is over.

6.5   *Toasting*

It is not surprising that in our society, speech from a man to a woman takes on sexual connotations (see also Chapter 9). Blacks have ritualized roles for males and females in the rapping form. The question naturally arises of why Blacks have done this. A reason suggested by folklorist Roger Abrahams is the Black preoccupation with speech as performance. Another is suggested both by Black toasts and ritual insults.

Toasts are actually oral epics like the *The Iliad* or *Beowulf:* long poems, originally intended to be spoken, that recount the magnificent deeds of a hero. The hero is a model epitomizing the way men are supposed to be. The epic not only entertains and thrills but teaches. Examining epic poems, then, reveals cultural attitudes.

Admittedly, most people would not think of epic poetry when they first hear Black toasts. The profanity and taboo subjects in the toasts so shock middle-class listeners that most cannot appreciate the skill it took to compose them. In recent years toasting has pretty much died out, so that younger Blacks frequently know no more than a verse or two, if any. Many middle-class Blacks are unaware that such poetry ever existed. Nevertheless, examining the toasts is a valuable lesson in the ways language activities mirror social realities and fulfill the need for ego satisfaction. The taboo themes and words used in toasting and in other Black and White speech activities are offensive to many, but they must be considered in a sociology of language. As will be demonstrated in this section and in those on ritual insulting and profanity, the very use of offensive language reveals social conditions and social attitudes toward those conditions.

The hero of the toasts is often a pimp or other lawbreaker. Even if he is not, he is overtly antisentimental and tough. Gambling, drinking, procuring, and prostitution are common themes. These were the facts of life to the anonymous composers of *The Fall, The Signifying Monkey, The Sinking of the Titanic,* and other tales of the Black folkheroes Shine and Stackolee.

Epic poetry sets its scenes in war. There heroes can exhibit the traits that society expects of its men. The battlegrounds of the Black epics are the slums of the large cities, as in these opening lines from one version of *The Fall*:

10. It was Saturday night, the jungle was bright
    As the game stalked their prey;
    And the cold was crime on the neon line
    Where crime begun, where daughter fought son
    And your mom lied awoke, with her heart almost broke
    As they loaded that train to hell
    Where blood was shed for the sake of some bread
    And winos were rolled for their port,

    .

    .

    .

    Where the addicts prowl, where the tiger growl
    And search for that lethal blow,
    Where the winos crump, for that can heat rump
    You'll find their graves in the snow;
    Where girls of vice sell love for a price
    And even the law's corrup'
    But you keep on tryin' as you go down cryin'
    Say man it's a bitters cup.
                              (quoted in Labov et al. 1968, p. 56)

This stark and graphic opener leads into a tale of a pimp who exploited a whore shamelessly, ending with his arrest:

11. Now as I sit in my 6 by 6 cell in the county jail
    Watchin' the sun rise in the east,
    The morning chills give slumber to the slumbering beast

    Farewell to the nights, and the neon lights
    Farewell to one and all
    Farewell to the game, may it still be the same
    When I finish doing this fall.
                              (quoted in Labov et al. 1968, p. 58)

In *Honkey Tonk Bud,* the hero is convicted of a narcotics charge. Before sentence is passed, he tells the judge:

12. He said, "I'm not cryin' 'cause the agent was lying'
    And left you all with a notion.
    That I was a big wheel in the narcotics field
    I hope the fag cops a promotion.
    It's all the same, it's all in the game
    I dug when I sat down to play
    That you take all odds, deal all low cards
    It's the dues the dope fiend must pay.
                              (quoted in Labov et al. 1968, p. 58)

"The game" is the way things are. Labov et al. point out that the toasts do not claim that the game pays off in any way. The satisfaction comes from playing with dignity, and according to the rules. The rules dictate that one never complains about what happens. Justice is not expected, nor is injustice bemoaned. Heroism consists of great courage as it does in the middle-class world, but, in the toasts, the courage consists partly of being willing to face the penalties of crime.

Certainly, these are poems of despair. Achilles had a battlefield with potential honor. Beowulf could become a bona fide hero by killing Grendel. These were heroes to their entire people. Blacks in the slums often saw no way to become the kinds of heroes general American society set up, at least not before the 1960s and the first glimmerings of the Civil Rights movement. This does not mean that all Black males sought their honor in playing the game of drugs and pimps. Most Blacks did not, and do not. But the message was the same to all: "You keep on tryin' as you go down cryin', You take all odds," and you don't complain.

The toasts taught other lessons as well. Clearly, throughout, no sympathy is to be shown, no self-pity, no pity for others. This is well illustrated in *The Sinking of the Titanic* when Shine, the hero, starts swimming across the Atlantic away from the disaster. He encounters several doomed passengers who plead with him to save them. Despite the rewards they promise, he rebuffs them all harshly and coldly. Finally, he meets a crying baby.

> 13. Shine said, "Baby, baby please don't cry.
> All little m – – – – – – – – – – – s got a time to die.
> You got eight little fingers and two little thumbs,
> And your black ass goes when the wagon comes.

Labov et al. (1968, p. 60) compare this to Achilles' speech in the *Iliad:*

> 13a. Ay friend thou too must die: why lamentest thou?
> Petroklos too is dead, who was better far than thou.
> Sees thou not also what manner of man am I for might and
> goodliness?
> Yet over me too hang death and forceful fate.

However, Achilles says this to another adult not a helpless babe. What can this mean, and why is it in the toast? Certainly, Blacks love their babies as others do. Clearly, Shine shows some feeling for the baby, "Please don't cry." In fact, the baby is the only one of the doomed that Shine speaks kindly to. To the others he is brutal. We have ample evidence from this toast and others such as *The Fall* that pity for others is to be squelched at all costs. Many verses in *The Fall* are devoted to first establishing that the prostitute served her man fantastically well. When she becomes ill, however, he throws her out and, again, several verses recount the particular heartlessness with which he does so, such as:

14. You had your run. Now you done.

.

.

.

I can't make no swag off some swayback nag
Whose thoroughbred days are past.
Why I'd look damn silly puttin' a cripple filly
On a track that's way too fast.

(quoted in Labov et al. 1968, p. 57)

My interpretation of passages like 13 and 14 is that they are intended to underscore an important message to the urban slum dweller. It is not good in that life to have too much pity for others. In a world as harsh as that pictured in these toasts, the only way to survive is to cut off compassion. The passage from the *Iliad* had the same message for the ancient Greek youths: in war one must not be compassionate. In essence, the world of the toasts is a world always at war. Just as Shine's swimming the ocean to safety is a tremendous exaggeration, so is his encounter with the baby. It is the message "be dispassionate" carried to the extremes, a tremendous exaggeration.

Black storytelling is suffused with tales that teach people not to trust, not to pity. This theme has even been grafted onto stories originally from Africa, such as the talking animal genre like the "Bre'r Rabbit" stories. The difference is that in Africa these stories were used to teach children to beware of antisocial creatures who disrupted friendship. In America, these were changed to teach instead that everyone must look out for himself or herself. Thus are the realities of society mirrored in speech activities.

6.6   *Black male attitude toward women*

The attitude toward women in the toasts goes beyond mere lack of pity. It is actively hostile. In one toast Stagolee casually shoots women on the slightest provocation. In another Shine makes the cruelest fun at the romantic notions of two young girls, telling them in the bluntest of terms that the sexual act itself, not love or romance, is all there is to relations between men and women.

In *The Fall,* the whore is called a "sex machine," and in the extended metaphor quoted in 14 she is likened to a racehorse. A general bitter vindictiveness characterizes all dealings of men with women in the toasts, a vindictiveness matched by the cruel insults hurled at women in verbal games like sounding and chopping long played by Black male adolescents. Labov et al. (1968, p. 62) point out that the hostility revealed in all such verbal activity makes it especially difficult for women teachers to deal with male members of this culture.

   The pimp as hero in the toasts and on the streets may be another expression of this hostility. Again, the reason is perhaps to be found in social values and conditions. Black culture is after all American. In our society as indeed in most, men are supposed to dominate women. Until recently this has meant that men should make more money than their wives and even control any earnings their wives bring in. During the years when the toasts were being composed, the ideal was that a man should be able to earn enough so that his wife did not have to work. That was a particular point of pride during my childhood in many families and still is. It must be emphasized that most Blacks have been and are raised in normal families with wage earning fathers. For many years, however, a larger percentage of Blacks than Whites came from families in which males were not the principal wage earners. Fathers in such families were absent much or all of the time or dependent on mothers or both. Such men suffered greatly in self-esteem. Yet, there was no alternative for many men, especially in the grim urban ghettos of large Northern cities. It was easier for women to get jobs. Furthermore, prestigious jobs such as teaching and nursing were open to Black women long before equally prestigious ones were available to men. For some men, the way to dominate women as well as to make a great deal of money was to pimp. Pimping is the rawest exploitation of women as sex object, of women being subservient to men (Chapter 9). In a horrible way, it allowed and allows some men in the ghetto to achieve the American ideals of making money and dominating women.

6.7   The toasts as art

   Before examining ritual insults, a defense is in order of the proposition that the toasts parallel the great epics of the past. It is very easy to look at the topics of the toasts: the profanity, the lawbreaking, the nonstandard speech forms, and dismiss them as being unworthy of scholarly attention. Examining such productions does tell us a good deal about the lives of the people who composed and recited them. It tells us how they saw the world they lived in and why they held certain attitudes. Granting all that, still, why call the toasts poetry? Yes, they have heroes of a sort. They tell their listeners how life should be lived: stoically, unromantically, unpityingly. This makes them epics, but does it make them poetry? Without any philosophical haggling about Art and what it is, we can see that the toasts make use of all the devices of poetry and do so skillfully. Poetry manipulates language while expressing even ordinary meanings (Keyser 1976). Often, this manipulation makes us see new relations between words, makes us see old things in new ways.

   Rhyme is a frequent but not a necessary feature of poetry. In order to catch rhymes, if they are used, poetry must be read in the dialect in which it was composed. For instance, in order to appreciate the skillful rhyming in 10–13 and 14, the reader must realize that the following sets of words rhyme in NNE (as well as in some other dialects, non-Black as well as Black): *odds, cards; cell, jail; wheel, field (fiel').* It is not easy in any dialect to find rhyming words that can fit in the rhythm of a poem as well as give the poet's desired meaning. Still, hundreds of lines of toasts and other Black oral activities manage perfect rhyme, many highly clever and unusual. This feat is all the more impressive when we consider the intricate rhyming scheme of the toasts. The basic schema of many toasts consists of a long line divided in two with internal rhyme, as illustrated in italics here:

> 15. She tricked with the *Greeks*, Arabs, and *freaks*
>   She tricked with the *Jews*, Apaches, and *Siouxs*
>
> *(from* The Fall*)*
>
> 16. He said, "I'm not *cryin'* 'cause the agent was *lyin'*
>   That I was a big *wheel* in the narcotics *field*
>
> *(from* Honky Tonk Bud*)*

These long lines formed four line sequences. A short line followed each long line. The last word of each of these short lines rhymed with the next short line. For instance, in 15, the scheme is completed by:

> 15a. To her they were all the *same*
>   She tricked with the Greeks, Arabs, and freaks
>   And breeds I cannot *name*
>   She tricked with the Jew, Apaches, and Sioux.

and 16 by

> 16a. He said, "I'm not cryin' 'cause the agent was lyin'
>   And left you all with a *notion*
>   That I was a big wheel in the narcotics field
>   I hope the fag cops a *promotion*

Lines 1 and 3 have internal rhyme, and 2 and 4 rhyme with each other. A very important feature of poetry is figurative language such as metaphor. The image of addicts in 10 as vicious felines is reinforced both by the metaphor of people as jungle animals (As the game stalked their prey . . . Where the addicts prowl . . .) and the rhyme of *prowl* with *growl*. The metaphor of the city streets as a jungle in which game stalks prey sets the moral tone as well as the physical aura of *The Fall.* "And the cold was crime on the neon line" emphasizes the misery and ugliness of the streets. Jungles can be warm and beautiful as well as vicious and unlawful, but these lines make it clear that only the latter meaning is to be taken. Images of heat are followed by images of cold throughout *The Fall.* The winos have canned heat, such as sterno, but still die in the snow. Even at the end the sun rises, but it is the morning chills that put the slumbering beast to rest. The word *slumbering* itself is one that even in Standard English (SE) is literary, even poetic. This is another instance of the supposedly unlettered being familiar with the language of books. Throughout, *The Fall* shows such skillful use of language, all bringing to us vividly, as only poetry can do, the terror and the feel of the city jungle, the contemptuous feeling for women, the bravery and resignation of the heroes.

6.8   *Profanity*

There is a great deal of profanity in the toasts, and swearing surely peppers the speech of the streets. Both profanity and taboo sexual subjects are so prevalent in all speech activities that it is impossible to represent such speech without including much that is highly offensive to many middle-class people.

As offensive as it is, still there is a reason for the profanity and sexually taboo speech, and frequently it is encased in brilliant phrasing and metaphor. Unfortunately, the gutter language so turns off middle-class listeners and readers that they often cannot analyze the speech dispassionately. In order to discuss everyday language activities and how these reflect social conditions, both the taboo speech and the discourses in which it is encased must be discussed. In deference to middle-class sensibilities, in this text the offensive words have been and will be, as often as possible, represented with dashes. However, in order to do justice to the subject at hand, some examples of sexual subjects have to be included, always with a clear explanation of their importance to a sociology of language.

Some people think that the members of the lower class, being uneducated, use profanity because of ignorance; that perhaps they do not realize that such words are vulgar and taboo. To the contrary, they are most aware of the impropriety. They realize very well that such language is shocking (or used to be) to the middle class. Its use was and is overt defiance.

Revolutions have been won on the premise that the poor are lacking because the more fortunate have taken from the less fortunate. The truth of such a position is beside the point here. What counts is that the poor feel that way. As we saw in Larry's argument that God must be White, many non-middle-class Blacks think that all Whites are privileged at the expense of Blacks. This is one cause of defiance toward middle-class Whites. Another more direct cause is that until relatively recently most authority figures were White. Blacks in the North especially were taught by White teachers, hired by White employers, visited by White social workers, arrested by White policemen, prosecuted by White attorneys, and sentenced by White judges. Even now, in most places, Whites are in the majority in all authoritarian roles.

One way to express defiance toward authority is to defy middle class mores about taboo words. Years ago, while teaching junior high in what is euphemistically called an "inner city school," after dropping a box of pencils, I muttered "damn," under my breath (I thought). The students heard and a really shocked cry of, "Oooh, what you said" arose. This from students whose most frequent epithets would be unprintable even in these liberal times. Obscenities or swear words, they felt, were theirs to be used as they wished; I as a teacher was not supposed to use them. Both in that school and as a teacher in an Upward Bound program, I frequently observed that students confined their profanity to teachers they disliked, never lapsing into it in front of those with whom they got along. Profanity can be a weapon, an overt expression of hostility.

This produces some problems for the female investigator especially. Many Black males who regularly use profanity cannot bring themselves to use such words in front of a middle-class female toward whom they have no hostility. The result is that it is virtually impossible for a woman to record a good deal of the speech activity common among Black street youth. They simply block and cannot get the words out. I had thought that middle-class Black males might be familiar with these activities and not be so prudish about sharing them with me for the sake of research. But alas, either the middle-class male claims unfamiliarity with the activities or simply will not make himself available. Some who admit to knowledge and do make appointments for taping cancel at the last minute. This reluctance has been found in Black males, middle class and not, from all parts of the United States. Such reluctance shows that users of taboo language certainly understand middle-class attitudes toward it.

Examining the most profane passages in the toasts confirms this. Such passages deny middle-class values. Recall Shine's plea to the baby. Extreme profanity characterizes Shine's denial of romantic love in a different toast. In *The Fall*, the pimp's profanity grows as he refuses charity to his old whore. He even couples taboo images with Biblical allusions, such as "Dig up Moses and kiss him in the crack of his a– –." The interesting thing here is that this is one of the few lines in *The Fall* that does not have a proper rhyme. It has clearly been thrown in for shock value. The passages in *The Fall* that set the scene and give the moral at the end (10 and 11 above) have no vulgarity, only poetry.

Profanity can also be a bonding device, a way of showing belonging. The following conversations were about the same event, told at the same location, a neighborhood YMCA, but to different audiences. The first was related by a Black teenager to two Black male friends. The second was the same story as related to a White teenager.

> 17. We's up to the Y, right? We was talkin' to these girls, and he pulled the van out an' he couldn' see 'im an' he almost hit my cousin and s– – –. My cousin said, "Hey, man, what you doin'?" So, he got out of the car, right? Said he was goin' to beat his a– –. Jumped out of the car called my cousin somethin'. Said I'm f– – –in' you up! Right ... My cousin went to karate. Right? Kicked that m– – – – – – – – – – in the n– – – and he... I broke it up because I didn' want

the White dude to get hurt. Right? I had my cousin. M– – – – – – –
– – – – snatched away ran back down there again. That m– – – – –
– – – – – – crazy.

18. Yeah [my cousin] had a fight with this White dude at the Y . . . The
    White dude came too close to my cousin with the van and my
    cousin got mad.

The greater detail in 17 is reminiscent of the sociolinguistic experiments in
which people are found to write more details if asked by a person with a
"proper" accent rather than by a person with the "wrong" accent (Chapter 7).
Another parallel can be found among middle-class women who wish to
emphasize that they are liberated and not docile housewives. Such women may
go out of their way to use once unmentionable words, especially to other women.
Sometimes this is done only once early in the acquaintance, as a way of
affirming their denial of traditional woman's role (Chapter 9). Profanity is not
just spoken. It is spoken under certain conditions and, like most language, has a
purpose.

6.9 Anti-middle-class feeling

Although far more data have been gathered on non-middle-class Blacks'
speech than from comparable Whites, what little has been gathered suggests
that similar attitudes toward middle-class values may also occur among at least
some non-middle-class Whites. There is verbal dueling, for example, which
deals wholly with taboo topics, including those rarely or never heard from
Blacks. As with Black ritual insulting (Section 6.11), what is said in the dueling
is not necessarily true. Rather, each person tries to build upon a previous remark
either by introducing a taboo subject or by insulting the other person, preferably
with his or her own words. Puns are not necessarily a feature of such exchanges.
The repartee can be between men and women, and the entire subject matter of
the discourse deals with subjects especially taboo in middle-class speech.
Although the subjects are taboo, interestingly, so far, few taboo words
themselves have been collected.
   A sample of such dialogue, gathered by a student Cynthia Marousis in an
urban coffeeshop after midnight started with a male customer's asking if a
waitress was married. When she responded "Yeah," he asked "How's your
lover?" The assumption, pretended as much as real, that she was immoral
enough to have a lover started an entire sequence of exchanges about
menstruation, incontinence, oral sex, and homosexuality. The waitress commented "My husband's good, but my lover's not doing good. He's got the rag
on." This comment about her lover shows that the object is to raise a taboo

subject somehow. It makes no difference how absurd, impossible, or bizarre the rejoinder is, just so long as the taboo subject is raised. Assuredly, such exchanges are displays of verbal skill, especially oneupmanship. The topics chosen indicate real hostility toward established middle-class values.

6.10   *Ego-raising through speech activities*

The men who created toasts could gain ego satisfaction from both their creation and their performance. As we have seen, Blacks overtly praise and encourage a man who is giving a good display of speech. In the toasts men could fantasize as they boasted about the great exploits of their heroes. Similarly, Black men exchange boasts about their prowess in fighting and other street activities. Muhammed Ali's rhymed boasts before big fights is a typical Black male speech activity. Italian-American working class youths in the Northeast also engage in boasting contests, although they do not seem as likely as Blacks to utilize rhymes for this purpose.

In a study of White bar flies, a student of mine, Robert Walling, found patterns of conversation also designed, in his words, to "reinforce and stabilize egos." Their pattern was simple. The conversation started with criticism of current government, society, or sports figures. This, apparently, served as a way of establishing the man's superiority over those in power. An unfavorable comparison of the present to the past was then made. This is not surprising since they always claimed that their glories were in the past. Finally, the bar fly gave a sketch of his past life, and, if he was a father, his children's past and present. This sketch proved to be untrue, though not wholly so. There was always some germ of truth in the tales. Unlike Black street youths, these older White men do not claim fantastic exploits; they only upgrade the past a few notches. The bars they frequented were in stable neighborhoods. Most of the men were lifelong residents, and the bartenders and other patrons could all verify the truth of each tale. Walling found no difficulty in getting the men to talk. Indeed, as soon as they saw a new face, they accosted him and insisted on telling him their tales.

One man who many years ago had driven a city bus for ten months, eventually getting fired for drunkenness, claimed:

> 19. I was a bus driver and a damn good one too. My wife used to work at the Outlet [a local department store] and now my two boys drive truck for them.

The bartender confirmed that his boys were doing no such thing, nor, as their father also claimed, was it likely that they could have gone to college. Another oldster who had been a janitor at an elegant hotel claimed:

> 20. I worked at the Biltmore. You name it and I did it. There wasn't much in that place that I couldn't do. That used to be the best hotel

in southern New England. All the big shots who came to Providence stayed at the Biltmore. [shows autographs from Jack Benny and Jack Dempsey.] Pretty impressive, huh? I talked to those two for about an hour apiece. Ya, they were great guys. I still remember what Demps told me, "You got to fight to win in this world." I'll never forget those words and that was almost forty years ago . . . When I had my big job with the Biltmore I never complained once.

Note the use of a pseudo-nickname, Demps, to indicate familiarity or intimacy with the great fighter. For these men, part of the reason for going to bars seems to be to have a chance to tell their stories, to present themselves as worthwhile people. Most people apparently use language somehow to boost their own sense of worth, to gain status and maintain their egos.

6.11   *Ritual insults*

Casual, rough talk can also be very revealing of social attitudes and conditions. Previously (Chapter 5), we got a glimpse of how society's values and the individual's needs combine to form utterance pairs like veiled commands and indirect requests for food. A more elaborate example is found in what Labov (1972) has termed ritual insults. Unlike true insults, ritual insults do not evoke anger or denials. Instead they evoke other insults, laughter, or occasionally a change of subject. Although probably all human societies have ritual insulting activities, some seem to indulge only sporadically. Others, such as American urban Black youth, have codified the activity. It is virtually an everyday business and, furthermore, one important in determining social rank. As with toasts, Black insults are often obscene, but the obscenities themselves are explicable by reference to the conditions that created the insults.

The frequency of ritual insulting changes throughout one's lifetime. There are times and situations when one is very likely to indulge in ritual insulting. Adolescence seems to call forth a good deal of play insulting. Examples are easily gathered from athletic teams, cafeterias, and schoolyards in the United States as well as other countries (see examples from Turkey in Dundes et al. 1972). Brothers and sisters often tease each other playfully but with a barb. College students tell me that insulting often reaches a peak in the dorms during exams. Some husbands and wives playfully insult each other. More rarely, and only in some really relaxed family situations, do children "bust up" their parents. In earlier times when children had to be far more formal with their parents than today, playful insulting to parents was unthinkable. Ritual insulting seems most acceptable when the participants are of equal or near equal social status, and it occurs most frequently at times of stress, such as adolescence in general and exams in particular. The business of living together as a family can create many small tensions. Thus siblings or college roommates or spouses insult each other jokingly, whereas casual acquaintances are not as likely to. When we see an entire cultural group regularly engaging in ritual insulting, we have good reason to suspect that they are under special strain.

Two cases in point are Eastern European Jews and American Blacks. Both groups have or had one thing in common: social circumstances that induce exceptional tension. Since ritual insulting allows hostility to be vented without disrupting social order, it is not surprising that both groups developed it to a high degree.

Ritual insulting can take on functions other than that of venting. For American Blacks and for Turkish adolescent males it has become a means of achieving status within the peer group. Eastern European Jews with their tradition of Biblical scholarship to determine status seemed to use insults only to lessen anger and hostility.

Black ritual insulting has shown growth in complexity and applications, nowadays being taken up by White youth as well. In contrast, Jewish cursing has all but died out in America, where the conditions that spawned it do not exist. Rather, America has allowed Jews to develop their tradition of scholarship. It is that which has grown in complexity and application in America. The kinds of ritual insulting that develop, and their subsequent history, are very dependent upon the social, physical, and cultural contexts of particular groups.

6.12   *Eastern European Jewish cursing*

Before most were exterminated in World War II, Jews of Eastern Europe were, for the most part, forced to live in very crowded impoverished ghettos or shtetls (literal translation: 'little cities,' from German *Stadt*). Even the relatively few who were able to leave the ghettos or shtetls always lived in fear of violence, even massacres, from their Christian neighbors. The tensions of such an existence are obvious. Living in overcrowded conditions with little mobility, as Jews were often forbidden to travel, overt quarreling or violence could destroy the community. Safer outlets were needed. In many villages and ghettos, a form of ritual insult arose that was a darkly humorous cursing. The cursing was always preceded by the formulaic "May you/your . . ." The curses themselves reflected Jewish social values. A representative few, translated from Yiddish, the language of Eastern European Jews, are:

21. May you be known for your hospitality to all God's creatures: rats, bedbugs, fleas, worms.
22. May you have all your dreams come true, all nightmares.
23. May you marry a raving beauty, live next door to the officers' club, and travel ten months of the year.

24. May you lose all your teeth but one—and have a toothache in that one.
25. May you be spared the indignities of old age.
26. May you make a widow and orphans happy—your own.
27. May your daughters' hair grow thick, black, and abundant—all over their faces.
28. May your son rise so high he becomes at least a bishop.
29. May you back into a pitchfork and grab a hot stove for support.
30. May you never have the problem of dividing your inheritance.

(from Singer 1977)

All of these are complex in structure. The real curse comes at the end of the statement, often after an apparently complimentary wish, as in 21–23 and 26–28. Others, like 25 and 30 do not state the curse overtly. The hearer has to ferret out the implications of the statements. In 25, if one is spared the indignities of old age, one has to die first. In 30, if one is childless, one does not have to divide one's inheritance. Ritual insults like 24 and 29 that begin with a curse, have a kicker at the end making them even worse.

These curses represent the most usual topics: cleanliness, death, and family pride. A curse is an insult only if it wishes something deemed terrible in a given society. To Eastern European Jews religion and family were what life was all about. Cleanliness and chastity were of the utmost importance. An unchaste daughter or wife caused ineradicable shame—hence curses like 23. All Jews were expected to marry and have children. Every community had its match-maker who ensured a spouse for all. Yente the matchmaker in *Fiddler on the Roof* was not a fictional creation. To be childless was considered a great tragedy, hence curses like 30. Today that curse might not be such an insult, since having children is, for many, a conscious choice.

To have children who brought shame was, if anything, a greater tragedy. Yiddish even has a word, *nachas,* that means 'the particular joy that one's children can give you' (see Chapter 9). A double shame and tragedy that could befall parents was for a child to convert to Christianity. If this happened, it was assumed the parents must have failed in the most solemn duty of giving religious training to their children. Given the isolation of Jews and the fact that so many of Judaism's rituals are family oriented, a Christian child was effectively lost to the family, which explains the curse in 28. Example 28 is included to show how social situation and cultural values determine what would be an insult. The attitudes expressed in 28 resulted from the bad treatment Jews had historically received from the Christian establishment. Of course, as in any kind of prejudice, there were individual Christians who treated their Jewish neighbors very well. Today in America 28 might not work as a curse at all. Many American Jews have never been faced with overt ill treatment by Christians. Therefore, they have to have the 'curse' explained to them, just as many have to be told that a wood stove is hot all over, not just on the burners. Otherwise, they miss the point of 29.

If one knew nothing about the Eastern European Jewish culture except the curses, one could reconstruct social values from them. If one knew nothing more about American Jews except those curses that no longer work as curses, one could reconstruct changes in those values in America.

It must be noted that these curses are indirect insults. They do not state that the person cursed has any failings beyond the general one of having aroused ire. The misfortune wished on others could as easily visit the curser. Both the indirectness of ritual insults and their centering on matters common to the group are also features of the very different Black ritual insults.

6.13   *Sounding*

Sounding, chopping, ranking, cutting, woofing, giving s– – –, giving S, and *giving J* are some of the local terms for the same activity: competitive insulting between males in the Black ghettos (Abrahams 1974). Hereafter, this form of ritual insult will be referred to only as sounding. Sounding arose from an earlier competition called "playing the dozens," rhymed couplets with four strong beats per long line. In 31, these strong beats are boldfaced. In my childhood neighborhood, one heard young men being "put in the dozens" with:

> 31. I **don't** play the **dozens,** I **don't** play the **game**
> But the **way** I had your **mother** is a **godd– –n** shame.

This started a round of such couplets, all insulting an opponent's mother, implying that she was promiscuous. By the early 1960s, perhaps because both the structure and topic of the dozens proved too limiting, they had given way to sounding. *Sounds* are unrhymed one-line insults on three general themes: poverty, the alleged sexual promiscuity of the opponent's female relatives, and their physical attributes or those of the opponent. Sounding often takes the form of a verbal duel between two boys. Onlookers overtly comment on the quality of each sound, much as onlookers to rapping might comment "Talk that talk" or "Rap City." The more original a sound, the higher it is ranked. As with the White repartee mentioned earlier, a sound that elaborates on an opponent's previous statement is considered better than an unrelated one. For street kids sounding and other verbal displays are the major determinants of social status.

As with any ritual insulting the topics of sounds are constrained (Labov 1972b). To overstep the bounds leads into genuine insulting. The limits shield participants from inadvertent hurt. However insulting the sounds may be, they are not calculated to bruise egos. To the contrary, the activity of ritual insulting provides ego-boosting for boys to whom the ordinary ego satisfactions are denied. The street kid who may never make it into college or a prestige job, who cannot participate in the American dream of upward mobility, can get proof daily of his intelligence and wit by these verbal duels. Abrahams (1974) says that verbal jousts are a safe arena in which to seek success and to exercise aggressiveness.

As with the Jewish cursing, the Black sounds are not true. Labov et al. (1968, p. 101–2) convincingly demonstrate that mention of a true incident is not taken as part of the game. Rather, it brings forth angry denials. For instance, although poverty itself may be sounded on, to mention something showing someone's actual poverty is taken as a grave insult. It is all right to say that the cockroaches in Junior's house are so bold that they pull a gun on you, but it is not all right to tell about the chair that broke when you sat on it. Labov et al. reported that when one boy mentioned that, the other hotly responded, "You's a damn liar, 'n' you was eatin' in my house, right?" In that community remarking that someone ate at someone's house implies hunger, a real need for food. Thus it is a true insult.

The reader may recall that asking for food is difficult for Americans in general (Chapter 5), calling for a ploy that doesn't make it seem as if one is really asking. With all the profanity and vulgar images that the boys proved capable of in the Harlem study, one of the worst insults that Labov et al. collected was "Yeah, but you sure be eatin'." It proved easy to determine true from ritual insults. The true ones were not only about highly plausible events, but the boy sounded on angrily justified what was said. Telling the truth about one boy's father, that he stuttered and had gray hair, evoked heated denials, even tears. This in itself shows the importance of untruthfulness as a component of ritual insulting.

6.14 Permissible truths

Nonetheless a germ of truth exists in the sounds. Poverty is sounded on; so are physical attributes like fatness or Negroid facial features. Although they have some foundation in fact, the sounds are saved from truth by being so fantastic that they could not possibly by true. Perhaps for this reason bizarre and absurd imagery abounds in sounding. For example, the following was recently collected from two college students by another student, David Aldrich. It is an excellent example of earthy, even raw use of language that in reality serves both social and psychological purposes for the speakers. As casual as it is, it follows the rules of the game. The taboo subject matter should not obscure the real wit of this spontaneous exchange:

32. *Craig:* Man, if I was a chick, I wouldn't kiss you with my dog's lips.
    Greg: With the size of your lips, you'd drown her for sure.
    Craig: I may not be the best kisser, but man, I'm hung like a baseball bat and swing it like Willie Mays.
    Greg: Well, you got your chance tonight. Baby, I got my goggles on, and I'm ready to do some heavy divin'.
    Craig: Just call me Jacques Cousteau.

The germ of the truth here is that Craig's lips are Negroid. So are Greg's.

Labov found a good deal of sounding on shared physical characteristics of Blacks. This does not necessarily indicate self-hatred as some suppose. Rather, it may be because things that are involuntary, short of deformity, can often be joked about. This seems to be true in many different cultures, although which topics are to be excluded are specific to the culture. Among most American Whites, teasing about freckles, red hair, and short stature is permissible, so that a short red-headed boy might be called "Strawberry shortcake" by his friends. If he were a genuine midget, his height could not be mentioned. Similarly, if a normal person trips, someone might joke, "Whatsa matter, forget your crutches?" but the same statement to a paraplegic would be outrageous.

Greg's retort is saved from being a true insult because lip-size is a permissible topic for sounds among Blacks. It is further saved by being absurd. Obviously, no one could drown in anyone's lips. Craig, who started the round, apparently just for the fun of the duel, quickly turns Greg's statement into a boast about his other physical attributes. In the verbal dueling and oneupmanship of ritual insulting, one can best one's opponent by taking another's insult and using it to lead into a self-glorification. Greg then shows his own skill by turning the sexual reference into a metaphor for deep sea diving. This also entailed a boast that he was going to score that evening, which may or may not be true. Truth is not the point here; besting the other in verbal play is. Craig's "Call me Jacques Cousteau" is a way of saying that he is the best "deep sea diver" of them all.

Comparing oneself to a famous historical figure or a modern celebrity is very common as a way of boasting in Black ritual insults. Making comparisons to figures who are not admired is a putdown. Although this exchange is undeniably vulgar as are many insulting rounds, it still is the subtle comment that wins the game (Call me Jacques Cousteau), and the entire discourse takes a good deal of wit and skill.

Labov et al.'s samples of sounding do include those about poverty, but they were all impossible exaggerations. They were collected on the streets of Harlem from boys who were really poor. Note the difference in the sounding on poverty initiated by Craig, a college student who is Black, and directed to Bill, his White roommate at college, as they were playing cards:

> 33. *Craig:*   Hey, man you got another trump card just as sure as a bear s – – t – in the woods.
>
> *Bill:*   I sure as hell don't got no trump card, just as sure as your mother s – – – – on the floor.
>
> *Craig:*   Well, Mr. Cool, at least we got a floor to s – – – on. They don't let you s – – – on the welfare office floor.
>
> *Bill:*   You're pretty bad with the mouth. How about the cards?

It is all right for Craig to tease Bill by implying that his family is on welfare, because it is neither true nor likely. To a genuinely poor person in an urban ghetto, this would be a true insult. Note that in this verbal gaming with a Black, despite his middle-class background and his college status, the White Bill uses the nonstandard double negative "Don't got no . . ."

The function of ritual insulting to vent hostility safely has already been mentioned. Another theory is that Blacks played the dozens as a way of turning their aggressions on themselves, since they could not compete with Whites. Nowadays many White males are very familiar with Black ritual insulting and engage in it themselves, although my consultants over the past ten years, White athletes mostly, all admit that the Blacks can easily best them verbally. In one of his most famous routines the comedian Gabriel Kaplan describes "ranking" in the New York City schools played exactly the same way that Blacks play it, primarily with insults against mothers and other female relatives. A White consultant who grew up in California told me that in the early sixties all members of the football team, White and Black, also regularly "chopped" by insulting mothers. So far, I have not been able to collect any admissions of sounding by White males before the early 1960s, even from those who were raised in racially mixed neighborhoods and attended integrated schools. Perhaps in some communities sounding by non-Black youths did occur earlier but has not been recorded. In any event the sociolinguistic literature has assumed that sounding began and remained a Black male phenomenon. In the absence of evidence to the contrary, we have to assume that Whites borrowed it relatively recently. Such borrowing from one group by another is always of sociological significance, as is the form of ritual insults within a social group.

As late as 1973, in my first sociolinguistic classes, the White males unanimously agreed with great vehemence that any slur on their mothers' or sisters' characters would be a grave insult. Now many are familiar with sounding and engage in it themselves; in 33 it was the White student Bill who initiated the first insult to a mother, and in 34 Bob, another White, simply laughed at the insult to his mother.

> 34. *Al:*   I can read 350 words a minute.
> *Bob:*   S––– —you can't even turn the pages that fast.
> *Al:*   I turned your mother that fast.

In view of the traditional psychological explanation for sounding, this is most interesting. Abrahams believes that the putdowns for women give Black males opportunity to assert their virility. Since they grow up in female-dominated households, often with highly authoritarian mothers and grandmothers, the insults are a way of asserting independence. Dr. Melvin Bell, a Black socialworker and colleague of mine, claims that toasting and sounding are necessary for Black youths to be able to cut the exceptionally strong Oedipal bond that forms between mothers and sons in fatherless homes. With the general disintegration of the family in America, there are now many more White fatherless homes as well. Perhaps this is one explanation for sounding among Whites (although both Whites and Blacks whose sounding is quoted here are from intact homes with fathers as the principal breadwinners).

The psychological explanations leave some questions unanswered. Why is Black ritual insulting going on between Whites and Blacks, contrary to claims that such insulting is a result of White's oppression of Blacks? The reasoning behind this interpretation is that Blacks turn their rage on to themselves. Why are middle-class males, both White and Black, indulging in the activity of insulting mothers, an activity that was highly offensive to their counterparts as recently as ten years ago? One reason, as Labov (1964) noted, is that Black youths have increasingly become the reference points for Whites.

Another possibility is the general devaluing of motherhood in this country in recent years. Jokes about "Jewish" and "Italian" mothers, meaning mothers very concerned with their children's welfare, abound on television and in the movies. Movies like *Harold and Maude* and *Where's Poppa* pan motherhood completely. Since women's liberation, girls often get the impression that a career is more important than motherhood, that motherhood is not a worthy way to spend one's time. It would be comforting to mothers to be able to say that sounding is innocent enough, just a way for adolescent boys to get things off their chests, but then it would have to be explained why it is not fathers who get sounded on, or other relatives or friends, or any of the host of possible topics that could be chosen for insulting. (In Turkey, for instance, adolescent males often insult each other by creating riddles that imply that the other is homosexual. In this country such allusions are taken as truly insulting.)

It seems to me that present social attitudes toward mothers and mothering allow a climate in which sounding can take place. It represents a very real devaluing of the feminine role. The word *mother* has even become by itself as obscene as the original unprintable compound. Note the difference in force between "That mother!" and "That father!"

6.15   *The real game and the verbal one*

We have already seen that ritual insulting provides two benefits to a social group: lessening of tensions and ego-boosting by besting others in competition, or at least by getting a good line or two in. It can also be used as a regulatory mechanism in conjunction with another activity. Examining such an occurrence is in itself a study in the sensitivity of language use to social needs.

In Black neighborhoods games of pick-up basketball are prevalent. They constitute a very important activity for the youths of the community. Since there is no referee at such games, the players have to keep score and generally regulate the game by themselves. Such a situation is potentially explosive: unsupervised boys playing a competitive game with no one to judge what is foul or out of bounds and scores kept only in the heads of individual players! Allan Baker, himself at the time a Black college basketball player, shows how the activity of sounding and general verbal gaming is used to regulate the game. The exchange in 35 occurred during a dispute about a score in a game played in a college gym between Black male college students from several Northern cities.

Baker was watching, taking down the exchange under the guise of doing his homework. A dispute was started when B called a foul on A. Because pick-up games are rough, fouls are not usually called. Baker says that the person who does call one can expect to be sounded on. Therefore, A says that B plays like a girl:

35. A: Look, man you play like my sister at your best.
    B: S – – – . Your sister is betta than me. She can dunk on Wilt! [referring to Wilt Chamberlain of the Los Angeles Lakers.]

B's response is typical, and, for the moment, gives him the advantage, since he turns A's words back into an insult about A's own sister. This exchange allows both players to shed their irritation with each other: B because he has a foul committed on him, and A because the foul is, in his eyes, unjustly called. Dissipating anger by verbal exchange works because both boys understand the ritual nature of the insults. An outsider, say a boy from Ireland, might be so incensed by A's remark or B's rejoinders that an actual argument might ensue. Then came the following sequence:

36. A: Look man, you cheatin'.
    B: Your a – – , I don't have to cheat-ya to beat-ya.
    A: I know we got more points than that.
    B: This ain't the welfare building; we don't give s – – – away here, sucker.
    A: You ain't givin' us nothin', we takin' it sucker!
    B: You ain't no d – – – go-rilla kool.
    A: Look man, we got ten baskets.
    C: Now, I know you jumped out of your tree, fool! You can't count on no f – – – in' ten!
    D: Look, man, give them ten and let's get it on. S – – – , we been arguin' all night. Other people wanna play.
    B: I ain't givin' them no ten, no way.
    D: OK. man! Let's start back at eight, tie score, all right?
    A: H – – – , yea! I just ain't gonna get beat out no points.
    B: Man, ain't no body tryin' to beatcha. You always cryin'. You got over this time, but I'm going to bust your a – – .
    A: Sure, man, you jus' keep talkin' that Jeff Davis s – – – .

During a pick-up game, each team keeps its own score. Although a running patter accompanies the game, whenever one team falls far behind, one of its members starts insulting the opposition. The point is to con the other team into thinking the losers have more points than they do. Allan Baker comments, "This is not to say that Blacks thrive on cheating, but rather that if the opportunity presents itself and debate occurs, the advantage goes to the most verbal." The technique that A uses in 36 is typical. He lures the other side into debate, thereby stalling the game. Baker points out that A sets the other side up by naming a ridiculous number of points, here ten baskets. In order to get the game going again, the opponents have to give A's team some points. Baker, sitting on the sidelines, had been keeping score. In actuality A's team had only five baskets, and B's had ten. A's ploy resulted not only in his team's getting more points but B's giving some up!

The reason that A's ploy is so successful is the shared cultural behavior of the participants. They know and understand that if an insult has been given, it must be answered, and that this will go on until one side can claim victory. The only way to stop the round before then is to at least partly accede to A's demands. A himself knows that he will have to give a little as well. In this particular round, most of the insults are not actual sounds. "You cheatin' " is a bald accusation. Baker emphasizes that because the participants are all friends they do not become angry at such insults. Within the context of the athletic contest, the insults are taken as ritual ones not real ones. The verbal requirements of the insulting contest take precedence over the game for these Black players. The entire sequence can be taken as a subcategory of sounding, one used to gain an advantage in a usually nonverbal activity. Baker comments that although none of these boys were professional players, they were all what he calls "professional talkers." Also, he notes that the verbal game is as important as the basketball game in pick-up matches.

Because ritual insulting can go on concurrently with the game, it has a strong regulatory function. It allows disputes over scoring to be settled on another plane by utilizing the well-known rules for ritual insulting. Here we see a beautiful example of what is probably a universal phenomenon, ritual insulting, as it is adapted to a specific social situation, the pick-up game. Verbal sparring takes the place of a referee and scorekeeper.

The apparently mundane matter of how people insult each other in a community is a highly complicated set of interrelated behaviors. To understand the workings of a social group, one must understand these behaviors. They reflect general social conditions as well as the requirements of particular social situations. As with Jewish curses, an examination of the insults alone would suggest a good deal about Black life even if the history books were silent.

6.16   *Jargons*

The sensitivity with which language mirrors society is highlighted in jargons. *Jargons* are varieties of language created for specific functions by the people who engage in them regularly. They are like minidialects, but used only for the activity for which they were created. Jargons are not only sensitive to the requirements of the activity but to the personal and social needs of the speakers. Jargons arise so rapidly and are so fitted to specific events that they give us insights into both the mechanisms and causes of language change.

6.17   *Bowling jargon*

The following dialogue was collected in Rhode Island by a bowler from that state, Timothy Rembijas. S is an experienced league bowler, but F is an outsider. The jargon, noted during a league game, is italicized.

37. S: Did you see that hit? I thought sure it was *buried,* but he left a swishing seven. He should have had a *turkey.*
   F: Yeah, I thought so too [bewildered].
   S: Roth's already over a *deuce.* He really got it *cranking.*
   F: Yeah, I noticed that [looks at Rembijas with smirk and shrugs].
   S: He has the advantage. He can play *inside* around the *fourteenth board.* The other guy can't get the *lift* and is *outside.* If he keeps *bellying* like that he's not gonna *carry.*
   F: I know it [with smile].
   S: Did you notice, he's rolling a *yellow dot.* A lotta the pros were using *gyros,* but this is a *plastic ball* house.
   F: Yeah.
   S: [looking at the action] What a *tap.*
   F: Yeah, it sure was. [glances over a Rembijas].

GLOSSARY:

buried 'perfect'
turkey 'three strikes in a row'
deuce '200 game'
cranking 'throwing ball with much velocity and curve'
inside 'left side of approach'
outside 'right side of approach'
fourteenth board 'position on lane— 14 boards from right'

lift 'curve'
carry 'get strikes or knock down pins consistently'
bellying 'too much curve'
yellow dot, gyro, plastic ball 'varieties of bowling balls'
tap 'perfect hit, yet pins left standing'

F was obviously thoroughly bewildered. Dell Hymes (1974) mentions two ways in which speech function can be mismatched to the participants in the speech event: (1) The intent is understood but not the actual words. (2) The words are understood by themselves but not the intent. The one-sided commentary just quoted is a beautiful instance of the first. The outsider F understood that the insider S was commenting on the play, but he had little idea what the words were referring to. Given the nature of jargons, the situation is not unusual. One function of jargons is to exclude lay people or novices, those who do not belong. It is well known that speakers adjust to listeners' needs (Giles, Taylor, and Bourhis 1973) defining words when they notice confusion, slowing down speech to foreigners, or speaking more loudly. Despite F's overt kinesic signaling that he was bewildered, S barreled on, piling jargon word on jargon word.

S behaves like those who display their brilliance by spouting jargon, cowing lesser beings who do not know it. Doctors and lawyers are often accused of such behavior, but the practice is not confined to them. Displays like S's commentary on the bowling game affirm that the jargon user is one in the know and, at the same time, underscores that those who do not understand are outsiders. In other words, jargons can be a way of playing oneupmanship, of saying 'I know something you don't know.' Tim Rembijas, the avid bowler who collected this conversation, explains that in order to be regarded as an expert bowler one must not only bowl well but be able to use the language. The bowler who cannot, even if he or she gets high scores, will be regarded by bowling peers as being simply lucky. We shall see the identical phenomenon with Black youths who consider anyone who does not know how to "talk that talk" a *lame*—an outsider to the Black ethnic community. Jargon is a clear case of language being used for social identification (Chapters 8–10).

The other side of identification is exclusion. Saying "buried" instead of "perfect," or "lift" instead of "curve" announces that one is a bowler.

It also serves the purpose of bonding friendships. Whenever people use special words to let others know that they share interests or background, this kind of bonding is achieved (Chapters 8–10). It is a way of saying "You and I have something in common." Style may be used similarly (Chapter 3). In both jargon and style, the choice of word itself, not its actual meaning, gives the social message. If jargon is used for bonding, it is a request for less social distance between parties. Claiming something in common is a request for at least some degree of intimacy. Also as in style selection, using features that heighten differences between speakers is a way of forcing distance. Thus the jargon word lessens distance between those who know it and heightens difference between the person uttering it and those who do not know it.

6.18   *Word creation in jargons*

Only words associated with the activity eliciting the jargon are used for excluding and/or identifying people as those who belong. In 37, all of the jargon words describe different aspects of bowling. This is hardly surprising. If the markers of a jargon center on the activity that calls for it, they will normally appear early on in an encounter. Thus, they are effective as signals for identification.

Another motivation of word creation is communicative efficiency. If something has to be mentioned often, it is more economical to have a single word to refer to it than a lengthy phrase. It is more efficient to say "carry" than "get strikes or knock down pins consistently," especially in the heat of a bowling contest when rapid encoding of the events is important. CB jargon, which is used

for quite different purposes, has a great many phrases as well as single words
peculiar to it.

6.19   *CB jargon*

38. T1: *Breaker 1-9* ["one, nine"] lookin' for a *southbounder* on this
95, come in.

   T2: You got a southbounder.

   T1: Hey, southbounder, what *be* your *twenty*?

   T2: I'm 'bout one mile from *that exit 23.*

   T1: *10-4, good buddy,* you got *the one "Outlaw"* here. I'm
'bout two miles past *that one exit 23*, so I *be takin'* the
front door lookin' things over. Eh-a, what *be* your *handle*
there good buddy?

   T2: You got *the one Happy Trucker* here, *closin' up on the
back door* and waitin' to *get an eyeball on* ya.

   T1: *That's a 4,* Happy Trucker. I *be* cruisin' in a blue *pick 'em
up truck.* What you *be pushin'*?

   T2: I *be* pushin' an eighteen wheeler.

   T1: Eh-a, Happy Trucker, what *be* your home *twenty*?

   T2: *That* Maine *Town.*

   T1: Hey, good buddy, you *be* cruisin' a long way from home
now. How long you *been* truckin'?

   T2: Too long. I'm 'bout ready to *catch me some Zs* now. Eh,
there, Outlaw, you wouldn't by chance know where I can *put
my nose in some pantyhose* for the night?

   T1: Sorry, good buddy, I ain't been truckin' that long.

   T2: That's a 4 Outlaw. Thanks anyway. I'll still be *on the beaver
hunt* till I come across *one eager beaver.*

GLOSSARY:
breaker 'I want to talk or interrupt'
southbounder 'someone going south'
twenty 'location'
10-4 or *4* 'affirmative', 'I understand'
good buddy general address form for CB'er's, like *man* or *Mack* in ordinary
   conversation
takin' the front door 'passing to the front of the chain of cars or convoy'
handle 'name', used on CB only, never speaker's real name; e.g., *Outlaw,
   Happy Trucker*
closin up the back door 'position at the end of the line of cars or convoy'
to get an eyeball on 'see'
pushin' 'driving'

pick 'em up truck 'pick-up truck'
catch me some Zs 'go to sleep'
put my nose in some pantyhose 'have sexual relations'
on the beaver hunt 'looking for a woman to have sex with'
eager beaver 'woman willing to have sex'

(courtesy of Amy Carrion)

39. A: How 'bout a *northbounder* on **this 95**?

B: Come on, you got a northbounder.

A: Yea, good buddy, how 'bout a *Smokey report*? How's it *lookin' over your shoulder*?

B: Hey, that 95 *be* lookin' good all the way to **that Providence town**, but you better *back 'em down*; around **that Exit 12** there *be* a *bear in the air with a picture taker*.

A: Hey, *40 Roger*, good buddy. What *be* your twenty?

B: I just *be* comin' up on **that Exit 15**. What be the handle *on that end*?

A: Hey, you got the Jungle Jim *on this end* and we *got your back door* for sure.

B: 10-4, Jungle Jim. You got **the one Rocky Raccoon** *on this side of the wavelength*. We'll just have that *front door* up to **that Exit 23**.

A: Hey, Rocky, *lay an eyeball on* that *seat cover* coming up in the *show-off lane*.

B: Oo-ee. That's a big 10-4 Jungle Jim; I wonder if she's *got her ears on*?

A: Hey, *negatory*. You can bet they'd be *ratchet-jawin'* if they did.

B: For sure, good buddy. You had better get yourself out of that *double nickel* lane. There *be* a *Tijuana Taxi with his snoopers on comin'* up your back door.

A: My god, someone must have *spilt honey all over the road*.

B: Hey, Jungle Jim, I best *be passin' you the good numbers*. I'll be comin' up *on that exit 23* in *a short-short*. I want to *feed the ponies* before I *press some sheets*. Now you be careful. Just *smile and comb your hair* 'cause that *pregnant roller skate* is a *brown paper bag giving out those green stamps* . . . for sure.

GLOSSARY:
Northbounder 'someone headed north'
Smokey report 'report to tell where the police [*bears*: Smokey the Bear] are on the highway'

looking over your shoulder 'road conditions behind you'
back 'em down 'slow speed down to speed limit or less'
bear in the air with a picture taker 'police helicopter with radar'
40 Roger 'affirmative'
'your *handle*' on that end, 'person to whom I am talking'
got your back door 'watch for police behind you'
on this side of the wavelength 'here'
lay an eyeball on 'look at'
seat cover 'pretty girl in a car'
show off lane 'high speed lane'
got her ears on 'equipped with CB radio'
negatory 'no'
ratchet-jawin' 'continually talking'
double nickel lane '55 mph'
Tijuana taxi with his snoopers on 'marked police car with blinking lights'
comin' up your back door 'coming up behind you'
spilt honey all over the road 'state troopers are everywhere'
passin' you the good numbers 'say goodbye'
short-short 'few minutes'
feed the ponies 'eat'
press some sheets 'go to sleep'
smile and comb your hair 'radar ahead'
pregnant roller skate 'Volkswagen'
brown paper bag 'unmarked police car'
giving out green stamps 'giving out traffic tickets'

(courtesy of Robert Marciano)

6.20   Differences between two jargons

Even a quick glance at the two CB samples shows two major differences from bowling jargon. First, the CB jargon has some special syntactic features, shown by the heavy italic type. Second, most of the special CB vocabulary involves phrases, often longer than the regular English words they replace. Both of these differences are related to the functions and conditions of CB converations.

CB radios began to proliferate in 1973 during the first energy crisis. At that time speed limits were lowered nationally to 55 miles an hour to save fuel, a real annoyance to drivers accustomed to higher speeds. Truckers and other drivers turned to CBs so that they could exceed the new limits without being ticketed by the police. Besides its function as a warning system, CB quickly showed its value for learning road and traffic conditions. Moreover, CB relieved the boredom of a long drive and relieved frustrations.

6.21   *CB grammar*

There are two major features of CB grammar. One is the use of *be* where *am, is,* or *are* would be expected: "I be pushin'," "What be your twenty?" "That 95 be lookin'." Another peculiarity concerns a group of words known as noun determiners (also known as articles and demonstrative pronouns); they precede nouns, giving warning that a noun may be coming. In CB jargon *this, that, the one, that one, one,* and [*the _____ town*] appear where one would expect no such word. For instance:

CB	*Regular English*
this 95	95
that exit 23	exit 23
the Jungle Jim	Jungle Jim (a handle)
the one Outlaw	Outlaw (a handle)
that Maine town	Maine

These differences are regular not sporadic. Dialogues 38 and 39 were collected from different speakers two years apart. One hears identical phrasing on CB all over the country. CB operators do use *a* and *the* as other Americans do, as in: "a southbounder," "the front door." In everyday English, *the* and *a* always tell us that a noun is coming; neither word can be used alone. They also serve the purpose of telling us whether the noun that follows is new or old information: "the dog" tells us it is a dog already known to the speakers, whereas "a dog" indicates one mentioned for the first time.

In CB we see noun determiners that in ordinary speech may also be used alone (*this, that,* and other demonstrative pronouns) becoming attached to following nouns just as *the* and *a* are. Why? Locations and exit numbers are extremely important to CB'ers when warnings about police or road conditions are being broadcast. An important function of CB, after all, is to locate the police and traffic jams. However, it is very difficult to decode messages on a CB. Not only is there a great deal of engine and road noise to contend with, but there is a tremendous amount of static on the airwaves. It takes many hours of listening before one can decode messages with any degree of accuracy. Even very experienced operators have difficulty decoding some messages.

This difficulty explains the *that, this* and [*that + town*] with exit and route numbers and locations. They have to be highlighted. The innovative use of old words, the demonstratives, warns listeners to be alert, that a location is about to be named. So, in CB, a *that* tells the hearer to pay special attention, an exit number may be forthcoming: "that exit 23," "that exit 15." Since exit numbers in non-CB talk are not preceded by noun determiners, using the *that* really marks them strongly, making the exit numbers stand out in the stream of speech on the CB. In 38 T1 says even more emphatically he is "two miles past that one exit 23."

Highway numbers are preceded by *this* ("this 95"). One also hears "on this Mass. Turnpike." In 39 "that 95" does occur, but it refers to a road already traveled. Actual place names receive double marking, the *that* before them, and *town* after ("that Maine town," "that Providence town"). This distinguishes them from routes, marked only by *this* or *that,* and exits, marked by *that* or *that one.* CB uses *one* instead of *a(n)* as an emphatic, as in "that one exit."

Since there is no way to know to whom one is speaking on CB, handles, or CB names, are extra important. Usually, several conversations are going on at once, making the generally noisy environment even more confusing. A listener has to be able to distinguish one speaker out of many in these co-occurring conversations. Hence handles are heavily marked in CB, although, in everyday speech, people's names do not take any noun determiners before them. One does not usually say "I'm the one Gregory" or "My name is the one Elaine." In CB, however, we do hear "the one" alerting listeners that a handle is about to be spoken. What is significant sociolinguistically is that we can correlate a change in grammar with a specific social need in a specific environment.

Perhaps *be* replaces normal *am, is* and *are* because *be* is more distinct on the airwaves. *Be* is certainly far more distinct than the usual contractions of *'m, 's,* and *'re.* The usage also seems to have a purpose related to the function of CB as an aid to illegality and an outlet for drivers' frustrations: it enhances CB's general aura of toughness. This usage of *be* does occur in many nonstandard English dialects. It may have been borrowed directly from the country and western music favored by the truckers who first made CB radios popular or from the speech of the truckers themselves. It has been borrowed by educated middle-class speakers, who are usually most careful about being "correct." The neat thing is that, again, we can correlate its borrowing very easily with the purposes of CB, demonstrating how social function determines the forms of speech.

6.22   *CB vocabulary*

The words and phrases in CB jargon differ considerably from those in the bowling jargon. CB terminology refers to driving, to road and police conditions, which, of course, are pertinent to drivers. Other spheres of CB lexicon are those marking entry into a conversation (*breaker*), ending of conversation (*passing you the good numbers*), and negative or affirmative responses. One does not find CB words for getting a strike in bowling or using a particular kind of ball, but one does find words for kinds of trucks and cars (*pick 'em up truck, eighteen wheeler, pregnant roller skate*); checking out conditions (*lookin' over your shoulder*); relative positions of cars (*front door, back door*); going to eat or sleep (*feed the ponies, press some sheets*); sex (*goin' on a beaver hunt, put my nose in some pantyhose*); and police activity (*takin' pictures, brown paper bag, givin' out green stamps*). Since CB originated with long-haul truckers whose activities on the road, except for driving, are limited to eating and sleeping and perhaps sex, having special jargon words for these activities is to be expected. Knowing special words for these common topics of conversation on CB helps mark a speaker as a true CB'er. Special words for 'yes' and 'no' also serve as useful identifying signals because agreeing or disagreeing with statements is frequent in conversation.

6.23   *Handles*

Sexual references in CB jargon are related to a curious quality of the CB handles: their lack of gentility. CB'ers do not use their real names. As Robert DiPietro (1977, p. 2) commented: "CB users often take care to insure their handles be devoid of any allusion to their own social status. Henry Ford II is reported to have rejected the handles 'The Chairman' or 'Hank the Deuce' . . . preferred instead 'Beer Belly'." Most handles are similarly rough and tough. "Outlaw" in 38 is a happily married college graduate, and "Jungle Jim" in 39 is a devout seminary student, destined to be a priest in a few years. The handle "Rocky Raccoon" is evocative of both toughness and thievery, "Rocky" being a common fighter's name (as in the movie *Rocky*) and raccoons being notorious thieves. The animal imagery also conjures up back-to-nature images with overtones of sexuality and toughness unrestrained by civilization. The CB allows speakers to hide their real identity and vent their most taboo fantasies. It is impossible to know who is actually saying what on the airwaves.

6.24   *CB accent*

Interestingly, CB jargon is spoken in its own accent, that of country and western music. Joe Williams of the University of Chicago commented to me that this feature may have originated because of the truckers' love of that music. One consultant spontaneously remarked to me, "You can't tell if someone comes from Boston or New York or the Midwest on CB." Adoption of a special accent helps to protect identity as license plates cannot be matched up to accents. Even those who normally speak with an Appalachian accent cannot be singled out by the license plates on their car since almost everyone speaks that way on CB. All of my consultants denied that they themselves use a CB accent while on air, yet all agreed that persons who do not are considered novices, not yet real CB'ers.

CB speech uses a number of markers of casual, masculine talk. One is the substitution of *-in* for *-ing*. Fischer (1958) showed that boys who wish to project a rough image were more likely to use the *-in* than girls or 'nice' boys. The *-ing* does not seem to be used at all in CB conversation, even in such an educated word as *contemplating*, as in "be sittin' here contemplatin'," collected by Lawrence Herman on the Massachusetts Turnpike. The use of *be* for *am, is* or *are* is generally associated with rough, uneducated speech.

Along with adoption of the nonstandard speech forms in CB goes dialogue many CB'ers probably would never dare initiate or participate in face-to-face. One hears operators on the airwaves threatening incredible bodily harm to each other. Women, as well as men, using very explicit and graphic language, offer or ask for sexual information and favors, often alluding to sexual practices considered somewhat irregular. Obscenity and vulgar racial and ethnic epithets prevail. There is no pretense of refined sensibility. CB handles and talk project an image of a tough, sexually active person, a macho man or his female counterpart. It is no accident that CB jargon, but not bowling jargon, has special dehumanized words for women, such as *beaver* and *seat cover.* It hardly needs to be pointed out that these words do not refer to female intelligence or ladylike behavior. CB'ers go on beaver hunts. The hunter is aggressive and masculine. The woman is the prey to be used for the hunter's pleasure. *Seat cover* seems the ultimate designation of women as passive creatures. As offensive as such terminology is to me, it cannot be denied that some women do not mind it. Women operators often offer themselves over the airwaves as completely sexual creatures. This does not mean that they necessarily intend to deliver sexual favors any more than men threatening violence on the CB really want to fight. The venting of taboo desires is often purely verbal, and those who do it may be quite respectable folk. They may talk quite primly and properly when not on the air. Considering that CB first attained widespread popularity as a means of lawbreaking, circumventing speed limits with definite hostility toward the police, the vulgarity of topic and speech is to be expected. The tough image co-occurs with hostility to police and breaking the law. The handles, hiding personal identity, are of importance in foiling the police. It is but a small step from there to other anti-middle-class talking, complete with vocabulary, pronunciation, and grammar. Note that even a college graduate, T1 in 38, uses the uneducated *ain't* just as in sounding middle-class boys adopt nonstandard speech. The requirements of the speech situation override the requirements of marking one's usual social status.

6.25   *Effect of motivation on creating CB words*

Bowling jargon clearly evolved for efficiency of communication. Its words are all short for the longer phrases which would have to be used by non-bowlers. CB jargon, on the other hand, is often longer than what it replaces: "bear in the air with a picture taker", "feed the ponies", "spilt honey all over the road." Patently, these are not motivated by considerations of efficiency, since non-CB words that give the same meanings are both shorter and more direct. Whereas bowling jargon is used under tense conditions of competition, CB'ers talk under relatively relaxed conditions. The CB'er has little to do except talk. Driving on the interstates is monotonous, so that drivers have to fight boredom. Efficiency is important to CB'ers mostly when discussing road or police conditions. Words for these are short and direct: *front door, back door, Smokey report, show off lane, double nickel lane, green stamps.* So are words for 'I want to speak' (*breaker*), 'location' (*twenty*), and 'driving' (*pushin'*).

Other words in CB jargon seem motivated by cleverness and humor, two good relievers of boredom. Who can fail to smile at *Tijuana taxi with his snoopers on,* or *bear in the air with a picture taker*? The rhyming and generally cute and colorful language of CB contrasts strongly with the terse efficiency of bowling jargon, a contrast wholly explained by the conditions each is spoken under.

6.26   *Recycling in language change*

Finally, it should be noted how rarely jargons use completely new words or constructions. Instead, they use items already in the language, then extend their meaning or function. In both bowling and CB jargon, just about all of the words are old but are used with new and different meanings.

The markings of locations and names in CB extend the regular system of noun determiners (*the, this, that, a*) to new uses. Human beings readily decode by checking with the context and figuring "What could the speaker mean by that in this context? (Clark and Lucy 1975; Chaika 1976). That is, normal and regular decoding practices make it easy to use old stock of vocabulary and grammar for new purposes. There is little need, if any, to stop to explain new words and constructions if old ones are simply extended so that their new meanings can be figured out from the environment. This does not mean that brand new words are never used, but that usually old stock is made to take on new functions. As one studies the history of a language, one discovers that much of the existing stock has been around for centuries but that it has changed meaning or function as society has required.

People are not conscious of the ways in which they create new words or new grammatical constructions in jargons or in any other language change. Nor are they always conscious of using new pronunciations. We do not know precisely how a particular group of people suddenly adopts a way of talking that tells who belongs to that group and at the same time fits the social situation of their speech. All we do know is that language is virtually instantly sensitive to social needs, and it changes in accordance with them. Such changes occur in jargons and, as the next chapter shows, in dialects as well. If there is a social need, language changes to serve that need. No one decrees such changes. They occur naturally in speakers. This is not to say that all language change is caused purely by social need, although a great deal of it is.

EXERCISES

1. If you participate in a sport or hobby, collect at least five words and phrases that are used only in that activity and have special meaning in the activity. You may collect such items during an actual game or discussion between afficionados or while reading an article on the subject of the game or hobby. Make a glossary as was done for the jargons presented in this chapter.

2. Can you find any other linguistic features of the jargon listed as exercise 1? Can you find a causal relation between the activity for which the jargon was created and the kinds of words that have developed for it?

3. If you do not engage in sports or hobbies that have associated jargons, make up a word for some everyday activity that you do in the company of at least one other person. Use the word as often as you can to see whether the other person will ask you what it means, or even start to use it.

4. Instead of the preceding exercises, you may prefer to scan the sports page, theater column, or other special section of the newspaper to see how many jargon words you can find. List the words and note why you consider them jargon. If you are unfamiliar with the topic, give the meaning that you assume to be true just by the context. Then, by consulting a dictionary or someone conversant with the activity, determine whether you decoded them correctly.

5. What insults can you throw at your siblings or your friends without getting them really angry at you? What would be taken as a real insult? Test your conclusions by actually insulting either siblings or friends. What kinds of responses do you get?

6. Does the pattern of insults in exercise 5 tell you anything about the values held by your social group?

chapter 7

EVERYBODY SPEAKS A DIALECT

It's hard to realize that our individual accents sound as different to others as theirs do to us. What seems only natural to our own ears may strike another as cute or harsh or suave or high class or brash or affected or something else. Words and grammar differ from dialect to dialect, as do sounds. Even in these days of mass communication, dialect differences are not necessarily disappearing. Dialect differences are important to social interaction itself. The tremendous concern of the middle classes with "correct" speech is explicable when the social functions of dialect are considered.

7.1   Dialect and accent

Dialect is the technical name for what Americans usually think of as an accent. Strictly speaking, **accent** refers only to differences in pronunciation between one variety of a language and another. Dialect refers to all the differences between varieties of a language, those in pronunciation, word usage, and syntax. Often, as indicated in Chapter 4, there are paralinguistic differences between dialects: timbre, tempo, and the like, as well as kinesic differences. These are usually ignored in traditional dialect studies, but that does not mean they are unimportant. To the contrary, they are often vital in rendering a dialect and in perceiving it. However, only the linguistic differences—the phonology, lexicon, and syntax—will be considered in this chapter. In themselves they are complex, and analyzing them serves to illustrate the important points about dialects and how and why they are used in social groups.

7.2   Language versus dialect

No sharp demarcation exists between language and dialect. As a rule of thumb, if two varieties of speech are mutually intelligible, they are considered dialects. If they are not, they are considered separate languages. In actual practice the situation is far more complicated. Today, partially because so many languages have become far flung all over the world, often one of the dialects of a given language is likely to be understood by all speakers of that language. Some of the other dialects, however, may be understood by relatively few speakers, or at least not by all. For example, in Barbados, the dialect of English associated with Blacks, like that used in the verbal contests of St. Vincent's described in Chapter 6, is called "talking bad." American and British visitors cannot understand it, although they have no problem with standard Barbados English, which is spoken by many Blacks and by White natives. Those Barbadans who speak the standard form of Barbados English report that "bad talk" is just another kind of English to them. In fact, several expressed surprise to me that English speakers from other places have any problems with it at all.

Some readers may think this Barbadan speech is not a fair example, because many scholars maintain that all Afro-English is a Creole, a mix of Africanisms with English. Perhaps a better example is Yorkshire English or the English of rural Ireland. A few of these dialects are either completely or partially incomprehensible to some Americans although apparently, not to the British or the Irish. There are probably American dialects that the British or Irish have problems understanding. Frequently the person whose dialect is incomprehensible to another can understand that other person. One of the worst nights of my life was spent in a charming pub in Cornwall, England. A Yorkshire man engaged me in conversation, apparently having no difficulty with my American-ese. Unfortunately I could not understand a word he said. I was not even sure when he was asking questions, as his intonation was completely different from any I had encountered. All I could do for hours on end was listen and say "Uh huh" politely, hoping I was not consenting to anything.

It is not only English that has such problems. In Italy, for instance, although bordering dialects are mutually comprehensible, those farther apart often become increasingly incomprehensible to each other. Speakers of rural dialects from the south of Italy often cannot be understood by speakers from the north.

One reason for the emergence in modern times of standard dialects, dialects that do not belong to any particular region, is the need for a speech variety that all people ruled by one national government can understand. As this need has grown in modern technological societies, the more widespread has been the development of national standards.

Political boundaries, in themselves, often determine whether two speech varieties will be considered different languages or not. For instance, some varieties of Swedish and Norwegian are mutually comprehensible, but they are considered different languages because they are separated by national borders. Conversely the so-called dialects of Chinese are as different as French from Italian, but being spoken in one country they are not considered separate languages. Sometimes ethnic and social factors determine whether or not speech is considered a separate language. Most of the Yiddish dialects spoken by Jews of Eastern Europe are mutually comprehensible with many varieties of modern German. Both Germans and Jews regard Yiddish and German as separate languages, however. This is a direct reflection of the separate religious and cultural affinities of Yiddish and German speakers. There are Jews who speak both, however, although they consider themselves to be speaking two separate languages.

Social factors can even determine whether or not speech is comprehensible at all. In Africa, the Kalabari are a powerful and important people, but the Nembe, who speak a closely related language are not. There seems to be no linguistic reason for the two speech varieties not to be mutually comprehensible. Yet the Kalabari claim that they do not understand the Nembe, and all communication between the two must be in Kalabari or Pidgin English.

A similar situation occurs in the United States. In public schools standard-speaking teachers confronted with nonstandard-speaking youngsters often claim difficulty in understanding them. The teachers complain that the students' speech is deficient or broken. As we shall see later in this chapter, however, nonstandard dialects are as systematically rule-governed as standard dialects. Standard speakers do not perceive this because of their attitudes to the nonstandard speakers.

7.3   Standard dialect

In modern countries the standard dialect can be understood by just about all speakers. Because it is also based upon the speech of the educated, which in most countries coincides with the written language, people often assume that the standard is the "true" language not realizing it is actually a dialect. Many people think that dialects are substandard, even defective. In fact, any variety of a language is technically a dialect, even the educated standard. Everyone speaks a dialect. Everyone has an "accent," except perhaps in those languages with so few speakers that there are no varieties at all. The dialect that becomes standard is an accident of history. It has nothing to do with intrinsic worth of the standard. All dialects are inherently equal, just as all languages are.

Socially however dialects are not all equal. A Briton might deliver a scientific paper in British RP, received pronunciation of English spoken by the educated British, but not in Cockney, the street dialect of London. However, Cockney might be better in a brawl. A Brooklyn accent does not seem appropriate for lecturing college classes, but it is very convincing for arguing the merits of a baseball team or even politics. Television commercials often gear the speech variety to the product being sold: *Shake and Bake* and a Southern accent; *Poland Springs* mineral water and a stage Maine accent; four-wheel drives and Texas accents. The accent suitable for a given purpose is related to the generally held image of people who speak that way.

Frequently, because we associate certain kinds of speech with certain kinds of activities, a dialect will take on a vocabulary especially efficient for those activities. Hence, educated dialects have developed a tremendous number of scientific and other learned words. These differ from jargon words only in that they are used by more diverse groups in broader social situations. Other dialects could as easily include the same words, but they do not because they are not used for the purposes that demand the particular expression.

Much of the ensuing discussion will be devoted to showing that nonstandard speech is as intelligent and complete as standard. This is essential to understand if nonstandard speakers are to be appreciated and respected. Effective education depends upon such understanding. This does not mean that I or linguists in general think that in speech anything and everything is all right. Even if one recognizes that all dialects are equally intelligent, equally rule-governed, and equally complete for their users' purposes, one can still recognize that educated dialects are necessary for many desirable kinds of social functioning. James Sledd once forcefully condemned attempts to teach standard varieties of American English in schools as "the linguistics of White supremacy." Such a view, in my opinion, ignores the functions of dialect and realities of social interaction.

It is necessary for students to be able to command educated varieties of speech if they wish to be able to hold certain kinds of jobs. However, any attempt to teach a standard dialect to a nonstandard speaker must take into account why people speak as they do. It must also take into account why there are different dialects of a language and what conditions favor dialect learning. Otherwise such attempts will fail, as indeed they usually do.

7.4   *Proper speech*

A good measure of the importance of speech variety is the anxiety it evokes. In the United States, because there is no one acknowledged standard as there are in countries like England, Italy, and France, the anxiety at times almost borders on hysteria. Proper speech is pursued with what can only be called religious fervor. Witness this advertisement for Fowler's *Modern English Usage*: "The most practiced writer will only too often find himself convicted of sin when he dips into Fowler." Clifton Fadiman, a respected scholar, author, and editor wrote of Fowler, that "it is the final arbiter of our language" and "it shows me how bad a writer I am, and encourages me to do better." The equation of grammar choice with sin, with being bad, makes it appear that *Modern English Usage* is on a par with the Old Testament. New Testament status has to be reserved for Nicholson's *American English Usage*, which is based on Fowler's.

For most Americans, however, the dictionary is the final arbiter of correctness. Fowler and Nicholson are reserved for the select few whose sins are too subtle for Webster's. In 1961 Webster's third unabridged edition innovated. Rather than acting as prescriber of "correct" usage and condemning "substandard" usage, it just listed how words are actually pronounced and used in American English. It lacked convenient labels like "vulgar," "preferred," and "slang."

Dr. Max Rafferty, then superintendent of schools for the State of California, said,

> If a dictionary doesn't exist to set standards and maintain them, what possible use can it have? ... when I go to a dictionary I want to

know what's right. I already know what folks are saying. What I want to know is what they should be saying.

(Pyles 1972, p. 167)

The intensity of concern about proper language forms is startling. Why can an advertisement promising to convict writers of sin sell a book? The ad for Fowler's reads like a call to that old time religion, not a reference book. Why should an exceptionally literate writer feel that Fowler had the right and competence to show him that he is bad? That word *bad* in itself in the context that Fadiman uses it has a strangely moralistic ring. Dr. Rafferty, an outspoken man, was certainly not one to be swayed by mere public opinion. Why then was he willing to take the word about his use of words from a dictionary? The answers to these questions are found when we consider the role of dialects in social functioning.

7.5   The decaying language

Edwin Newman, the TV newsman, has had great success castigating the educated for their writing. He is a modern hair shirt. The fans of Newman's book *Strictly Speaking* object, "But he's trying to save the language from decay." He is far from alone in his concern.

Jean Safford, a Pulitzer prize author, wrote an article in 1972 for *The Saturday Review* entitled "The Decay of English." She claimed that English was in imminent danger of collapse because of the improper, loose, and wanton ways of its users. She proceeded to give several examples, all completely comprehensible, like the metaphoric "Her hair haloed her face" meaning 'Her hair framed her face like a golden halo.' Although the meaning was perfectly easy to grasp, Ms. Safford was outraged because the noun *halo* was being used as a verb. Much of her contention that English is rotting away was based upon the fact that writers ignore the distinctions between nouns and verbs.

The problem with her reasoning is that English has always done this; nor is the practice confined to English. Surely even Safford herself has used words like *love, group, kill, hunt,* even *man* or *police* both as noun and verb and for that matter as adjective. Most and probably all languages allow words to cross part-of-speech boundaries in some way. If a language did not allow slipping across categories, many of the meanings one wished to convey would need at least two distinct roots: one for a noun, another for a verb. It is much more economical to use the same root as a noun, verb, or adjective simply by changing the grammar slightly. This may be done by changing endings or prefixes or by using other syntax markers like sentence position or *the* before a noun. To give an English example, there is no confusion in interpretation of *love* or *group* in any of the following:

1 a. The *love* I had for him is gone.　(noun)
  b. I *love* candy.　(verb)
  c. That was quite a *love* tap.　(adjective)

2 a. That's a good *group*.　(noun)
  b. Let's *group* them this way.　(verb)
  c. It's a *group* project.　(adjective)

Using *halo* as a verb is a creative extension of this regular practice. Great poets often demonstrate their artistry by using old words in new ways, helping us to make new connections by just such violations of part-of-speech boundaries. Think of Shakespeare's "But me no buts" or Dylan Thomas' "the cargoed apples" or "the sweethearting cribs."

Not only do poetic new coinings communicate meaning, but they do so with images more vivid than ordinary language can convey, which is the point of such communication. All of the examples presented by the doomsayers as evidence of language rot communicate meaning, too. Newman cites passage after passage as evidence of breakdown in communication and then tells us what they mean. If he knows what they mean, are they not communicating? In fact, think of language forms that are generally considered wrong, like *ain't, he don't, didn't do nuffin'* (for *nothing*), *trow* (for *throw*), and *duh* (for *the*). These are all perfectly comprehensible; their use in speech or writing would cause no breakdown in communication. Many have been around for years, even centuries, without causing the collapse of English. Why then are they wrong? Why are boards of education willing to spend millions a year on classes designed to stamp out such errors—errors that do not hamper communicability?

7.6　*Language change and language decay*

It does make sense to suppose that changes in the language could lead to its decay, except that all language is always in a state of change. That is what makes it such a delicate social instrument. In the past 1000 years, English has changed so that its earliest writings have to be studied as if they were written in a foreign language. At no time has such natural change led to a breakdown in communicability, at least among those living at about the same time and in the same regions. Someone who does not understand a new coinage can always ask the speaker who uttered it to paraphrase it. It takes centuries of change before incomprehensibility sets in.

Many historians of the language have taken special delight in poking fun at the preachers of the doctrine of correctness and their followers. This is easy to do, especially since many of the supposed sins of language are among the oldest forms in English and have been found in the best of English writers: Chaucer, Milton, Shakespeare. Stranger still, there is no justification in the history of the language for many of the rules prescribed by those who would save our speech. They were made up out of whole cloth by self-styled educators like Bishop Robert Lowth of the eighteenth century or writers like Jean Safford who have never examined language objectively. Such criticisms of the purists miss the mark, though, for historical justification has nothing to do with what should or should not be considered correct.

Neither, apparently, does it make much difference who is telling us what is or is not all right. Who was Fowler that he could condemn speakers of verbal sin? Who are writers of dictionaries? Why are they privy to divine revelation denied the rest of us speakers? Scholars like Thomas Pyles, W. Nelson Francis, Elizabeth Traugott, or Joseph Williams who are authorities on the history of the language are far less likely to be heeded than prophets like Fowler, Nicholson, Safford, or Newman. Who ever asks the qualifications of an arbiter of language? What is perhaps most puzzling is that people who so unquestioningly accept the authority of the arbiters of language are often precisely those who have been the best trained in questioning what they read, examining all arguments for flaws, or accepting nothing without empirical proof. All this training flees when they hear a lecturer or a writer criticize middle-class usage, prophesying doom and decay. Even the best educated leap into the lap of the saviors of language. It is they who equate language with sin, who want to be told how to talk, who seek some authority who will tell them what is correct and, even better, what is incorrect. Others may not notice if you use phrases correctly, but they will notice if you do not. For an educated person publicly to commit a grammar error is profoundly humiliating, like being caught slobbering over food. The heretic few, mostly linguists, who scoff at the doomsayers and linguistic saviors are themselves scoffed at.

Since those who delve into dictionaries, flock to Fowler, and kneel to Newman are clearly among the best and the brightest, they cannot be dismissed as unintelligent. For that matter both Newman and Safford, like most who plead for correct speech, are highly intelligent, perceptive, and literate. Newman is correct, I think, in his judgments about the clumsiness of academic and government writers, but this is not necessarily indicative of mind mold or of language decay. Language is patently an emotional issue, not wholly an intellectual one. As we shall see in this chapter and the next, the concern with keeping language pristine (if in fact it ever was pristine) stems from social psychological needs. More is at stake in the forms of language one uses than communicating per se.

7.7   *The function of correct speech*

Dialect studies show that how one speaks is inextricably bound up with one's identity. Who one is, how one may be treated, and how one may treat others are all proclaimed in one's speech. In earlier times in stable societies people in a community knew one another and knew where everyone belonged on the social scale. When there is little social mobility all one needs to know to assess another's social rank is what family the person belongs to. In many cultures there are other indications as well: clothing, hairstyles, jewelry, dwelling place, automobile. Today in America none of these is exclusive to any one class or group. The son of a janitor might be a college president. An eighth grade graduate may own a home next door to a high-ranking business executive with two masters' degrees. Even occupation fails as a guide. Your local woodcarver might hold a Ph.D., and the driver of your cab might be an expert on Jane Austen. Nowadays, rich or poor, lawyer, doctor, plumber, or ditch digger all wear the same sorts of clothes ("Forever in blue jeans!"), wear the same gold chains, and style their hair the same ways. Because of the homogeneity of other aspects of culture, speech is likely to be the most reliable determiner of social class or ethnic group.

This is a matter of great concern to the educated middle class, which above all wishes to be identified as educated. Its members' being recognized as those to be listened to hinges strongly on language. When people say they want to know the right way to speak, they do not mean the right way to communicate their ideas but, rather, the right way to announce that those ideas are to be respected, to be listened to. To some degree, perhaps, people who fear innovation and change in language may really fear that they will no longer know the rules. That is not as petty as it may sound. Not to know social rules is a serious business to eminently social creatures such as human beings.

7.8   *Proof of the need to speak "properly"*

The rebels among us might ask, isn't it irrational to dread not speaking right or being caught in a solecism (a mistake)? Several experiments suggest that the fear is well-founded. Using incorrect—that is, nonstandard—forms can have consequences that strike right at the heart of middle-class privilege. Recall that the discussion of field methods (Chapter 2), especially the matched guise technique, showed that the dialect used in asking patrons to fill out a survey questionnaire was a prime determinant of whether they would comply.

Crowl and MacGinitie (mentioned in Giles and Powesland 1975, p. 91) had six White and six Black speakers read identical answers to two questions. The Blacks spoke in NNE, Nonstandard Negro English, the Black ethnic dialect of English that is considered nonstandard. It must be emphasized that not all Blacks speak NNE, and many who do also speak SE, Standard English, switching dialects according to the situation. The abbreviation NNE is used to refer to speech identifiable as Black English, but at no time is it to be assumed that all Black Americans speak the same dialect. It must also be emphasized that unless Blacks are speaking NNE, they are not identifiable on tapes or on the phone as being Black. Crowl and MacGinitie apparently chose NNE for its value as a nonstandard dialect in America. The Whites recorded spoke one of the educated standard American dialects, hereafter termed SE.

In Crowl and MacGinitie's experiment Whites acting as judges heard one NNE and one SE speaker give an answer to two questions. Although NNE and SE speakers read exactly the same answers, the judges consistently rated the SE answers as better. It is not what is said but how it is said that counts. Intuitively you probably already knew that. Imagine, for instance, a philosophy professor lecturing, "Ta tell ya duh trut' duh problem of good 'n evil ain't gone away," as opposed to "A consideration of the problem of good and evil entails a realization that definitive answers may well be impossible."

Speech variety may also influence how willing people are to help. Gaertner and Bickman (1971) had both Black and White callers telephone 540 Black and 569 White subjects, pretending to get the wrong number. The caller told each subject that he was stranded and had used his last dime. He then requested that the subject call another number to send help. At this number there was a confederate of the caller who recorded which subjects had responded to the caller's request for aid. Black subjects helped Black and White callers equally. Whites helped Blacks less frequently than they helped Whites. This, of course, might also be explained on the basis of racial prejudice; however, it does show that the dialect used does, in and of itself, affect how others treat you.

Giles, Baker, and Fielding (1975) developed an experiment to test the effect of nonstandard English (NSE) that did not entail racial differences. Theirs was based upon SE in its British RP form and the NSE of Birmingham, England. They used a matched guise technique, having had a male speaker who was equally proficient in both dialects address two groups of high school students. The students had to write letters of recommendation stating their opinion of this speaker as a suitable candidate to lecture high school students about the nature of university studies. The students also had to evaluate him on traditional rating scales. Giles et al. based this experiment on earlier findings that subjects write longer letters about someone they like than about someone they do not like. Also, it had previously been demonstrated that subjects speak more when they are conversing with someone they imagine they like than with someone they do not like.

Giles et al. figured that if more students wrote letters for the fake candidate and wrote longer opinions when he was speaking in one guise than in the other, that would constitute proof that the dialect alone caused him to be rated differently. What happened was that the high school students to whom the speaker had used SE wrote 82 percent more about him than those who heard him talk in NSE. Furthermore, 24 percent more students who heard him speak in SE wrote about him than those who heard him in NSE. On the rating scale, he was judged significantly more intelligent by those who heard his standard speech than by those who did not. Finally, 13 out of 18 found him "well-spoken" when he spoke as a standard speaker, but only 2 out of 28 who heard him speak NSE described him that way.

7.9   The case for nonstandard speech

It must be emphasized that the task in the experiment by Giles et al. is one in which standard speech is considered suitable. One expects educated speech from a man lecturing students about preparation for the university. Nonstandard speakers are judged higher on some traits, such as being humorous, hardworking, sincere, and being more trustworthy in a fight (Lambert, Giles, and Picard 1975). Gary Underwood (1974) found that Arkansans prefer their own supposedly nonstandard speech to that of other regions, even that of the supposedly standard Midwest.

There is strong evidence that the "in" group of Black urban youth prefer those who use their NNE, calling others "lames" (Labov 1972). Similarly, the college students who have done rating tests for me rank NSE speakers as being hardworking, sincere, and trustworthy.

Like the Arkansas speakers who are regularly mocked by television comedians and by tourists, Eastern New England speech is often disparaged by outsiders. Yet Eastern New Englanders do not downrate their own accents when judging them from a tape recording. Interestingly even those from other regions rate educated Eastern New England speech highly, despite all those jokes about "pahking the cah in Hahvahd yahd."

Many of our judgments about the relative impact of standard versus nonstandard speech are based on studies from Great Britain or from French versus English speakers in Canada. Too many of the studies in the United States have pitted NNE against SE, thus adding a component of racial prejudice. The very fact that nonstandard dialects survive even the massive onslaught of television implies that they have a value for their speakers (Chapter 8). Furthermore, the very fact that middle-class SE speakers adopt NSE at times shows that nonstandard speech is positively valued for some purposes.

7.10   The American standard

Many Americans ask me, "What is the right way to speak?" or "Which region has the right speech?" In England one knows that RP is the right speech. This is a social class dialect not a regional one. In that country anyone with education, regardless of regional origin, speaks RP at least some of the time, and the regional dialects are all considered nonstandard to some degree.

The United States, being a considerably larger and more culturally diverse country and one without the traditional sharp class divisions of England, has always had several regional standards in speech. One can sound educated in any of the regional standards. There has always been an educated variety of New England, Southern, Midwestern, Southwestern, or Northwestern speech. For many years, Eastern New England educated speech was considered especially fine, probably because of its similarities to British RP. Virtually all radio announcers and movie stars, even those who hailed from other parts of the country, learned to speak like New Englanders. A crash course in the late night show, or tapes of old radio shows will confirm this. Even in her earliest films, Joan Crawford, for example, spoke a flawless Eastern New England dialect, although she came from Texas. Katherine Hepburn's aristocratic tones are another example. Nowhere does she ever pronounce the /r/ before a consonant, although she came from the /r/-pronouncing section of Connecticut. Judy Garland in *The Wizard of Oz* switches between the Tinman's "heart," pronounced with her native /r/ and "hot." Apparently, she had been coached not to pronounce those /r/s.

There is a noticeable change in the dialects used by announcers and actors starting in the mid-1950s. With respect to the /r/ rules, especially, New Englandese is no longer the prestige dialect taught in broadcasting and acting schools. It is not necessarily nonstandard, though. Educated people all over the country are sounding more and more alike, although some regional differences, particularly in vowels, persist.

It appears as if in time the British situation may develop in the United States, with regional dialects being preserved mostly in blue-collar and lower class speech. It is dangerous to make any predictions with certainty, however. Sturtevant in 1921 predicted that the entire country was going to speak like Eastern New England within a generation or two, which indicates how prestigious that dialect was then. Then came World War II and changes that reversed the trend. These changes in American society and even some in international politics have changed the dialect patterns of this country permanently.

7.11   *Dialect as marker*

Dialect overlaps with style of speech to announce the relative social status of participants in an interaction. Dialects can be used deliberately by speakers as a way of marking style, as when middle-class males in a macho mood adopt NNE or NSE. Dialects differ from each other in the same ways as styles: phonologically, lexically, and syntactically. There are variant ways of pronouncing the same sound, of naming the same thing, and of creating sentences that mean the same thing, just as there are for styles.

As with style, very few variants are used for markers and these can be perceived by listeners in as little as 10 seconds. Like stylistic markers, dialectal ones are perceived independently of linguistic message, and the information they provide often is backgrounded in normal interaction. Some dialect messages, especially those that only give information about regional origin, can be overtly commented on. Those that give social class information, however, usually are not. You might say upon meeting a doctor or lawyer from Chicago "Oh, you're from Chicago," but you would hardly comment, "Oh, you're educated" or "Despite your education you probably were raised in a poor neighborhood."

Although some dialects are used as styles as well, most stylistic markers in American English do not overlap with dialect. For instance, recall the /t/+/y/ as an indication of formality, anger, and authority, as in "won't you" instead of "woncha". Although the precise enunciation signals formality, it is not a feature of any dialect in this country, even the most aristocratic. All dialects of American English use [č] for /t/+/y/ in casual speech.

Accents, different ways of pronouncing what speakers of a language perceive as the same sound, seem to be the prime determinant of or clue to dialect. Sounds rather than words or sentences serve as the clue because there are fewer elements of sound than any other kind of language element. Thus, the chances of a sound's having to be emitted in a brief encounter of any kind are quite good. The chances of hearing a particular word or sentence form are not so good. Since dialect gives important social information to all parties in an interaction, its signaling function is well served by variation in pronunciation. Style is also crucial to interaction, but style concentrates word and phrase differences in openers.

Information about style has to be reassessed at every meeting. Information about dialect is a more general statement of a person's identity. The phonological variants of style in English, at least, are concentrated in a few key positions that are likely to occur at the start of interaction. The [č] and [ǰ] variants of /t/+/y/ and /d/+/y/ occur frequently in questions that include a *you*. The auxiliaries *did, won't, must, can't should,* and *would* coming before *you* in a question force the choice between [č] and /t/+/y/ or between [ǰ] and /d/+/y/. It is very likely that one of the variants will appear in commands, invitations, and requests: "Won't you meet me?" "Why did you do that?" or "Can't you come?" The differences between dialects pervade the entire speech pattern, whereas the differences between styles are concentrated at the outset of social interaction. The markers of style and the markers of dialect neatly correlate with their functions, illustrating for us how finely tuned a social instrument is language.

7.12   *Status-marking in written language*

For people in authority—scholars and bureaucrats, doctors and lawyers—written language can be made to serve the same function as dialect markers. Edwin Newman in *Strictly Speaking* is correct that much government and scholarly writing is overblown and unwieldy. It is not because English is decaying, as he asserts, however. Such inflated writing is a signal that the author is educated. An idea expressed directly and in the simplest possible terms just does not sound cerebral enough to many writers. For instance, consider from a sociology article:

3a. Showing that will involve us in indicating the important sense in which this paper is necessarily a study in the methodology and relevance of members' activities of categorizing members.

(Sacks 1972, p. 92)

What this means is:

3b. Showing that will indicate that this paper is a study in how and why members of society categorize each other.

A second example from the same page is:

4a. It seems the simplest way to show the generality of the categorization problem is by showing that no uncategorized population may be specified such that only one categorization device is available for categorizing the population's personnel.

In other words:

4b. The simplest way to show the scope of the problem of categorizing is to show that no group can be categorized in only one way.

A large part of becoming educated is learning to handle such overblown language.

Samuel Keyser's (1976) comment that poems say quite ordinary things but in unusual and artistic ways can be applied to scholarly and government writing as well, except that *learned* should be substituted for *artistic*. The educator who writes (or speaks) of *positive* and *negative reinforcement* rather than of *praising* and *punishing* is really letting readers (or listeners) know that he or she has had special courses in education that included scientific consideration of ordinary behaviors. It is not only English that is replete with scholarese and bureaucratese. It is the bane of modern industrialized societies. Any reader who has had to suffer through courses that included eighteenth- or nineteenth-century essays knows that the problem is not all that modern. The overblown Latinate writing of the twentieth century descends from overblown Latinate writing of the past.

One reason such writing seems so prevalent today is, undoubtedly, that, with the advent of typewriters, word processors, and cheap and easy copying devices, more writing is being done today and more rapidly, hence more carelessly, than in earlier times. Another reason and perhaps the prime one is that the need for signaling status in sentence structure and word choice is tremendous in a world in which almost everyone can write. This is not a defense of such writing, only an explanation. It is easy to accuse writers of being obscure because they want to hide their ideas or lack of them in a barrage of verbosity. That may well be true. What may be equally true is the principle that Bales uncovered (see Chapter 4, Section 4.13): He who speaks most is considered smartest, no matter what his ideas. There seems to be a rough equation between obscure but plentiful phrasing and the spreading of semantic content over as many words as possible with the appearance of intelligence. If people are hard to understand but not apparently bizarre or incoherent others may assume that they are hard to understand because they are brilliant.

7.13   *Phonological variations*

Phonological variants in dialects are more diffuse than are those that operate stylistically. That is, in dialects, phonological variants occur in large sets of words, not limited environments like the /t/ + /y/ in casual speech turning to [č] at word boundaries. In Chicago for instance the /a/ in words like *back, tag, Barry, that,* and *sad* is pronounced [ɨ], whereas some Southerners and most Southern New Englanders pronounce the same /a/ as [æ], more like Chicago's /o/ in *John* or *clock.* Yet speakers of each dialect perceive speakers of the other to be pronouncing the vowel in *back* or *tag* as /a/. The Los Angeles /a/ 'ah' in *talk, walk, saw,* and the like corresponds to the New York City and Southern British /ɔ/ 'aw'. 'Ah' and 'aw' are different ways of pronouncing the same sound in those two dialects. Generally speaking, the differences between dialects of American English are differences in the pronunciation of vowels. No two dialects have quite the same vowel systems.

Consonants, which seem more crucial to identifying spoken words themselves, show fewer dialectal differences than vowels do. There is one major difference in consonants between most British and American dialects. Virtually all American dialects pronounce the /t/ and /d/ in between vowels the same way, as a light /d/-like sound, so that *latter* and *ladder* are pronounced the same, as are *better* and *bedder.* Many British dialects still make a clear distinction between the /t/ and /d/. Furthermore, they hold the /d/, as in *ladder* or *Daddy,* longer than Americans do. The pun advertising water beds as "off track bedding" would not work in British newspapers as it does in American.

Another major consonant difference among English dialects is the presence or absence of /r/ before consonants as in *park* and at the ends of words. In so-called /r/-less speech the word-final /r/ is dropped only if the next word starts with a consonant or at the end of an utterance. For example, *four* and *farmer* are pronounced "faw" and "fahmuh" if said alone or before a word starting with a consonant. Before a word beginning with a vowel, some so-called /r/-less dialects pronounce the /r/, so that there is an alternation of word-final /r/:

> 5a. [fɔroklak] "four o'clock"
> b. [fɔboⁱz] "faw boys" (four boys)
> 6a. [famər ɪn ðe dɛl] "fahmer in the dell" (farmer in the dell)
> b. [faməčiz] "fahmuh cheese" (farmer cheese)

Some /r/-less dialects never or only occasionally pronounce the word-final /r/ even before a word beginning with a vowel. They even omit the /r/ in between vowels. In these dialects *parents* is pronounced "pa'ents," and *four o'clock* is "faw o'clock." In America both Southern White and NNE dialects are likely to omit this /r/ between vowels, although some Southern New England speakers do so as well. In Great Britain some RP speakers omit it.

7.14   *Lexical variation*

There are small differences in lexicon from dialect to dialect. Since these differences involve the names of commonly used items, misunder-standings can and do occur, even in this land of television and national advertising. Recently, in a Providence, Rhode Island, supermarket, a male customer just ahead of me in the checkout line asked the boy packing groceries to place a large box in a "sack." The boy looked puzzled, then said dubiously, "I'll have to ask the manager." The customer reddened angrily. I intervened, hastily explaining that in Eastern New England, as in many other regions, groceries are placed in *bags*. *Sacks* are made of cloth. The customer, from Oregon, said, "I never heard of such a thing," and the boy had never heard *sack* for *bag*. Usage of these words varies considerably all over the country. Some regions reverse the usage just mentioned, so that *bag* means a cloth container, as in *burlap bag,* but *sack* for one of paper. Tuscaloosa County, Alabama uses the two words interchangeably.

At O'Hare airport in Chicago a thirsty woman with a strong Boston accent asked an attendant where the bubbler was. The attendant kept saying "What?" to which the traveler raising her voice, kept answering "The bubbler!" In parts of Eastern New England, a public drinking facility is a *bubbler*. Since Wisconsin speakers also drink from bubblers, it is surprising that Chicagoans are not familiar with the term. Perhaps it is equally surprising that the traveler was unaware that most of the country calls it a *fountain, drinking fountain*, or *water fountain*. To those who call it a *bubbler*, a fountain is one of the big, gushing water decorations in parks or in front of buildings. *Water fountain* seems redundant. *Fountain* may also refer to soda fountain, a bar, usually in a drugstore, where ice cream sodas and cokes are dispensed.

Other terms for common items that still cause confusion across regions are *soda, soda pop, pop, soft drink,* and *tonic.* In parts of the Midwest and Far West, if one orders soda, one is served an ice cream soda. On the East Coast, if one orders pop, one is likely to be greeted with "Huh?" There, except for Boston and vicinity, the term is *soda. Tonic* is peculiar to the Boston area. In New York City and environs, the bottled stuff is soda, but a drink made at a soda fountain with chocolate syrup, milk, and soda water is an *egg cream,* although there is neither egg nor cream in it.

There are also regional differences in the name of the drink made from ice cream, syrup, and milk beaten together. Most of the country calls this a *milkshake* or *shake.* Other terms are *frappe* and *cabinet,* the former from Boston and vicinity, the latter in Rhode Island. Because of national fast food chains, *shake* has come into those areas as well. Often, customers order *cabinets* at a *creamery* (ice cream parlor), but a *shake* at a fast food place. Since the fast food shakes typically contain gelatinous thickeners, whereas cabinets are only milk, syrup, and a scoop or two of ice cream, the two drinks are not alike. With the advent of two Massachusetts ice cream chains into Rhode Island, *frappe* is creeping into Rhode Island, although there is no sign of Massachusetts *tonic.*

Eastern New England dialect differences have been stressed so far for the following three reasons (beyond the practical one of the ready availability of data to me as a resident of the region): (1) Concentrating on one area illustrates the dangers of speaking of broad regional dialects. There is really no one Southern or New England or Midwestern dialect. Each region is characterized by several interrelated dialects. Although the lack of homogeneity within a regional dialect is also true with respect to accent (sounds) and grammar, it is most easily demonstrated by discussing words. (2) Concentrating on the speech of one region illustrates the complexity of dialect differentiation. (3) It illustrates a related fact about dialect change. Namely, it is not the case that each dialect is sharply split off from all others. Rather, dialects are alike in some features and different in others. The more closely related, the more features alike, of course, but differences remain. For instance, although Eastern New Englanders share *bubbler,* they split on *tonic* vs. *soda.* Although *frappe* is moving to former *cabinet* towns, *tonic* is not moving along with it. Despite the entry of *shake,* visitors to Massachusetts and Rhode Island from outside the region are often disappointed to discover no ice cream in the shakes or milkshakes they order at a soda fountain or creamery. For Eastern New England a milkshake is literally that: milk shaken up with syrup. It has long been considered by linguists that as one travels from the East Coast to the West, there is more and more ice cream in the milkshake.

Chocolate bits on ice cream are *sprinkles* in New York, but *jimmies* in parts of New England, and *shots* in some other areas. A huge sandwich on a roll is a *submarine* or *sub, hero, grinder, hoagie,* or *poor boy,* depending on where you eat it. Local terms are retained even in regions close to each other both geographically and culturally. The persistent differences in regionalisms between Rhode Island and Eastern Massachusetts are interesting because not only are the states adjacent to each other, but many people commute to work on both sides of the border.

It is not only foodstuffs that retain local terms. Some regions call *stockings* what others call *hose.* The latter, common in the Midwest, is often not comprehended in the East, where *hose* refers to the long snaky thing used to water a garden. The newer *pantyhose* is used alongside *stockings* for many Eastern women. They put on their *stockings,* even when their stockings are pantyhose. In a store, however, they will distinguish between the two if they wish to purchase some, as in "Where are the pantyhose?" or "I want two pairs of stockings."

In building, Northwesterners put *shakes* on the sides of their homes, but Northeasteners put *shingles,* referring to the same item: wood squares, usually made of cedar. There are variations on this theme all over the country, with some also putting *shakes* on their roofs, whether or not they are wood, and others putting *shingles* on if they are not wood. Yet others use *shingles* for both sides and roofs, wood or not. Others put *shakes* on the side, and *shingles* on the roof, and for others just the reverse occurs. As with *sack* vs. *bag,* the material used may affect the word, so that cedar *shakes* can be used for either roofs or sides, but asphalt will be *shingles.*

In mobile societies words from one dialect may conflict with words from others. When conflict occurs, two things can happen. Either one term drops out, or each word starts to refer to slightly different aspects of the thing originally designated. English *shirt* and *skirt* are old examples of this, originally having been British dialect variants for the same article. In the United States, the hardware on a sink from which one gets water is called a *faucet, tap,* or *spigot.* In areas where all three or two of the three terms compete, people will assign a slightly different meaning to each, so that *faucet* is what is in the house, and *spigot* is outside. Even within the same area, interestingly enough, different speakers may reverse the meanings. Even members of the same family may use the terms differently. Sometimes the same speaker uses all of the terms for any kind of faucet.

A number of vocabulary differences distinguish British from American English, British *lift, hire, lorry* vs. American *elevator, rent, truck,* for example. One British term, *bunk* meaning 'escape' or 'leave someplace without telling others' is used in parts of America, but only in the meaning of 'stay out of school with no excuse.' In Philadelphia that would be to *bag* school, and in other areas it would be *play hooky*.

Such examples could go on endlessly, but the point should by now be quite clear: mass culture has not obliterated local terms. Despite the invasion of television and the general mobility of Americans, regionalisms survive. This is an attestation to the supremacy of the social marking function of dialects and further proof that language usage is not simply imitation.

Many readers may feel a bit disgruntled at this point, wishing to complain: "Hey, how about my dialect! You didn't mention the words *I* use." English is too widely a spoken language and there are far too many dialect differences in word choice for anything approximating a comprehensive discussion here. The purpose here is to illustrate principles and, of course, to whet the reader's appetite for more.

7.15   *Syntactic variation*

Dialects differ in syntax as well as phonology and lexicon. Americans are generally familiar with the well-known signposts of uneducated dialects, such as double negatives and lack of agreement in number of verb to subject. The dialect markers that signal social class distinctions often occur on common constructions of the type that crop up frequently in conversation. This is another manifestation of what we have already seen with both style and dialect marking, that the markers must appear early on in an interaction, or else they would not be reliable.

Oddly, syntactic markers center on marginal constructions, grammar rules that are relics of bygone days. This is the counterpart of the marked sounds used as phonological markers. Consider the major differences between educated and uneducated American dialects. The educated ones use the forms of *be* (*am, is, are, was,* and *were*) that agree with the subject of the sentence in which they appear.

7.   *Singular*   *Plural*
     Present tense   *Present tense*
     I am (1st person)   we/you/they are
     you are (2nd person)
     she is (3rd person)

     Past tense   *Past tense*
     I/she was   we/you/they were

These different forms for one verb are a relic of the **inflections** used long ago when the English language had a widespread system of verbs agreeing with their subjects in both present and past tenses. Besides the inflected *be,* the only other survival of that older system is -*s* that marks the present tense in the third person singular, as in the singular forms of *go*:

8. I go (1st person)
   you go (2nd person)
   she goes (3rd person)

Be usage is a particularly effective marker of social class in both American and British English because it is hard to talk for very long without one of its forms cropping up. Whether or not a speaker uses the correct form of *be*, hence whether or not he or she is middle-class educated, is quickly evident. This is because almost none of the nonstandard varieties of English uses the inflected forms of *be* in the standard way. Some speakers say "I is"; others say "I be," "you is," "you was," or "you be." Some do not say the *be* at all, as in "he good." There are differences in *be* usage from one nonstandard dialect to another, but all seem to differ from the standard varieties of English, whether British or American. In this respect, the standard, educated dialects of English are alike.

Similarly, although all educated dialects still use the -*s* number agreement marker in the present singular, nonstandard speakers often omit it there, saying "He go" or "He don't." Some nonstandard speakers do use the -*s* agreement marker but not necessarily on the third person singular. Rather, they say "I sits," "we sits," "you sits," and/or "they sits."

Verb inflections work beautifully as signals because they stand out in the stream of speech in English, which has long since shed the large system of inflection and agreement its words once had. The very fact that the *be* forms, relics of the old system of inflections, no longer fit the general grammar of English means that people will notice how they are used in speech. That these relics remain suggests to me, at least, that they may have survived because they are so useful as social class markers.

Another social class marker that is a relic of a former stage in the language is the past tense of irregular verbs. Here sometimes the older form is now nonstandard while the newer regularized one is standard. Appalachian *holp* was the original past tense of *help*. In fact, *helped* originally must have been the kind of kiddie error we saw in Chapter 1, like *sitted* for *sat*. *Have went,* which is today nonstandard, reflects the original past participle of *wend,* as in "She wends her way." *Wend* used to have the past tense *went,* thus "She went her way," and the past participle *went* as well, just as today we still have *spend, spent, (have) spent.* For some reason the present tense of *wend* was replaced by *go,* but the past tense of *wend,* replaced the old past tense of *go.* The old participle of *go*—*gone*—was retained, resulting in the present **paradigm** (the set of forms) *go, went, gone.* When the paradigms of two words *collapse* (coalesce) this way, the process is called **suppletion.** The process typically affects common words in the language; we see another example in the paradigm *good, better, best,* where the *good* clearly comes originally from a different set than *better* and *best.* The speaker who today says "have went" is just using the old participle form of *wend,* although it is not clear whether this is a survival in that speaker's dialect or just a new formation on the model of *spend, spent, (have) spent.*

Once English had several classes of irregular verbs, each class inflected differently for the different tenses. Most have since become regularized, and almost all have changed in some way from their original patterns. Some differ regionally, even among the educated. One example is the participle of *wake,* the form used with *have,* or *had.* In "I had just _____," do you say *woken, awakened,* or *wakened*? Since the irregular verbs are all common everyday words, and the system they were once part of is now moribund, they serve well as signals of social class. This is not to say that all language change or preservation of older forms is dictated by the need for status marking. When change or preservation is related to the need for status marking, however, I have noticed that it seems to center on commonly used items in the language that are no longer parts of regular paradigms or are in some other way unusual.

Negatives also have to be used frequently in conversation. They are, by their nature, not part of large sets so that they too stand out in the stream of speech. Negation in English has become a social class marker and by extension a stylistic one as well. Double negation as in "I didn't do nothin' " signals the blue-collar and lower classes, but "I didn't do anything" signals the formally educated middle class. Double negation sometimes is affected by educated speakers as a marker of casual, informal style as they attempt to emulate the naturalness and informality they presume to be characteristic of less-educated classes. Therefore, speech forms readily identifiable as belonging to the blue-collar and working classes, especially double negatives in the United States, have become stylistic as well. Again, as it happens, the blue-collar and lower class practice is the older one in English, and the educated *anything* is the newer.

Some regional grammatical differences are unrelated to social class. These are more subtle, not concentrated in constructions that have to be used a great deal. People are frequently unaware that these differences exist, just as they are often unaware of lexical differences.

Prepositional differences are a case in point. Prepositions have a habit of slipping and sliding around over the years. Often, prepositions in themselves have little meaning, and the selection of one over another has little consequence for meaning. Old English prayed to God "on heaven" rather than "in heaven." Today, *in* and *on* vary regionally. New York City and the Hudson Valley wait *on line* instead of the more common wait *in line.* In the South, *wait on* means what Northerners mean by *wait for.* In the North, *wait on* refers to serving another person, as in waiting on a customer. In Pennsylvania and parts of the South, one might hear *sick on his stomach* and *sick in his stomach.* More commonly, in the South one hears *sick at his stomach* as opposed to the usual Northern *sick to his stomach.* Appalachians speak of *at the wintertime,* rather than *in.* Rural Maine often stays *to home* rather than *at home.* The Midlands tell time with *quarter till* instead of *quarter to* or *quarter of.* Some speakers in New York City, parts of Wisconsin, and Pennsylvania *stay by* someone when they visit, rather than *stay with,* perhaps because of the influence of German or Yiddish on those areas.

Because choice of preposition is determined by arbitrary grammar rules rather than by selection on the basis of meaning alone, much preposition use is considered syntactic. Prepositions in many European languages have replaced old endings on nouns that tell how the noun is being used in a given sentence. For instance, in English, the one surviving inflectional ending on nouns, the possessive *'s* is also paraphrasable by using the preposition *of.*

7.16   *Anymore users*

For most English speakers, or at least those who use *anymore*, it can be used only when preceded by a negative word, as in

9a. He doesn't come here anymore.
 b. He hardly comes here anymore.
 c. If he comes here anymore, I'll beat him up.

In some parts of West Virginia, Pennsylvania, Delaware, New York, Ohio, Kentucky, Indiana, and South Carolina (Parker 1975), it appears affirmatively, as in:

10a. Things are getting busier for me anymore.
  b. Boy, it sure gets dark here anymore.
  c. You really talk a lot anymore.
  d. Most people get married around the age of twenty anymore.

Speakers unfamiliar with this *anymore* often are not too sure of what it means. They are likely to assume that it has some relationship to *still.* Actually, it means 'nowadays.'

Even more subtle syntactic differences occur in the verb system. An educated Detroit consultant says "That squirrel *is keeping on getting* into my bird feeder." Eastern New England consultants only allow *keeps on getting.* British RP allows *wanting to know*, which sounds odd to many Americans. One hears "We are married for five years" from New York City speakers, probably because of the influence of foreign languages like Yiddish and Italian.

7.17   *Dialect difference is rule difference*

An accent is what someone else has. People do not notice their own speech variety, only those different from their own. Their own sounds natural;

other kinds, especially those with which they are least familiar, may sound cute or quaint or harsh or ugly. They may even sound as if their speakers are making mistakes.

For instance, speakers of the /r/-full dialects often accuse those of the misnamed /r/-less dialects of putting /r/s where they do not belong as well as leaving them out where they do belong. The /r/-less dialects are misnamed because they do have /r/, at the start of a word (as in *ran*) and, for most such dialects, between vowels.

The American /r/-less dialects share rules for /r/ with the British /r/-less dialects. Yet /r/-full Americans do not perceive the British /r/-less dialects, especially RP, as being wrong, although they may perceive some of the American ones that way. In the United States, the coastal South, New York City and environs, and New England east of the Connecticut River have traditionally dropped the /r/. Australian and South African dialects of English also drop the /r/.

Is /r/ dropping a kind of carelessness? Since educated speech, even upper class and aristocratic British, Australian, South African, and older East Coast American speech, drops the /r/, there must be another reason.

The following explanation for /r/ dropping shows how general constraints on human language production influence language change, which then may become implicated in social marking. The /r/ used in English does not occur in too many languages. Sounds that are not commonly used in the world's languages are called **marked** sounds. Linguists think that such sounds are, in some sense, difficult to produce. Languages and dialects seem to be roughly equal in difficulty, so that if a language is more complicated or difficult than other languages in one feature, it will be simpler in another.

The English /r/ is a case in point. Dialects that retain /r/ in all positions often compensate by collapsing at least some of the older vowel distinctions before the /r/, frequently rhyming *your* with *sir*. To such speakers, *current* is [kərnt] 'kernt' with the 'cur-' rhyming with *sir*. They also may pronounce *Mary, merry,* and *marry* alike.

The so-called /r/-less speakers usually preserve most of the vowel distinctions shown in the spelling, although each /r/-less dialect uses different vowels. In Southeastern New England, for instance, *your* is [y: ɔ(r)] 'yaw(r)'; *sir* is [s3 (r)], or, as in Britain, [sə] 'suh', as in 'no suh'; *Mary* is [mɨri] 'Mary'; *merry* is [mɛri] 'mehry'; and *marry* is [mæri] 'maery.' So, there is a balance in the number of features: many /r/ full speakers drop vowel distinctions, and /r/-less speakers drop /r/. Each drops some sounds and retains others. Neither is more careless nor more precise than the other.

Yet another aspect of /r/ pronouncing worth considering illustrates the complexity of factors that cause dialect differences. This is the so-called intrusive /r/ of many /r/-less dialects that occurs at the end of words like *saw* or *Cuba*. Many people think this is a case of "putting in an /r/ where it doesn't belong." Actually, there are some good reasons for the appearance of this /r/, and we shall see that it is not an intrusion.

Wherever two or more consonants come together, there is a tendency for speakers to drop one of them. Two consonants together, consonant clusters (CC's), are also marked constructions. In English, consonant dropping is done especially at the ends of words, as in "roas' beef." The /r/-less speakers, by dropping /r/ in words like *park* have simplified their language in two ways: they have reduced the CC in *park* and gotten rid of the marked sound /r/. The same explanation holds for the dropping of final /r/ before a word that begins with a consonant, as in "four please." By saying "faw, please," the speaker gets rid of the difficult /r/ as well as the CC.

7.18   *"Intrusive"* /r/s

If /r/s are so tough to pronounce, what about the "intrusive" /r/s? These occur in many Northeast American /r/-less dialects, as well as some British ones, including RP. Examples are seen in the alternations between italicized words in columns 1 and 2:

> 11a. I got a new *sofa*.   but   My *sofer* is new.
>   b. Let it *thaw*.   *Thawr* it out.
>   c. What an *idea*!   The *idear* is good.

It must be emphasized that the /r/ in column 2 sounds intrusive only to those speakers who do not have it in that position. An Ohio speaker finds it intrusive. A New Hampshire or London speaker does not even hear it (unless it is pointed out). But, then, the Ohio speaker does not hear his or her own intrusive /r/ in [wɔrš] 'warsh' (*wash*) and [sarks] "sarks" (*socks*) (Shuy 1967). I do not know the reason for the Midwestern instrusive /r/, but those in 11 are explainable. They are not mistakes, as many people think, but occur regularly under certain conditions.

If simplicity is the reason for dropping /r/s, then why add one where it does not belong? If there is anything more difficult to pronounce than two consonants together, it is two vowels together. Most languages have some way to alleviate that condition. In English, in phrases like *see it*, we insert a /y/, actually saying "seeyit." This breaks up the vowels, giving the consonant–vowel–consonant (CVC) pattern that is preferred in the languages of the world. In the same way *co-op* gets a /w/ glide, so that it gets pronounced "cowop." The /y/ glide appears in between two vowels if the first of these is made with the tongue bunched toward the front of the mouth, as when saying "I ate," "Mr. Shea ate," and "he ate." You will feel the /y/s as your tongue glides into *ate*. The /w/ glide appears between two vowels when the first is made with the front of the tongue down, and the back of the tongue humped up. This happens in phrases like "who is," and "Mo is." Again, if you say these aloud, you will feel yourself making a /w/ as you glide into the "is." The reason that /y/ and /w/ work as glides is that the tongue is in the position for making them after making certain vowels. Say

"I," but leave your tongue up as you finish articulating. Do not relax it. Note that it is in position to start a /y/. Do the same for "ooh." Note that the tongue is in position for /w/. The /r/ glide is caused by the same sort of situation.

There is more than one way to make /r/. The most common American way is to curl the tongue tip up, making what is known as the retroflex /r/. However, many /r/-less speakers make it somewhat differently. They hump their tongue up in back, and although the tip is lifted it is not usually curled. As a result, when /r/-less speakers pronounce the mid vowels, their tongues are in position for /r/. Speakers of some of those dialects, such as American Northeastern and British RP, use the /r/, then, as a glide, one that completes the system of the /y/ and /w/ glides. They can break up any sequence of two vowels with a glide.

The /r/-full speakers do not get an /r/ glide, of course, so they break up sequences with the /y/ and /w/ vowels when appropriate. In other instances, lacking the third glide, they often get rid of the unhappy sequence by leaving out the second vowel, so that *thaw it* sounds like "thought," *sofa is* become "sofas," and *idea is* becomes "ideas." When that is not possible, they add a glottal stop. That is the sound that many /r/-less Americans (and British and Scots) use instead of a /t/ in words like *bottle*. Often when comparing two dialects (or languages) we find that both actually make use of some of the same elements. They just use them differently.

It is hoped that the foregoing has made it clear that even though different dialects sound different, no one variety is necessarily better or worse than the rest. There are many equally good and logical ways to speak a language. For each dialect's rules there are equally logical and sensible explanations.

7.19   *The verb system in NNE*

Another example of the systematic differences between dialect, this time an example from syntax, comes from NNE. One charge against that dialect is that its speakers do not use verb tenses at all or do not use them correctly. NNE speakers, for instance, often say "play" for *played*. They may use other forms unusual to SE speakers as well, such as "I done sung" or "He been gone." At other times, they seem to be leaving verbs out altogether, as in "I goin' " or "he busy."

Closer investigation reveals that far from being mistakes, these are part of an intricate verb system different from that of SE. Like SE, NNE is a collection of related dialects; like most dialects in America today, NNE is showing change. The following NNE verb system represents at least one conservative dialect of NNE (based on Bolinger 1975, p. 339). It illustrates how systematic a dialect is, even one in which speakers are considered to be making mistakes. Far from being a collection of mistakes, the following paradigm shows that the dialect is not only well ordered, but makes very fine discriminations in its use of verb forms:

12. *Present*   *Habitual*   *Complete Past*
    I singing   I be singing   I done sung
    I do sing   I been sung

    Future   *Incomplete Past*
    I'ma sing   I sang/sung
    I'ma gonna sing   I have sung
    I gonna sing   I did sing
                       I sang

As indicated by the headings, this NNE verb system indicates aspect as well as tense. *Aspect* is concerned with such matters as whether or not action is completed and whether it occurs habitually or just once. *Tense* is concerned with the time of action. Many NNE dialects mark aspect in their verb forms somewhat differently from the ways that SE does. They make more distinctions in aspect than does SE.

The *done* and *been* forms do not always appear in the speech of younger Blacks in Northern cities (Wolfram and Fasold 1974, p. 152). It should also be noted that the *done* and *been* auxiliaries appear in other English dialects as well in much the same meaning as in NNE. These words, which indicate completed action in the past, are not necessarily exclusive to Blacks. Appalachian English (AE), among other English dialects, uses the *done* form extensively, for instance (Wolfram and Christian 1976). The *been* has been found in Newfoundland speech (Williams 1975).

Some scholars claim that *have* is not an auxiliary in NNE dialects (Stewart 1965, p. 17; Dillard 1973, p. 48), which use only *done* and *been.* Bolinger does not include *have* as an auxiliary, nor does he include the simple past forms, such as *sang.* I have included them because both are regularly heard from many NNE speakers, even those who use the *been* and *done* forms (Labov et al. 1968, p. 152; Herndobler and Sledd 1976). Other NNE speakers use *ain't* as an auxiliary similar to SE *have* (Labov et al. 1968, p. 255).

When NNE speakers do use the auxiliary *have,* they tend not to contract it to *'ve.* Furthermore they stress it. For instance, Larry (Labov 1969), a definite NNE speaker, while discussing the existence of God, said "I have seen all kinds gods."

Although NNE uses the full form of the auxiliary *have* where SE rarely does, as SE speakers are quick to notice, NNE often has no *be (am, is, are),* as in "I singing" or "She busy." SE speakers hear this as a mistake, as if something was left out. On this premise, some have even based claims that Blacks have defective language. But the *be* is left out very systematically and with reason. Forms like "I singing" and "he busy" refer to right now only. They correspond to SE "I'm singing" and "I'm busy." "I be singing" and "I be busy" indicate that these events are true always. These correspond to SE "I sing" and "I am busy all of the time." NNE has a contrast that SE lacks in its verb tense system between present habitual and nonhabitual actions or states. SE can express the same idea, but by using words and phrases like *all the time, usually,* or *frequently.* NNE can use these words as well but also can encode the notion just by the form of verb used.

Some researchers believe that this contrast is a survival of the verb systems in West African languages. They believe that the original slaves imposed the African verb system on the English that they were forced to learn (as bilinguals sometimes do; see Chapter 10). One problem with this view is that there was a durative *be* in Old English that has been found again in Newfoundland White speech. Since Newfoundland speakers also have the *been* meaning 'completion of an action in the remote past' (Williams, 1975), it may be that Black slaves learned English from those who spoke the same dialect as that in Newfoundland (see Section 8.28).

NNE present and future tenses do not quite correspond to those of SE. For instance, in SE "I do sing" is emphatic. In NNE, it means "I've been singing just before now and up to now." Both NNE and SE use *going to* (often pronounced "gonna" even by SE speakers) to indicate indefinite time in the future, although NNE does not use *be* with it as SE does. NNE has two other futures as well, *I'ma,* which means 'immediate future, right away', as in "I'ma leave you alone, baby." Then NNE also has *a-gonna,* which indicates 'not right away, but soon'.

NNE past tenses are similarly finely differentiated. The *did + past* ("did sing") refers to slightly longer ago than *do sing.* It should not be confused with SE *did sing,* which is an emphatic meaning 'any time in the past'. *Done sung* is longer ago than *did sing* in NNE, and does not impinge directly upon the present. *I did sing* could mean 'I sang yesterday, and the activity is still relevant today.' *I done sung* means 'I sang last month or even six months ago, but I'm not necessarily going to do it again.' *I been sung* is the time longest ago, not recent at all.

Readers should not get the impression from the above that NNE is superior to SE in its use of verb tense. Both systems work equally well and are just as logical and useful. Examination of SE verb tense also reveals complexity.

7.20   *Classroom application*

It is not only NNE that differs from SE in verb tenses and other facets of grammar. The problem with such differing systems is that schoolteachers typically are SE speakers. Even if they started out as non-SE, they usually think that the NSE dialects, their own original one and everyone else's, are full of mistakes. As we have seen and as could be illustrated many times over, this is not true.

It is not fair or sound to isolate one form from a dialect and then compare it to a different dialect. It is this practice that leads one to think the other dialect contains errors. Teachers confronted with speakers of dialects different from their own should listen carefully and try to ascertain the ways the other dialect operates. Then they should try to analyze exactly how it differs from their own accustomed usage.

In foregoing examples, notice that even when NNE and SE use the same forms, they sometimes mean quite different things. An investigator should never assume that the identical forms in two separate dialects mean the same thing or can be used the same way. Remembering this can be crucial in teaching reading. Everyone who reads well translates the printed sentence into his or her own dialect. NNE-speaking children are not likely to come across their own dialect's verb system in the reading textbooks. The teacher can point out to a child, "Oh, this 'I did sing' means 'I really DID do it' not 'I did it yesterday' " or he or she can say " 'I will go' is the same as your 'agonna go.' "

Some immediately object with horror: "But isn't that reinforcing the nonstandard speech?" Not really. The next chapter examines what leads to a child's picking up new dialects. Here, note simply that it is impossible to learn to read unless one knows how to relate the printed page to the speech one already has. Middle-class children know this from having been read to all of their lives. No dialect of English is spoken the way the language is written. We all had to learn how the written language corresponds to our spoken language. For instance, British and other /r/-less speakers learn to consider *ar* as /aː/ 'ah', and *or* as [ɔː] 'aw'. For them, the /r/ is just another silent letter like the *k* in *knee*. Grammatically we learn that the printed *have* in *They have gone* is really the *'ve* we are accustomed to hearing for the same sentence, which is pronounced "They've gone." In order to learn to read the NSE child must learn the correspondences between his or her dialect and the written one (Labov 1967; Baratz 1969).

Reams have been written about NNE and a fair amount about Appalachian English (AE) and Chicano English. Unfortunately, precious little has been examined in other NSE dialects. The teacher faced with these others simply has to learn to be sensitive to students' speech, being alert to sources of conflict between it and SE. It also helps if the teacher has had enough linguistics so that he or she can analyze contrasts between dialects (DiPietro 1971).

EXERCISES

1. Find at least two examples of regional or social dialects being used in TV commercials. Explain why you think each particular dialect was chosen for the product it sells.

2. Is there any TV show whose characters seem to you to have accents? If you know of one, watch and list the name of the show, the character(s) who have the accent(s), and the role of the character(s). What kind(s) of accent do you think are being used? Does the accent

itself affect your feelings about or judgment of the character? In each instance determine whether the character's role in the show is emphasized by the accent or if the accent just seems to be an accident of casting.

3. Are you aware of any word(s) in your dialect that differ from words for the same thing(s) in other dialects of your language?

4. Do the TV announcers in your area speak with the local accent? If it is the case that some do and some do not, is there a difference in what is announced by those who do speak with the local accent?

chapter 8

SOCIOLINGUISTIC INVESTIGATIONS

Traditional dialect investigations were concerned with regional differences, especially with making maps showing the distribution of dialect features. These still provide some social and historical information about people of different regions. With the discovery that the dialect a person uses correlates with his or her feelings of identity, dialect investigations within a community have been developed that give important sociological insights. Insight is also garnered by examining how people feel about the speech of others and how they think they themselves speak. People are often quite unaware of how they actually speak, thinking they sound like those they profess to admire. Discovering both present social stratification and changing conditions can be done via dialect investigations. The implications of such studies for education are followed by a discussion of how dialects arise within a society and whether some dialects can be more restricted than others.

8.1   *Traditional dialect studies*

Traditional dialect studies concentrate on fine points of pronunciation and lexical differences in different regions. If syntax is noticed at all, it will be with respect to those items that are most closely related to word choice, such as *you-all* or the selection of *dived, div* or *dove* as one of dialectal variants for the past tense of *dive.* Such studies do not treat the topics discussed in Chapter 7: entire verb tense systems or interrelated rules of pronunciation, like the /r/ rules. This is probably because traditional dialect investigations were best at eliciting single words from consultants, not entire sentences, much less discourses. They were concerned with linguistic geography, the regional distribution of differences in speech (McIntosh 1952; Bloomfield 1965). Since the earlier investigators were scholars thoroughly trained in the history of language, they were also very interested in the spread of words and sounds from one region to another because of cultural influence or migration. Their aim was to prepare linguistic atlases of the speech of various countries. Such maps have been partly made for nearly all the European countries, including Germany, France, Italy, Switzerland, and the Slavic countries.

Linguists in North America began the painstaking work for such an atlas in 1931. Raven McDavid, Jr. as principal field worker for this project, entitled *The Linguistic Atlas of the United States and Canada,* explains its purpose as follows in 1958: "Thus, the American Atlas seeks to record data illustrating the social differences, the dimension of time, and the process of language and dialect mixture that has been going on everywhere since the New World was settled."

8.2   The methods of the Linguistic Atlas

As with the European studies upon which it was based, the American linguistic atlas was concerned with the differences in speech between educated and uneducated speakers. To this end, field workers trained to transcribe speech selected at least two speakers from each area: an older, uneducated speaker and a younger (middle aged) speaker who usually had at least a high school education. The field workers asked for information from questionnaires prepared for the atlas survey, such as the names of certain activities or items, noting the word choice itself as well as the pronunciation used. The three examples below are typical atlas questions, still pertinent today. The words in parentheses are some of the answers one might expect:

1 a. [What do you call] The place to which children run in a tag game. (goal, guwl, base, home den)
   b. Someone who won't change his mind is _____? (bullheaded, contrary, sot)
   c. A large, open metal container for scrub water is a _____? (pail, bucket)

(Shuy 1967)

The questionnaires listed 520 to 850 items. All responses had to be transcribed carefully in the International Phonetic Alphabet (IPA). Competent field workers were always in short supply. In the days before sensitive tape recorders, workers had to be able to discriminate fine phonetic differences on the spot.

After the painstaking work of collecting the data, they had to be sorted and classified. Maps showing both pronunciation and word choice had to be prepared. Thus it took years to complete the investigation of each area and even longer for the publication of results. The New England Atlas, known as LANE (Linguistic Atlas of New England), was begun in 1931 but was not completed until 1943. In rapidly changing countries as large as the United States and Canada the first part of such an investigation is likely to be outdated long before the last is completed. Very little of the United States and Canada was ever covered by the atlas at all. The field work was completed for New England, the Middle and South Atlantic states to the northeast tip of Florida, the North Central States, and the upper Midwest. The field work has been completed and the linguistic atlases have been published for the first three of these regions (O'Cain 1979). This does not mean that there are no linguistic geographies of the rest of North America. There have been studies in selected areas throughout, but a complete atlas is far from a reality. The original plan was logical enough: start with the areas of first settlement and move westward as migration did. In 1931 the East Coast seemed entrenched as the cultural and educational center of the country. It was hard to foresee that influence would start flowing West to

East, with important consequences for linguistic geography. The fact that /r/ pronouncing in words like *park* is becoming the American standard is a prime example of this shift.

Although the concerns of dialect geography and sociolinguistics intersect, a complete discussion of the former is really outside the province of this book. Here, we are mainly concerned with the two facets of dialectology considered the province of sociolinguistics, although, admittedly, it is sometimes difficult to draw a hard line between the fields:

- The ways that speech shows the social groupings within a community;
- The social markers for which people listen, no matter how subconsciously, in their social dealings in a community.

8.3   Problems with the atlas investigations

More recent investigations have uncovered some problems with the kind of traditional study represented by the atlas efforts. The first is that people in interview situations use their most careful speech, what they think is correct, not what they ordinarily use. McDavid (1979) objects that some of the field workers did manage to get casual style from consultants. However, there was no regular attempt to get more than one style from them. Formal style is as necessary to a sociolinguistic investigation as casual style is. Comparing both styles for any given speaker reveals crucial sociological information. Such comparisons are missing from earlier studies.

Furthermore, for the most part, all the atlases give us is a record of single words. There is virtually no information about sentence structure or the forms of discourse, much less the purposes for which they are used. To be fair, linguistics itself as a social science had not yet begun a serious interest in such matters at the time of the atlas studies. One example will suffice to show the limitations and yet the need for atlas studies. Linguistic geography shows that the working class in Eastern New England and New York City share the same /r/ rules as speakers of southern British dialects. That tells us a great deal about the history of the dialects and their range, but it does not tell us anything about the social worth of the /r/ rules in the different countries and the social purposes for which they are used.

An atlas can provide a framework for future study. It shows us what we might start looking for and gives a historical framework for interpretations of linguistic differences. That is the function of traditional dialect studies, and it is not fair to criticize them for not being what they were never intended to be. Hence these comments should not be taken as a criticism of the tremendously careful, detailed work of dialect geographers.

The biggest problem with the atlas—one that renders it of dubious value even as a framework—is the paucity of speakers interviewed in each region. The danger with an inadequate sample in any social survey is that subjects may not be representative of the entire population. Linguists have long known that anyone in a given locale may idiosyncratically use words or pronunciations somewhat differently from others in the locale to denote the same things. If too few consultants are used, one such idiosyncratic speaker can throw off the study, giving a false picture of the area.

Another sampling problem with the atlas is that it did not include subjects of enough different ages. Today, we know that there must be several representatives of different ages for every potentially significant social group in an area. For instance, it appears that upper middle-class adolescents in many formerly /r/-less areas are pronouncing at least a light /r/ before consonants. It is hard to know exactly what to make of this. The atlas workers often transcribed the speech of only two or three consultants. Therefore, we do not really know if this is an innovation, indicating that /r/ pronouncing is coming into an /r/-less area. If it is, what does it mean? Is it merely a reflection of a lessening of the cultural influence of Great Britain? Could it represent a reaction to the rise of the immigrant groups who first imitated the speech of the descendants of original settlers then usurped their political power? Has this population had the /r/ for years, but atlas workers just did not happen to catch it in the few consultants they interviewed? Today we know that sociolinguistic survey is extremely important in discovering the attitudes in a community, but it must be based upon adequate data. My own investigations in this area suggest that the atlas was correct in delineating Eastern New England as /r/-less. The speech of older residents, regardless of social class, is completely /r/-less, but the atlas alone is shaky evidence for this assertion.

8.4   *The newer studies*

The methods of collecting data of the atlas are not completely outmoded. Many valuable studies are still being conducted in essentially the same manner, as even a casual perusal of the journal *American Speech* will show. Rather than trying to blanket large regions, however, recent studies have concentrated on smaller areas and within those areas have studied more subjects from more social groups than older ones did.

One massive effort now underway is the U.S. Dialect Tape Depository. This is most ingeniously blanketing a large area: the entire United States. Its director Joseph Mele is taking advantage of tape recorders. He has contacted linguists all over the country. They select whomever they think is representative of social and ethnic groups in their region and tape record their speech. The linguists have their consultants read a collection of sentences sent by Dr. Mele and also tell a brief anecdote about an exciting or happy event in their lives, tape recording the entire interview. Undoubtedly, the quality of the tapes is not consistent and perhaps occasional investigators may not be wholly familiar with the social structure of their respective communities. Still, many are native speakers of the areas in which they are collecting, and most of the tapes should be of high quality. Certainly, this is an excellent method for getting representative speech from an entire country. Had the atlas workers possessed the abundance of tape recording equipment available today, their own work would have been far more extensive.

Quite a different approach to dialect study was pioneered by William Labov. His inspiration, in part, appears to have been a small study by John Fischer (1958) investigating the use by schoolchildren of *-in'* and *ing,* as in *runnin'* vs. *running.* Each child was found to use both pronunciations, but the percentage of times each was used varied according to how genteel or rough the child was or wanted to appear to be.

8.5   *The Martha's Vineyard study*

In the early 1960s Labov (1963) noticed that there was a great deal of variation in pronunciaton of various sounds on Martha's Vineyard, an island off the coast of Massachusetts that was and still is a playground for Bostonians. The native dialect was quite different from Boston's. The original settlers, apparently unlike the Southern British who settled Boston, were strong /r/-pronouncers. Being an island, Martha's Vineyard had not generally succumbed to Boston speech. Labov noticed that native Vineyarders pronounced the /r/ before a consonant but that there was variation both in how sharply the /r/ was pronounced and how often.

He also noticed that the vowel sounds usually spelled < i > and < ou > as in *right* and *house* were tenser and made more toward the center of the mouth than their Boston counterparts. The Vineyarders used an [əⁱ] in *right* and an [əᵘ] in *house* at least some of the time.

The reader without a background in phonology can approximate these sounds by saying "uh-ee" for the vowel in *right* and "uh-oo" for the one in *house.* To some degree Americans from many regions regularly produce these vowels before /p/, /f/, /t/, /č/, /s/, /š/, and /k/. You can test your own speech by contrasting *right* with *ride* and *louse* with *lousy.* If you have used different vowels in each set, chances are the one in *right* and the one in *louse* are the tense central vowels that Labov noticed some Vineyarders producing. The fact that many other American dialects, including many in New England, have those tense central vowels shows that these are not peculiar to Martha's Vineyard. The point is that Boston, the nearest large city to the island, does not have that pronunciation or the /r/. Some Vineyarders used the Boston pronunciations and some did not.

Wanting to know who spoke with a Vineyard flavor as opposed to a Boston one and why, Labov conducted a survey that asked subjects to read passages that had plenty of words calling for the /r/s and the diphthongs /aⁱ/ and /aᵁ/. He also asked questions loaded so that the answers had to contain words with those sounds. Like Fischer he found that it was not a case of using a pronunciation or not. All the Vineyarders tested varied somewhat in their pronunciation of these sounds. What was significant was the percentage of times each person used the Vineyard sound as opposed to one more like Boston's. Most amazing was the correlation between Vineyard pronunciation and the attitudes of the speaker. Labov found that the old line Yankees, who felt that the island belonged to them, pronounced the /r/ most frequently and used the Vineyard vowel quality for /aⁱ/ and /aᵁ/.

As the traditional livelihoods of farming and fishing declined, more and more of the descendants of the original settlers found that they had to cater to tourists from Boston or leave the island. Those who had decided to stay, often in the face of financial hardship, signaled their loyalty to the island by a strong Vineyard flavor to their speech. The Gay Head Indians, who also felt that the island belonged to them, but who did not have quite the assurance of the Yankees, used the Vineyard pronunciation just a little less. Third and fourth generation Portuguese used Vineyard /r/, /aⁱ/, and /aᵁ/ just a little less than the Indians. These Portuguese were well assimilated into the island, and felt a part of it, but had even less assurance that they really belonged than did the Indians. The first generation Portuguese did not use the Vineyard pronunciations at all. Not surprisingly, they showed overtly that they were unsure of themselves and their place on the island.

The pronunciation of high school students was a direct reflection of their career plans. If they were going to leave the island, they talked like Bostonians. If not, they spoke like Vineyarders. Two important results of this study were:

- Each social group used a key pronunciation a certain percentage of the time with no overlap from group to group.
- Attitude can be precisely correlated with fine points of pronunciation.

Phonological variables, different ways of pronouncing the same sound, appeared to be a potent tool for sociological investigation.

8.6 *The New York City study*

In his later New York City study, Labov (1966) proved even more conclusively that examination of phonological variables is a remarkably exact way of analyzing a community's social organization. Furthermore, it reveals attitudes unerringly, attitudes that people often would never admit to having. New York City, being sociologically more complex than Martha's Vineyard, has more phonological variables.

Labov investigated the following:

- Whether or not /r/ was pronounced before a consonant.
- Whether the /θ/ <th> in words like *thing* was pronounced as [θ] or [t].
- Whether the /ð/ <th> in words like *the* was pronounced as [ð] or [d].
- How high the front of the tongue is when pronouncing the <a> in words like *bad* and *dance*. Labov found that there were five ways of pronouncing this <a>, ranging from the tongue being held low enough to produce a very low [æ] to a high [ɨ] 'ee'.
- How high the back of the tongue is when pronouncing the <o> in *more* and *coffee,* producing sounds from [ɔ] to [ʊ].

Just because a feature is sociologically significant in one area does not mean that it will be in another. In both Martha's Vineyard and New York City, by coincidence, /r/-pronouncing is important, but it signifies quite different things in each place. The raised /æ/ sound, disvalued in New York City, is quite normal for most of northern America and much of Canada. The most educated and refined speakers in the Great Lakes cities like Chicago, Buffalo, Cleveland, and Detroit may show far more raising of /æ/ than any New Yorker. However, in those cities, that raised /æ/ sound does not mark social class. In the Midwest the person who pronounces *bad* as [bɨd], *that* as [ðɨt], and *happy* as [hɨpi] is showing a regional not a social pronunciation.

Similarly, using an [ʊ] 'oo' for <o> in *more* and *coffee* may not denote lower class speech outside of New York City. It appears in the speech of those with impeccable ancestry and schooling, even one Harvard Ph.D. of my acquaintance, a Philadelphian by birth and graduate of a fine prep school, who always asks for "some cuwafee" [kʰʊwafi] not "cawfee" [kʰɔfi] or [kʰafi] "cafee."

Substituting [t] or [f] for /θ/ and [d] or [v] for /ð/ marks social class throughout most of the English-speaking world. For centuries, saying "duh" for *the* or "ting" for *thing* has marked an adult speaker of English as uneducated, as has pronouncing *mouth* as "mouf" and *mother* as "muvah." This does not mean that there is anything intrinsically wrong with /t/, /d/, /f/, or /v/. They are all just fine in other words, those in which we feel they belong as in *tine, dine, fine,* and *vine.*

Swedish, which like English once had /θ/ and /ð/, has long since converted, so that the Swedish counterpart to *that there* is "dat dere" for all speakers, and it sounds right to even the most educated Swede. Those sounds are not social class markers in Swedish as they are in English. The two sounds spelled <th> in English fit all the requirements for workable social class markers. They are unusual, marked sounds, appearing in few of the world's languages. When they do appear, as in Swedish, they have a tendency later to disappear.

In English, these sounds have disappeared in most dialects. Although they appear in only a few words even in the dialects that have retained them, those few words must be used frequently. One can barely complete one sentence without having to use *the*. The sounds are rare enough to stand out and cannot be avoided even in casual conversation. Like agreement markers, they may have survived mainly because of their utility in social class marking. This does not mean that all marked sounds that survive do so only because they are social markers. Sociolinguists do not know that, at least not yet. However, it is remarkable how frequently social class markers are either marked sounds or irregular relic forms in English (Chaika 1973). If the same is found to be true in a wide variety of languages, then we can claim that social marking is a major factor in retaining such sounds and forms.

8.7   *The uses of style in sociological investigation*

Elaborating on the methods he pioneered in Martha's Vineyard, Labov elicited speech in all styles from formal to casual. The pronunciation that people use in formal styles indicates what they think is correct in formal situations. If the same pronunciation is typical of a particular group or social class, we know that that group is admired, the *point of reference* for the society being investigated. Copying the speech of another group for other purposes, as when being supercasual or recounting a fight (Labov 1964) reveals points of reference for those situations as well. Everyday, casual speech reveals an individual's true feelings of social identity. Labov (1966) proved this by correlating pronunciations that occurred only in casual speech with membership in ethnic and social classes.

The most careful, formal style can be elicited by asking people to read lists of words that contain the variables suspected of being important in a community. When possible it is fruitful to include **minimal pairs,** pairs of words that differ by just one sound, especially a socially significant one. For his New York study Labov included pairs like *guard* and *god,* because he felt that pronunciation of the /r/ was socially significant, although many New York City speakers would not pronounce it in casual speech. Many speakers did pronounce it in a reading task he presented. Labov considered that this showed that the /r/ before consonants, as in *guard,* has become the prestige pronunciation in New York City. Whether or not someone attempted to pronounce that /r/ in the reading task depended strongly on the person's social class. This in itself is significant.

Labov used another reading task as well, one that yielded a slightly less careful style. As in Martha's Vineyard, he asked subjects to read passages loaded with **variables,** sounds that are articulated in more than one way by different people in the community. The passages formed a story, with each paragraph concentrating on one phonological variable. For instance,

2a. We always had chocolate milk and coffee cake around four
o'clock. My dog used to give us an awful lot of trouble . . .
b. We used to play *kick the can.* One man is "it." You run past him as
fast as you can, and you kick a tin can so he can't tag . . .
c. I remember when he was run over, not far from our corner . . .
d. There's something strange about that . . . how I can remember
everything he did: this thing, that thing, and the other thing . . .

One warning to the reader who wishes to use such reading passages. Many
subjects get "tipped off" to what you are after very soon, and either become so
tongue-tied that they stumble over every key word, or they turn it into a joke.
Perhaps the reason that this did not happen to Labov is that in the Lower East
Side of New York, in the early 1960s, people were not so overtly aware of which
pronunciations were socially disvalued.

Besides the reading tasks, Labov also noted responses to questions in an
interview. The pronunciations in the responses were usually careful but not as
careful as those elicited in reading. He found that it is possible to elicit informal
and casual speech in an interview, however, by asking subjects to describe
games that they played when they were children and to recall childhood rhymes.
The rhymes often work only in a casual style with nonprestigious pronunciations. Both the rhythms and pronunciations of careful speech ruin such
rhymes, as in the jumping-rope rhyme:

3. Cinderella, dressed in yellow,
    Went down town to get some mustard
    On the way her girdle busted.
    How many people got disgusted?
    1, 2, 3, 4, . . .

The only way that this works is without the /r/ in *mustard.* Labov found that
even when the disvalued pronunciations were not important to the rhyme
scheme, subjects resorted to them when reciting rhymes. For instance,

4. I won't go to Macy's any more, more, more,
    There's a big fat policeman at the door, door, door,
    He pulls you by the collar
    And makes you pay a dollar
    I won't go to Macy's any more, more more.

Labov found that people used the high <o> in *more* and *door* even when a low
one would fit as well. This shows the degree to which style may be determined
by what is being talked about. Childhood rhymes call for nonstandard speech
even in an interview.

Sometimes other questions, such as those dealing with sports or hobbies, will yield casual speech in an interview. Shuy, Wolfram, and Riley (1967) in their Detroit investigation relied on a variety of questions, being careful to pick cues up from their consultants about what they were interested in. They asked about TV shows, fights, and personal aspirations. They even asked questions about others in the same social group, such as "Is there one guy everyone listens to? How come?" In order to get casual, unselfconscious speech samples, interviewers must induce consultants to lose themselves in a topic.

To achieve this end Labov relied most heavily on a "danger-of-death" episode. Consultants were asked to relate a personal experience in which they had felt themselves to be in danger of death. While recounting the episode, people became progressively less formal, lapsing into their normal, everyday speech. Labov was also able to check on everyday speech by carefully listening to conversations between subjects and their families before the interview started. Sometimes people switched from talking formally to him to talking informally to their children and back again. He also observed speech in the streets during neighborhood games to get a good idea of usual informal modes.

8.8   Correlating variables with social stratification

Since he had at his disposal the results of a previous sociological study, Labov was able to correlate his findings with information about social class, occupation, education, income, and personal aspirations. If a preexisting study is not available, however, a researcher determines the social status of consultants by using the Index of Status Characteristics (ISC), a common sociological measure that divides populations according to occupation, education, income, and residence. These criteria have repeatedly been found to be important in uncovering the division of communities into groups. Such groups are called **strata**, hence the term **social stratification** of an area. Since language is social behavior, the ISC is useful in deciding which groups to study to uncover dialect differences within a community or society.

Labov found in his New York City study (1966) that use of variables within a community accurately reveals the actual social stratification of the community. It reveals changing patterns of stratification as well. Each social division that he found was characterized by distinctive pronunciation of at least one phonological variable. Although each group varied in the utilization of variables according to style, there was no overlap between groups in their total behavior.

Among older speakers, the speech of ethnic Jews and Italians was marked out by the pronunciations of two of the variables. Jews used the [ʊ] "oo" sound in words like *coffee* and *more;* Italians used the [ɨ] "ee" sound in words like *bad* and *can.* The [ʊ] "oo" for *o* was a signal that one had Jewish identity, but the [ɨ] "ee" was a signal that one felt Italian.

These differences showed up most in casual speech. In formal situations, all speakers tried to keep their tongues low when articulating <a> and <o>. All raised their tongues for these sounds as the speech became more casual. However, when articulating <a> Italians raised their tongues higher than Jews, even in the formal styles. In informal styles, the Italians were still higher than Jews for the <a>. The reverse of this pattern was shown with <o> pronunciation, the Jews raising the tongue higher for that sound.

Significantly, younger speakers (age twenty to thirty-nine at the time of the study) did not show the clear ethnic differentiation. This finding mirrored changing social stratification. By the time of Labov's study the older social stratification of New York City into ethnic groups like Jews, Italians and Irish was giving way. The new stratification was by rich or poor, White, Black, or Puerto Rican, educated or uneducated. There were also differences between men and women, but these may have always existed.

8.9   *The birth of a variable*

The oldest consultants did not vary their /r/-pronouncing according to style. Whether it was a formal task or an informal one, they made no attempt to pronounce /r/. This indicates that for them /r/ was not socially diagnostic. Labov surmised that they placed no importance on pronouncing it, and they did not consider it necessarily correct or upper class. Younger speakers clearly did. They made a maximum effort to articulate all /r/s in the word list and reading passage tasks, pronouncing /r/ less when they were using casual speech. The percentage of times /r/ was pronounced in all contexts varied according to social class, but the higher the social class, the more /r/s in every context.

The lower class produced no /r/s in casual speech, or almost none. Although they did produce more in formal tasks than in the casual, they still pronounced it the least number of times overall. One interesting exception to this rigid social class differentiation in the use of /r/ was the lower middle class. They actually out /r/-ed the upper middle class in the most formal style. The lower middle class **hypercorrected**. This is typical of lower middle class behavior. That class is often extra careful to be correct. They do not have the assurance of the middle and upper middle classes, who feel that they are the ones to set the standards. Unlike the poorest classes, however, members of the lower middle class believe that it is possible for them or their children to move upward. The lower classes do not attempt to pronounce the variables that signal middle class-hood, as it is not likely that they will have a chance to become middle class.

What all of this indicates is that /r/-pronouncing was and probably still is a clear social class marker, with /r/-full speech a prestige pronunciation. The prestige of using /r/ is shown by the trend toward increased /r/ pronunciation as styles become more formal. It is also shown by the fact that the higher the social class, the more overall use of /r/.

Since the oldest speakers did not share in this pattern of /r/-pronouncing, Labov concluded that variable was a relatively new one in New York City. Articulation of /r/ as a prestige factor apparently emerged shortly after World War II. At that time the social stratification of New York City began to show changes as the flight to the suburbs began. Also a good number of children and grandchildren of immigrants began to "make it" during those years.

Social class became more important than ethnic group. Many people needed a badge to proclaim new status. That badge, apparently became /r/-pronouncing. What is ironical is that in older New York City speech, /r/-lessness was considered upper class. However, once all classes were /r/-less, or because they were, it could no longer serve as a status marker. Labov noted that /r/ more than any other feature correlated with earned status. Furthermore, it was a feature that many in his study adopted after adolescence. Adoption of /r/ as a social marker is another example of the sensitivity of language change to social needs.

8.10   *Putting people into cubbyholes*

People categorize each other according to the phonological variables they use. If they did not, there would be no reason for the systematic way that variants of sounds are pronounced in a community and their tight correlation with social facts. In New York City hearing the preconsonantal /r/ pronounced by a speaker a high percentage of times allowed hearers to peg the speaker as upper middle class. Conversely, hearing a high percentage of [ɪ]s for <a>s classified someone as being lower middle to lower class, and, for older speakers in particular, as Italian. Labov's New York City study, even more than his Martha's Vineyard one, showed that it is the percentage of times that someone uses a variable in each context that reflects social class. It is not a case of uttering a particular sound as opposed to not uttering it at all. Virtually all speakers occasionally used disvalued pronunciations, and all occasionally used valued ones.

8.11   *Classification is a game of percentages*

In some way, listeners must be tuned in, not only to the presence or absence of an articulation, but to the frequency of its occurrence. Why? It would seem to be more socially efficient to have either/or situations. Yet upon deeper consideration, it would be less efficient to have social identifications on the basis of absolute differences in sounds between social groups. It is true that Labov showed no overlap in percentage of certain pronunciations from one group to another, but each group in the community did use the same sounds as identity markers. It was how often the sounds were pronounced in each of their possible variations that yielded the social identification. In order to understand why frequency of usage of some feature works better as a social class marker in a society, one must bear in mind also the number of markers that would be necessary in a society of any complexity. Listeners would have to be aware of too many features if each group's speech was marked by a unique set of features.

Consider the implications of the claim that an individual's different way of pronouncing words is a reliable signal as to which social group he or she identifies with. It means that there must be separate pronunciations for every significant social category. In other words, if, in a given community, some factor is important in social grouping, then that factor should be reflected in a feature of dialect. Thus in New York City when earned status became more important than birth status, a new variable arose that cut across ethnic groups to signal earned status. In Martha's Vineyard, when a need to signal allegiance to the island became important, sounds already in the dialect began to function as markers of that attitude. Stewart (1972) says that in Appalachia, where age is especially important to social groupings, children signal that they are not yet adult by using infantile pronunciations long after children in less age-graded societies do.

8.12   *Why variables: why not constants?*

Why are social differences so often indicated by frequency of usage rather than by absolutely different pronunciatons between groups? Why is the middle class in New York City, for instance, marked out from the upper middle by using a smaller percentage of /r/s? If the upper middle class is delimited by /r/, why isn't the middle class designated by another sound, say /l/, and the lower middle by yet another, say/m/?

Any answer is purely speculative, but it seems to me that this phenomenon is related to what we saw in jargons. Old material in the language is frequently made to do new duty. Human beings are already geared to handle flexibility, matching what they hear to the social context and deriving meaning accordingly. Variables in pronunciation fit into regular decoding strategies, demanding no new techniques.

Marking social groups by percentage of times that a feature is used may well be more efficient than having separate markers for each group. In a complex speech community, there would have to be a great many markers floating around, one for each group. Instead of having to listen for five or six markers, noting frequency of usage in order to categorize people correctly, residents would have to listen for as many separate markers as there are separate groups. Add to this the burden of recognition of regional markers, attitude markers, and purely stylistic markers, and the whole becomes so complex that efficiency in social functioning could well be impaired. In order for social interaction to proceed smoothly, categorization of all sorts has to be swift. Perhaps this is why dialect markers themselves are sometimes used stylistically, as when middle class youths lapse into NNE on appropriate social occasions.

Obviously people do not attend conventions to decide how to use speech socially or what markers to adopt. In fact, pronouncements by experts who have tried to legislate speech have rarely if ever been successful. Any teacher who has struggled valiantly with trying to get pupils to speak "correctly" knows how little such effort helps. Yet, patently, people do change their speech patterns. What does make them do so?

Rarely are people wholly conscious of all that they are actually doing with speech, much less why. All of these signaling behaviors seem to be inborn in humankind, as is speech itself (Lenneberg 1967). Social markers on language are not products of formal instruction. Rather, they seem to have developed as language itself developed, in response to social need, a product of a finely tuned evolution.

8.13 *Evaluation*

The preceding discussion lacks one important proof. How do we know that people really do categorize each other on the basis of dialect features? Readers should always question such assertions.

The same ways that sociolinguists use to ascertain how people evaluate voice quality can be used to discover how they evaluate various pronunciations. In his study of the social stratification of New York City speech (1966), Labov took one sentence from each paragraph of the extended reading passage, as read by five separate speakers. Each way of pronouncing the five variables was included. For instance, Labov included one of the sentences that tested for /r/ pronouncing as read by each social group. He also included speakers who read the "kick the can" passage with the lowest [æ] to the highest [+] for <a>. Then he asked the participants in the study to listen to the tape, pretending that they were personnel managers interviewing job candidates for a large corporation. They were given a rating form on which to indicate which job would be suitable for each speaker on the tape. The jobs listed ranged from TV personality to factory worker.

The results matched those of the original interviews, hence confirmed those results: the variables rated as appropriate for the highest ranking jobs were exactly the ones people tended towards in the formal reading tasks. Speakers with a very high <a> in <can> were consistently selected for the lowest jobs. Those who used the lowest <a> were deemed suitable as TV personalities and executive secretaries at the top of the occupational scale. Recall that participants in the study lowered their tongues when pronouncing <a> as the task originally given them became more formal. Significantly, no matter how they themselves regularly talked everyone rated speakers on the tapes the same way. Just because someone habitually says "dese" for *these* does not mean that he or she has values in speech different from the values of those who use the standard pronunciation. Labov pointed out that all members of a speech community share the same linguistic values. If they did not, then speech variables would not be useful for signaling social class and ethnicity.

Moreover, Labov found that, even more than others, speakers who used a disvalued pronunciation the most downgraded speakers on the tape who used the same pronunciation. What we dislike most about ourselves is what we so often dislike the most in others.

8.14   *Subjective reaction tests*

If everyone shares the same norms and if users of generally disvalued speech dislike their own speech why does anyone speak in a nonprestigious manner? The answer is that people are not aware of how they are actually speaking. They think they sound different than they actually do. In fact, one sure way to get people angry is to tell them that they are using a particular pronunciation that they criticize in others.

Again, it was Labov who showed that people's evaluation of their own speech is not accurate. He played a tape with different pronunciations of seven words: *card, chocolate, pass, thing, then, her,* and *hurt.* Each word was pronounced four different ways, and subjects were asked to circle the number that correlated with their own pronunciation. In most instances, people reported themselves as using prestigious pronunciations even if they really used them no more than 30 percent of the time. They monitored their own speech according to community norms. That is, they thought they were talking according to the community's standards of prestigious features. However, the way they actually talked correlated with their social class or ethnic group. In other words, people talk according to their feelings of identity without realizing it.

8.15   *The street gangs*

Nobody is immune to the community's values. Even tough street kids who rebel against established institutions in every way can show a surprising concern with correct speech. In the Harlem study Labov et al. (1968) got some unexpected results from a subjective reaction test. Because Black youths respond best in competitive situations, the test was given to the whole gang at once in the form of a **vernacular correction test.** One of the Black field workers read sentences to the group, having asked them to correct the sentences to make them conform to the boys' usual way of saying them. If the sentences were correct according to the Black dialect they spoke, the boys were to make no correction. When reading the following examples remember that the entire exchange was performed out loud, so that all could hear and verify the truth of the responses. One sentence read to the boys was:

5. That's Nick boy.

One feature of NNE is that it does not ordinarily use the possessive *'s*. Even so, Boot, one of the toughest, roughest members of the group, one who spoke virtually "pure" NNE, shouted out

> 6. That's Mr. Nick's son. That's Nick's son right there. Do you know that's Nick's son?

Later, the field worker gave:

> 7. She a real stab bitch.

Again, Boot was on his toes with a response:

> 8. She a real [laughs]—she *is* a real stab bitch.

That *is* was important. Boot started to affirm 7, then caught himself and inserted SE *is*. Although, as we have already seen, NNE does not use it in such a sentence, Boot reported himself as using the SE form.

Then the worker asked, "What does *stab* mean?" Boot answered, "She bad." He left out the *is* when caught off guard. Boot talked NNE but reported himself as using SE because he knew that there is such a thing as correct speech, as is shown by his response to the field worker's sentence:

> 9. Why he do that?
>
> | | |
> |---|---|
> | *Boot:* | Why did he do that, man? |
> | *Interviewer:* | Don't people say, "Why he do that?" |
> | *Boot:* | Some people that don't speak correc' English do. Calvin little brother do. |

Here he failed to use the possessive that he reports himself as using in 6! Wolfram and Fasold got similar results with other populations of speakers of nonstandard English elsewhere in America.

8.16   *A counterexample*

Trudgill (1972) got reverse results from working class men in Norwich, England. They reported themselves as using stigmatized (nonprestige) forms more than they actually did. He felt that this showed that working class values have, in his words, covert prestige there. That is, although people are supposed to admire middle and upper class ways, in Norwich men really prefer the working class as their standard. Trudgill concluded that in Norwich the norm at which men are aiming is nonstandard working class speech.

We have seen some of that in America as well, as when middle class men adopt NNE or AE speech for various activities. In fact, one wonders if Labov would have gotten different results had he asked consultants to select the pronunciation they used in situations such as parties, sports events, and work.

8.17   *The sociolinguistic survey versus conventional sociological studies*

Sociolinguistic surveys are especially valuable for determining social stratification of a community for three reasons. First, a tremendous amount of pertinent information is obtained in every interview, as much as 400–500 pieces. Therefore, only ten to twenty representatives of a given group need be interviewed to obtain reliable data. Second, subjects do not usually know what is being looked for if it is looked for skillfully, although one does tell them that it is a language survey. I have found that the only tipoff to the particular features being sought is the reading passage, but other investigators have used reading passages successfully.

Labov found that subjects' unconscious use of phonological variables was more consistent with their social and ethnic group than were their answers to any single question on the original sociological survey that he used for selecting subjects. As has been shown, one's speech is more revealing of one's identity with a social group than are one's stated attitudes. Moreover, people asked directly what their attitudes or feelings are often give the answer they think is correct or say what they think the investigator wants to hear. Of course, they do the same in a language survey as well, but the very lie contains valuable information about social attitudes. It reveals what is considered the prestige speech and the points of reference within a community. It also reveals the criteria for social identity within a community and shows how these are changing.

It reveals who is admired and for what purposes. Frequently, for example, lower and working class White boys live in open hostility with Black youths, engaging in urban guerilla warfare with them. The Whites express open disdain and even hatred for Blacks. Yet when discussing fights the same White youths frequently lapse unconsciously into Black dialect (Labov 1964, p. 493). In their field work, my own students have frequently gathered samples of White youths lapsing unconsciously into NNE when discussing sports, especially basketball and football. When discussing nonclassical music—jazz, blues, bluegrass, disco—SE speakers often substitute NNE or other nonstandard forms for SE ones. Much general American slang, like "real cool, man" or "groovy," seems to have entered the standard dialect of the language by such borrowing.

8.18 *Dialect copying in popular music*

With the advent of the 1960s, and the accompanying questioning of middle class values and new admiration of naturalness, nonstandard dialects took on new value for American youth. This was reflected in the increased use of NNE and other NSE dialects in popular songs, even those sung by SE speakers. Today many middle-class SE speakers sing with overtones of AE, NNE or working class dialects. Bob Dylan and James Taylor come to mind. Compare them with Frank Sinatra, who was one of the biggest teen idols ever at the start of his career in the 1940s and who has always rendered song lyrics in SE. The converse of today's singing dialect was found in the 1940s and 1950s with many Black singers, such as Lena Horne, Nat King Cole, and Johnny Mathis singing in SE, adopting pronunciation virtually identical to White singers. Some, like Sam Cooke, switched from NNE to SE in different songs. Charlie Pride, a Black singer who prefers country and western to traditional Black music, sings in a dialect completely indistinguishable from other Nashville performers. One has to see him to realize that he is Black; one cannot hear it.

8.19 *Negative attitudes in dialect copying*

Not all copying of others' dialects is so benign. Negative attitudes can also be revealed by dialect copying. Labov (1964, p. 492) cites the example of a Black consultant, Mr. McSorley, who spoke SE in a "quiet, pleasant, and cultivated manner." There were no traces of NNE in his normal speech, and on tape he was not identifiable as Black. However, in the danger-of-death episode, Mr. McSorley recounted a frightening experience he had had as a guard at a YMCA, when he had to investigate a man who was threatening others with a gun. In imitating this gunman, Mr. McSorley used NNE. When asked what the man's background was, Mr. McSorley answered, "I don't know. Some kind of Hungarian, I think." Labov explains, "In this incident, we see a process of unconscious substitution taking place in accordance with the value system of the speaker." For this speaker, rough, uncultured speech was associated with NNE.

A similar kind of dialect copying is often heard in ethnic jokes. If these are about Jews, for instance, joke tellers frequently lapse into a pseudo-Yiddish accent. Although the telling of the unflattering or derogatory joke itself may be sufficient to show prejudice, the dialect copying underscores the teller's feelings that Jews are foreign, or, at least, different.

The accents used in ethnic jokes are rarely accurate. Typically, stage dialects are employed for such tales. A *stage dialect* is an inaccurate rendition of the speech alleged to typify a given group. However inaccurate, the stage rendition is so commonly associated with the group that if a truly accurate dialect were used, the audience might not recognize it. Although few American-born members of different ethnic groups speak with foreign accents today, most Americans have little difficulty identifying a performer as using the supposed Italian accent, the pseudo-Irish brogue or mock Chicano lilt, for example. Stage dialects too often are used for ridicule and derogation. The fact that they are used can tell more about true attitudes than do proclamations favoring brotherhood.

8.20   *Hidden attitudes in a dialect survey*

The subjective reaction part of a sociolinguistic survey can also uncover hidden attitudes. When Rhode Island and Eastern Massachusetts /r/-less speakers are asked to identify the ethnicity of speakers on a tape, with uncomfortable frequency they misidentify /r/-full Christian SE speakers as being Jewish. To these speakers, /r/-full speech is foreign. It indicates those that do not belong. Yet if asked, those same speakers will mouth words of brotherhood, never admitting their prejudices.

Although few Northern college students would seriously venture to claim that Southerners are stupid, lazy, and intolerant, when asked to evaluate a woman speaker with a strong Alabama accent, Northern subjects consistently pegged her as having those traits. The woman in question is in fact a practicing medical doctor, comes from a definitely upper middle-class family and is most tolerant.

Feminism has made enough strides so that college students would not claim that women are more emotional and less intellectual than men. Yet their true feelings surface when they are asked to evaluate a man and a woman with the same accents, reading from the same speech. In such a test the two read different paragraphs, but the paragraphs are matched for various speech features. The woman is consistently rated by listeners as less intelligent, more emotional, and less logical.

If subjects are asked to check off the character traits of speakers they hear on tape, clear pictures of stereotypes emerge. We discover what speech and what groups are associated with intelligence or toughness, with sincerity, honesty, humor, diligence, or laziness, and even general attractiveness. Lambert, Giles, and Picard (1975) studied attitudes toward French Canadians, both in Canada and in Maine. They found that in the St. John's Valley in Maine both those who were and those who were not Franco-Americans evaluated French speakers favorably. In contrast, Quebec French Canadians are inclined toward self-deprecation, mirroring the prejudice of those who are not French. The explanation for the difference in self-evaluation between the two Franco-American populations is explicable by the attitudes of those in power. In Canada there is considerable disvaluing of the French (Lambert, Giles, and Picard 1975). In Maine there seems to be none or little. Carranza and Ryan (1975) found that in Chicago, Mexican American adolescents assigned Spanish speakers the same social rank as non-Hispanics did. Both groups evaluated the Spanish speakers lower in status than English speakers.

Just as people evaluate their own speech according to community norms, they seem to evaluate themselves and their ethnic, racial, or social group. People see themselves in terms of society and their speech as an integral part of their individual character and worth. Many Americans when asked overtly what they think about a particular group answer in terms of brotherhood. When the question is concealed by asking the same subjects to evaluate speakers on tape, however, their true feelings emerge.

8.21   *Hypercorrection*

It is easy to make fun of people who make mistakes because they are trying too hard to be correct. For example, one hears schoolteachers ridiculing parents who say things like

> 10. We wants the best for our children. They tries hard, but that Mr. S. he give them bad grades.

Such speech is often associated with NNE, but one hears it in other varieties of NSE as well. Nonstandard speakers who do not share the SE agreement rules of -*s* on third-person singular present tense are nevertheless aware that such a rule exists. The problem is that, since it is not a part of their dialect, they are not sure exactly how to apply the rule. In formal situations, when trying to be correct, as when talking to education officials, NNE speakers may sporadically stick in the -*s* as in

> 11. He don't belongs with them.

(Labov et al. 1968)

As in 10 they may formulate their own rule. Knowing that -*s* marks the plural on nouns, they assume that it also marks the plural verb rather than the singular. This is certainly a logical assumption, even if it is not correct from an SE viewpoint.

Some speakers are not sure which person gets the agreement marker, so they put it on all, or all but the right one, as in the paradigm

> 12. I trusts my friend.
> You trusts my friend.
> He trust my friend.
> We trusts my friend.
> They trusts my friend.

Virtually all NSE speakers do realize that the *-s* goes on the present tense. Even SE speakers occasionally put the marker on the wrong person, especially in narrating ancedotes as in "I sits myself down . . ."

The important thing to remember is that the very fact that a speaker is hypercorrecting means that a person does perceive social norms. Moreover, it means that he or she wishes to be well thought of by educated speakers.

Some kinds of hypercorrection are a direct result of the features of a particular dialect. NNE is reputed to drop final consonants more than most other varieties of American English. All dialects drop the final consonant in some circumstances, as in *roast beef*, which gets pronounced as "roas' beef." The SE rule is that a final consonant in a CC is dropped if the next word begins with another consonant, but not usually if the next starts with a vowel, as in *roast in the oven*. NNE does permit consonant dropping before a vowel, as in "roas' in the oven." Those dialects that do simplify CC's before both consonants and vowels are actually more systematic than those that do not, since the latter drops in some instances (before consonants), but not in others (before vowels).

This kind of consonant dropping may not be as exclusive to NNE as investigators of that dialect think. Examples such as "lef' in" for *left in* and "mine another" for *mind another* have cropped up in my own collecting from speakers with little contact with NNE.

However, such dropping may result in some conflicts. In reading classes, for instance, if a child pronounces *cold* as "col' ", the teacher might say that the word was not read correctly, thus baffling the child who has indeed read it correctly for his or her dialect. Worse yet, because NNE speakers frequently do not pronounce the final consonant that indicates past tense, saying "kick" for *kicked* or *love* for *loved* for example, SE speakers have assumed that NNE is lacking in verb tense. This became a political issue when researchers like Bereiter and Engelman and Deutsch concluded that NNE speakers are therefore verbally deprived and that their speech is too defective for its speakers to learn to do well in school with it, a claim hotly disputed by linguists (See Chapter 6 and Sections 7.20 and 9.1). However, NNE speakers do use a past tense, especially in the irregular verbs, so that one hears

> 13. I lef' it.
> We play' ball yesterday.

With irregular verbs like *leave–left*, the past tense is preserved even though the /t/ is dropped, but with *play*, it is not. NNE speakers often seem to be aware that such consonant (or "past tense") dropping is disvalued by middle-class speakers. Therefore, in careful speech, they may hypercorrect by adding an extra past tense ending, as in

> 14. I loveded it.
> But it did tasted like chicken.

(Labov et al. 1968)

8.22   *Middle-class hypercorrection*

Lest we chuckle, we should be reminded that SE bears traces of the same kind of hypercorrection. The modern English *children* actually has two plural endings on it. Originally, the plural of *child* was *childer.* English once had several different plural endings. Different nouns pluralized differently according to the category to which they belonged. Apparently, over the years, children learning the language failed to learn the correct endings, just as children today say "foots" or "feets." One by one, the nouns with -*er* and -*en* plurals, as well as those which formed plurals by changing internal vowels like *mouse~mice,* took on the -*s* plural. Finally, the only survival of -*er* was on *childer.* Since -*en* was also a highly unusual ending by that time, surviving only in *oxen, brethren,* and *kine,* speakers endeavoring to be correct put both plurals, the -*er* and the other irregular -*en,* on *child.* We have evidence of this as early as the thirteenth century. The double ending on *children* remains to this day.

There is another hypercorrection rampant in SE today.

> 15a. between you and I . . .
>   b. He gave it to John and I . . .
>   c. He saw Mary and I . . .

In all of these, *I* should be *me.*

The system of signaling subject versus object pronouns has been dying out for centuries in English, The old *ye/you* distinction was moribund for Shakespeare. The original object of *it* was *him,* but this died out shortly after *ye.* NSE speakers often got rid of the rest of the alternations, uttering sentences like "Him and me went." Even SE speakers followed a general rule of using the object form after any verb, as in "It's me." Generations of schoolteachers railed against such barbarisms, stressing "He and I went" and "It's I." Since the old subject~object alternation is not really a part of the language anymore, speakers who did not quite understand why the *I, we, she, he* or *they* was preferred began to hypercorrect by putting those forms in even where *me, us, her, him,* and *them* are correct.

Perhaps because so many doctors, lawyers, teachers, and businessmen in this country rose up from the lower middle class whose native dialect actually included "Him and me went," the hypercorrections of 15 have become widespread. Even children whose parents do not hypercorrect seem to be learning the forms in 15 from their peers. In a generation or two "between you and I" may be SE.

It can easily be seen that the fate of a hypercorrection depends upon who is doing it. That, in general, is true of speech. Errors are what the socially disvalued or politically disenfranchised make.

It is also humbling to realize that SE speakers hypercorrect when they try to imitate nonstandard speech. One example is the pop song "Baby, I'ma want you; Baby, I'ma need you." Unless the singer, David Gates, means that he will want and need her in the immediate future, not now, this is an error in syntax. Apparently, he was trying to sound cool and sexy, two traits associated with NNE. Noting that dialect used the *-ma* form, but not quite understanding it, he used it incorrectly. Another example is Sha Na Na's incorrect "youse." The dialects that have this, have it as a plural beside singular *you*. Sha Na Na's performers consistently fail to make this distinction, constantly saying "youse" when addressing an individual person.

8.23   *Lames*

The way people speak tells us where they come from and who they are. It also tells us who they are not. As mentioned earlier, NNE has a term for the person who does not belong, a *lame*. The term does not denote a true outsider, but a person who should belong but does not. A lame might be a Black youth who rejects the street life and attempts to be middle class or it can be a rough, tough NNE speaker who simply prefers to go it alone. Females can be lames as well, as seen in one line of *The Fall:* "Girl, you ain't no lame, you know the game."

There is convincing evidence that lames in Harlem literally do not sound like gang members (Labov 1972a). They use phonological variables quite differently from gang members. Both by the percentage of times certain pronunciations are used, and also by using other pronunciations entirely, lames are differentiated from gang members. For instance, lames, but not gang members, occasionally pronounce the ending *-ing* as "-ing", not "-in" in words like *running*. Lames also used the verb *be (am, is, are)* more than twice as frequently as gang members in sentences of the "He (is) good" variety. Those who do not belong signal that fact by their speech as much as those who do.

Recognizing this can be important to teachers, socialworkers, or therapists. Well-socialized children speak like their peers not their parents, often to their parents' distress. Fortunately perhaps, dialect is not set until one's early twenties, if then. Children and adolescents may persist in peer group language when interacting with nonpeers. In adolescents this can be seen as an assertion of individuality, of breaking away from the dominance of elders. Some children switch dialect according to the person they are speaking with.

Children or adolescents who do not talk like their peers may well be the ones in trouble, as much as their speech may please elders. Consider the case of L. Although he was raised in New England, he sounded like a visitor from Brooklyn, his parents' original home. He consistently pronounced his <a>'s in words like *bad* and *Alaska* as [+]. He even pronounced *time* as "toym," as well as saying "on line" instead of "in line." He always chose New York local terms, such as "sprinkles" on his ice cream, rather than the localisms of his own community. His parents, not realizing that he (and they) were using pronunciation and vocabulary both stigmatized and ridiculed in their adopted state, were proud of the fact that L spoke as they did. However, they were upset by the fact that he was a complete outcast. Other children mocked him and overtly disliked him. The parents attributed this to his superior intelligence, although many intelligent children, including L's own brother, are very well accepted. L's speech was a reflection of the fact that he was an outcast.

Well-socialized children may switch dialects many times through their growing years as they move from region to region or social group to social group. Some are bidialectal, switching dialects according to the group or situation in which they find themselves.

8.24   *The development of an American standard*

The fact that one's personal feelings of identity are signaled in speech has ramifications for language change. In the United States people traditionally signaled their allegiance to a region or at least signaled that they came from a particular region. Thus, there were and still are regional dialects. Since World War II, however, migration from birthplace has become so common that regional loyalties have been weakened. This seems especially true for people most likely to move: the educated middle class who go where their jobs take them. More and more, at least on the East Coast, educated speech is losing its regional qualities. Many middle-class speakers seem almost aggressively pleased if they can claim, "no one can tell where I come from." Although this is truer of younger speakers, those under about forty-five, occasionally consultants as old as seventy make this boast. When East Coast middle-class speakers are asked to participate in a dialect study, they frequently respond, "Yes, but I don't have a [name of locale] accent."

Whether or not this is true throughout the country is not yet certain. Perhaps the East Coast has been hit first because of the myth—and myth it is—that there is a general American accent, one in which only the South, New York City, and Eastern New England do not participate. Midwestern and Far Western consultants are often surprised when I am able to pinpoint their regional dialects. The almost archetypal response is "Do I sound to you as if I have an accent?"—always uttered in absolute amazement.

The converse is that many Northeastern and Southeastern educated speakers are convinced that whatever they learned in childhood is not "general American." Truthfully even those of us most dedicated to our regional dialects find ourselves modifying our native speech when at academic meetings or their equivalent. Our children, Northern or Southern, even those who do retain some regional "flavor" to their speech, still have modified their parents' speech considerably. Increasingly, for example, high school children of educated middle-class parents are not completely /r/-free in words like *park,* even in a backwater like Rhode Island. Ted Kennedy, unlike his late older brothers, puts in that /r/ when he is speaking on national television. Much of the ribbing on "Saturday Night Live" that Barbara Walters had to take about her speech is clearly because the younger speakers on that show do not even recognize that her speech is actually a once aristocratic Eastern New England dialect. In that region /r/s, when they are pronounced at all, are typically a light, almost /w/- like sound. The so-called general American sharp /r/ was once highly disvalued, especially on the East Coast.

Perhaps the most startling examples of loss of Eastern regional speech are heard from college students from cities like Atlanta, Georgia; Boston, Massachusetts; and Bangor, Maine, who in less than a generation have lost virtually all trace of what once were considered the accents of those regions. Some of these speakers insist that nobody they know at home talks the way people from those regions are portrayed on TV. Always, these are children of educated professionals: headmasters, college professors, Episcopal ministers, and the like. They have apparently become dialect deaf to their own native dialects, unable to hear the distinctiveness of the speech of local residents of their own hometowns. Certainly, walking on the streets of those cities, one hears regional dialects including their educated versions.

The nitty-gritty of dialect geography is not the subject of this book, except insofar as it affects social perceptions. Since educated people expect to move about a good deal during their lives or to be in contact with those who have, it is more important to them that their speech signal that they are educated and middle class than that it signal loyalty to a region. So long as television and movies portray East Coast and, perhaps also Texan, regionalisms as belonging to rednecks, farmers, and other quaint but not prestigious types, then more and more speakers will be likely to disdain what they perceive as local accents, even accents once considered quite aristocratic. Of course, this is the reverse of what happened during the heyday of moviedom when East Coast accents were the ones to copy.

Blue-collar and lower class speakers who are less likely to leave their native regions or to come into frequent contact with outsiders whom they might wish to impress with intellectual attainments, retain regionalisms to a far greater degree than do the educated. Moreover, many regionalisms carry positive connotations of toughness, sincerity, down-to-earthness, and the like, making people want to use them. Finally, regional dialects also serve as a signal of bonding among members of a social class.

8.25   *Implications for education*

We have already seen that people not only announce who they are by their speech variety but also the positions they may take in society. Blacks overtly recognize this by the label *lame,* but it is true of society as a whole. We have also seen that people unhesitatingly assign others to particular job categories according to their taped speech categories. Bowlers, CB'ers, and other jargon users consider only other speakers of the jargon as really belonging, as being "in the know."

One implication of all this is that there can be no equality of opportunity unless all English speakers can handle standard English of the sort necessary to enter higher level jobs or professions. Labov (1966) tells the tale of a Ph.D. who could never get a university appointment because he never lost his original working class accent, specifically pronouncing /θ/ as [t] and /ð/as [d]. This is not a peculiar instance. How trusting would you be of a professor who said "dese" and "ting" for *these* and *thing*? Of course, that can work both ways. A person doing unskilled factory or construction work would be ridiculed for using refined, educated speech.

Public schools traditionally try to resolve dialect problems by giving regular grammar lessons and having teachers correct pronunciation sporadically. None of this helps. As we have seen, children and adults speak like those with whom they identify. If they do not identify with the teacher and the middle class in general, nothing will make them talk that way.

Since they do not identify with the middle class, students whose parents are of the blue-collar and lower classes are not likely to identify with the values of school, that archetypal middle-class institution. Even those who do are often under peer pressure not to conform to the demands of school, including "proper" speech. When teachers correct their speech, many pupils feel insulted, as if they themselves have been attacked as individuals. Considering the close connection between speech and identity, such feelings are justified.

Yet once they reach their twenties, some of these pupils will change their minds. They will start to see some value in middle-class ways and want to become better educated or to get higher level jobs. American Indians, by tribal custom, frequently do not start preparing for adult roles until their late teens or early twenties (Ohanessian 1972). Black youths frequently make no attempt to adopt middle-class speech until their late teens or early twenties either. The same probably holds true for other youths. The biggest problem for education is that sometimes it is very difficult by that age to begin to use certain sounds and constructions with any consistency (Labov 1966). Unfortunately, the sounds hardest to change are often just the ones most implicated in social class marking, such as the *th* sounds.

There is one way out of this dilemma, a way that does not insult students or get their backs up so that they refuse to learn standard speech forms. We can play on the students' natural ability to switch speech style. One technique is to use sociodrama. Students can be asked to act out natural situations, such as being interviewed for a job, lodging complaints with authority, or impressing a schoolteacher. They should be directed to speak appropriately for the roles. They usually do surprisingly well, and in their roles are willing to take correction if given politely.

This technique can be adapted to writing as well. Inner city high school students with reading achievement scores as low as second grade proved able to write coherent newspaper articles for teachers in a college workshop that I guided (Chaika 1978). Students worked in groups, correcting one another's work, with the teacher floating from table to table to give help with mechanics.

Teachers are pleased to find that such students show a hefty passive knowledge of standard speech and writing forms when these are not elicited in a punitive manner.

Other tasks which allow students to practice standard speech include putting on plays in which the characters are middle class, having students write and produce mock TV shows, and even asking them to instruct their classmates.

8.26   *The origins of dialect*

We have seen the almost incredible sensitivity with which dialect usage mirrors social realities. It reveals who individuals think they are, how a community or a country is stratified socially, where allegiances are, and what covert aspirations people may harbor, as shown by hypercorrection.

Where do the dialects come from in the first place? In America English dialects were brought by the early settlers who gave their dialects to the Eastern Seaboard communities. Later, as members of these communities moved westward, they took some dialect features with them. To this day, early migration routes can be traced on dialect maps.

Some linguists have claimed that the first settlers were /r/-pronouncing but that in the nineteenth century East Coast speakers began dropping the /r/ out of admiration for the British, whose dialect had dropped it. Supposedly, the Easterners became /r/ droppers because they had more contact with the British than those further inland. As it happens, there is evidence that the original settlers brought the /r/-dropping rules with them. Even if there were not actual evidence, however, sociolinguistics would tell us that this must be the case, for there is no other way that the entire Eastern seaboard would have adopted /r/-dropping rules after independence from Great Britain.

Study after study has confirmed that people speak like those with whom they wish to be identified. There is no reason to suppose that early Americans, striving for their own nationality, were likely to adopt innovations in British speech. Even if a few wealthy East Coast families did remain in contact with Britain, this would not have affected the speech of the large working class, artisan, and farming populations. Similarly, it is not likely that the upper and middle classes copied the /r/-lessness of Cockney sailors visiting coastal towns as some have posited. The prevalence of /r/-less speech up and down the East Coast by speakers of all classes argues strongly that the original settlers were already /r/-less. After they had established the local dialects, later comers conformed to what was already there. The reason that the speech of other areas, such as Pennsylvania, the Appalachian mountain regions, and Western New England (west of the Connecticut River), is strong in /r/-pronouncing is that the settlers of those areas were in fact British /r/ pronouncers. For instance, the Quakers who settled Philadelphia came from northern England, which was strongly /r/-full (Williams 1975).

In order to prove that the East Coast settlers were /r/-less, it has to be established that there were British /r/-droppers before and during the initial colonization of these shores. There is such evidence, much of it derived from examining rhymes, puns, or spelling errors. Schlauch (1959) points out that the Pastons, a married couple who kindly left us some of their fifteenth century correspondence, made spelling errors that showed that the /r/ was already being dropped. For example, they spelled *answer* as < arnswer >. We know from older manuscripts that the word never had an /r/ after the /a/. Why, then, would a writer suddenly insert an *r* where it never existed before and where it is still not pronounced? That would happen if the /r/ after an /a/ as in *park* was no longer being pronounced. The /a/ in *answer* originally was pronounced as [a:] 'ah'. If an < ar > was already being pronounced as [a:] 'ah' as it is today in /r/-less accents, then the misspelling < arnswer > makes good sense. Similarly, /r/-less speaking children today often misspell words like *socks* as < sarks > because either would indicate the same pronunciation in their dialects. The Pastons were writing well before colonization of the New World by the British.

Kokeritz (1953) pointed out that Shakespeare rhymed *John* with *forsworn, death* with *earth, dyrst degree* with *high'st degree.* He also made a pun of *food* with *ford.* Such rhyming and punning shows that Shakespeare, and by implication his audience, was familiar with /r/-less pronunciation, although he himself was /r/-full. Shakespeare was writing just before and at the time of original colonization.

On the other side of the Atlantic, colonists were keeping records. Often, they spelled as they pronounced, as people still do today. These spellings provide us with definite clues as to articulation, as do sporadic misspellings today. For instance, in contemporary America one occasionally sees a misspelling like < ornch > for *orange.* This only occurs from strong /r/ pronouncers who leave out the vowel after the /r/ in *orange,* just as the < sarks > misspelling comes from /r/-less speakers for whom < ar > indicates [a] 'ah'.

Celia Millward (1975) delved into colonial records and found convincing evidence that the Eastern New England /r/-dropping rules in colonial times were the same as they are today. She found:

16. *Misspelling*	*Word Intended*
brothe	brother
therefo	therefore
Arthu	Arthur
administe	administer
furthe	further

Examples 16 show that the writers did not pronounce /r/ at the end of a word.

17. Mach	March
Osbon	Osborne
orchad	orchard
Sanphod	Sanford

Examples 17 show that the writers dropped /r/ before consonants.

>   18. piller   pillow
>   Marthere   Martha

Examples 18 show the /r/-glide on words ending in /ə/ 'uh'.

The reader may have noticed that some /r/s that would not be pronounced by /r/-less speakers today do occur in the spellings. Does this mean that /r/-dropping was more sporadic than it would be today? Probably not, for there is no reason to suppose that the colonial record keepers always spelled everything phonetically. After all, they were not using a scientific transcription like IPA. Although spelling was not as standardized as it is today, there were spelling conventions. Literate people were familiar with spellings of words that represented pronunciations different from their own. Therefore, the mis-spellings are not wholly consistent.

Furthermore, spellings represent different pronunciations to speakers of different dialects. That < ar > stands for /a:/ 'ah' for /r/-less speakers has already been noted. Hence, to a consistently /r/-less speaker, the < ar > in *Arthur* or *Marthere* could simply have been a way to spell an [a:] 'ah' with no /r/ intended. Similarly, the *er* in *therefo* and the *or* in *orchad* did not necessarily represent an actual /r/ pronunciation. For /r/-less speakers, the *r* in such spellings is a silent letter indicating an /r/-less vowel pronunciation of a particular vowel.

To give a modern example: for /r/-less speakers < or > spells /ɔ:/ 'aw'. Therefore, in *Winnie-the-Pooh,* the donkey's name is Eeyore, that is, 'ee-aw' (*heehaw*). He is a cockney donkey, one who doesn't pronounce his /h/s, but most Americans miss the joke entirely, because they do not realize that the < ore > spelling in Mr. Milne's British accent represents an 'aw' (as in *heehaw*).

So strong is this connection between that spelling and the 'aw' pronunciation that many /r/-less speakers think they are hearing an /r/ in an /ɔ/ 'aw'. For instance, a South African /r/-less speaker complained to me that in London he was disgusted with the way people put /r/s in where they do not belong. Thinking that he meant the /r/-glide, which he certainly used, I asked him for examples. He said, "Why the /r/ they put in *off*!" Bewildered, I asked, "What /r/ in *off*?" He proceeded to use a strong /ɔ/ 'aw' for the vowel in *off,* with nary a trace of an /r/.

The Virginia Tidewater and Eastern New England were settled by colonists from the East Midlands and Southeast of England. These settlers already were using /r/-less pronunciation. They also pronounced the so-called broad *a* [a:] 'ah' in words like *half, calf, ask,* and *can't.* The Middle Atlantic states were settled by Quakers from the North of England who had a strong /r/. Western New England and the Great Lakes also were settled by Northern Britishers.

A second source of dialect features in this country is migration from East to West. One can trace old migration routes on a map that shows dialect features. Marietta, Ohio, for instance, was colonized by New Englanders and until recently speech there contained vocabulary features of the New England dialects, such as *pail* rather than *bucket*. Los Angeles speech shows some features of Oklahoma dialect because of the great migration from that state during the Depression. The strong Los Angeles /a:/ 'ah' in words like *talk* and *law* has been traced to that source.

Above all, however, dialects develop for purely social reasons. The New York City development of /r/-full pronunciation to mark out the educated middle class has already been cited. One might well ask why in America /r/ has virtually become the locus of dialect change, when in fact there are many other differences between dialects, especially in the vowels used in different words. For instance, because /l/ is a sound phonetically similar to /r/, it is no surprise to a linguist that in those dialects in which /r/ is dropped before a consonant, so are many /l/s. After <a>, /l/ is not pronounced for most English speakers, at least in words like *half*. In the Deep South one also might note its lack in words like *help*, which ends up as "hep." In some strong /r/-pronouncing regions, /l/ is pronounced in words like *talk* and *calm*. This last is homophonous with *column* for some Midwestern speakers. My favorite hypercorrection came from a most uptight Eastern New England couple who asked me if the fish on the buffet was "solomon." I finally managed to understand that they wanted to know if it was *salmon*. Noticing Midwestern broadcastese "column" for *calm*, they had assumed "solomon" for "salmon."

Even so it is /r/ that remains the focus in the United States. Most laypersons (that is, nonlinguists) are not aware of the differences in /l/-pronouncing. They are not too sure of vowel differences between dialects, either. For example, East Coast speakers seem wholly unaware that the Midwestern accents they think are "correct" are just those that use some of the locally most disvalued pronunciations. Unless it is pointed out to them, such speakers rarely have processed the fact that Chicago and Cleveland speakers (among others) who put in the prized /r/s also use the not-so-prized (on the East Coast) [ɨ] in words like *bad* and *aunt*. Many New York City and Southern New England speakers also have never noticed that which they disvalue in Boston speech, "tock" for *talk*, is prevalent in the Western and Midwestern speech that they assume must be correct. Pronouncing /r/ or not is clearly the focus of conscious dialect differentiation in the United States today.

8.27   *Why /r/?*

As part of the myth that there is a general American dialect out there somewhere in the great Midwest, people associate /r/-full speech with being American. After World War II America rose as a world power, and Great Britain declined. In national terms, so did Eastern New England. Southern dialects, the other /r/-less dialects, had lost their prestige in the aftermath of the Civil War. No longer was /r/-lessness associated with power in America, nor, with the phenomenal growth of the great Midwestern and Western universities, was the East any longer considered the repository of learning and culture. The /r/-full pronunciation prevalent in most areas of the States and Canada already was a natural candidate for new prestige marking in formerly /r/-less areas. Thus, although the educated /r/-less accents are far from dead in America, the encroachment of a new /r/-pronouncing standard is evident up and down the Eastern seaboard. This is little different from the use of NNE or NSE by SE speakers in informal situations. A given pronunciation becomes associated with a given trait; it becomes copied when the image associated with that trait is projected.

8.28   *Creoles*

A third source of dialect differentiation is Creolization. This results when two languages mix together to form one new one. NNE possibly had such an origin. Creoles typically develop in a situation in which an upper status group must deal with a distinctly subservient group that speaks a different language. This was the situation with the first slaves. They spoke a variety of West African languages. Their masters spoke one of the European languages: English, French, Spanish, or Portuguese. Upper status people do not copy the speech of those lower unless there is some admired trait in the lower group. Then borrowing occurs only in situations in which that trait is pertinent. Today's borrowing of NSE forms by middle-class youths has been already noted. Even their borrowing never occurs in learned or formally polite language but only when the borrowers are partying, playing sports, or displaying macho traits.

In any event, masters were (and probably are) not about to learn their slaves' speech. Indeed, many of the languages of Europe were originally the languages of conquerors. The languages of the conquered often died out because the conquered had to learn the languages of their new masters. Prime examples are the Romance languages—Italian, French, Spanish, Portuguese and Rumanian—which replaced the earlier languages spoken by peoples conquered by the Romans. In Great Britain, Germanic speaking conquerors obliterated most of the original Celtic languages. These Germanic dialects eventually developed into what we now know as English. The loss of both North and South American Indian languages to those of Europe is another example.

In the New World slaves did not have daily contact with their masters as a rule. Therefore, opportunity to learn the language of their owners was often limited. What develops in such a situation is first a **Pidgin**: a partial language with limited vocabulary and grammar, sufficient to communicate the business at hand. In much of the Orient, for instance, there were trade Pidgins between Chinese and Europeans, although that situation probably was caused as much by Chinese reluctance to learn European languages as the reverse.

The slave Pidgins in the United States and the Caribbean eventually became the first language of the children of the slaves. When this happens the Pidgin grows up, so to speak, into a full language, a **Creole**. Some scholars trace differences between NNE and SE to West African blending into English (Stewart 1968; Turner 1971; Dillard 1973; Dalby 1971). Certainly, there are similarities in words. To *badmouth* is a direct translation of a Vai expression meaning 'to curse.' NNE *dig* 'to understand' seems to be derived from *dega* 'understand.' Words like *goobers, jazz, banjo,* and *okra* are clearly derived from African languages.

Gullah, spoken on the Sea Islands of Georgia and South Carolina, is a distinct Creole. And if we can believe the literary representations of Black speech in the eighteenth and nineteenth centuries, it was far more different from SE than it is today, much more of a Creole.

One apparently clear influence of West African, at least on older NNE speech, was the substitution of a [b]-like sound for /v/ in words like *river* and *devil.* West African languages lack a /v/, so that the original slaves must have substituted the closest sound in their native speech. The sound must have been unfamiliar to English speakers, who, in turn, when imitating slaves, substituted the closest sound that English speakers used, a /b/, thinking their slaves were saying "ribber" and "debbil." Because they were socially and psychologically isolated, many NNE speakers kept this *b*-like sound for generations. It is not a feature of most NNE dialects today, however.

One problem with the Creole theory is that just about every feature of syntax in NNE that has been claimed to derive from West African languages can also be traced to some British dialect or other. Even if the feature did not appear in the slaveowners' dialects, often slaves could have picked them up from overseers.

Two good examples are the NNE verb forms of durative *be,* meaning 'all the time', as in "He be good," and the *been* indicating completed action long ago. Much of the claim that African origins of NNE cause its difference from SE rests upon these two forms. The *be* is supposed to be an English translation a West African durative *blan.* Such carryovers are quite usual in bilinguals (Chapter 10).

One problem with this interpretation is that there was a durative *be* in Old English, too, and one has been found in Newfoundland White speech. Joseph Williams (1975) believes that it must have submerged into a lower or lower middle-class social dialect in England, so that it did not appear in writing for many centuries. Then it must have been brought to this continent by such speakers where it surfaced again. He argues, and I believe correctly, that the Whites in Newfoundland were not likely to have learned this form from southern Blacks. Furthermore, it strains credibility to believe that the same meaning could have independently developed in exactly the same form in the two dialects. His arguments are bolstered by the fact that the *been* meaning 'completed past' has also been found in Newfoundland. More than likely, the slaves learned English from those who spoke the same dialect as that from which Newfoundland English is derived.

English has, and has had, so many dialects that one must be most careful when claiming that a certain form is unique to a given group. One must look not only to extant American or British dialects but also to those of Ireland, Scotland, and Wales and to older dialects of rural Britain.

The ardent proponents of the Creole theory of the origin of NNE do not tolerate suggestions that NNE is just another form of English. They insist that it is a whole different language system that should be recognized as such. Perhaps they think that NNE would have more prestige if it were recognized as a blend of West African and English than it does as a derivative of other English dialects. One Creolist accused a nonbeliever of senility and the respectable scholarly journal *American Speech* of irresponsibility because it published the non-believer's data showing that the NNE durative *be* could have come from old Irish rather than from African tribal languages (Dillard 1979). There were Irish overseers and plantation owners whose Irish English could have contained such a survival; through them, it could have been transmitted to the Black population. That population, in turn, could have been receptive to the durative verb forms because they already had them in their native African tongues. This is not to say that the Creolists are right or wrong, however. The issue of the development of Black speech is clearly a complex one, complicated by the conditions of the original slavery, then the years of social and psychological isolation of Blacks themselves, an isolation attested to by the fact that a distinct NNE group of dialects still exists all over the United States. The isolation is probably what is important, not the specific origin of verb forms. But then scholars are a feisty lot, always ready to defend their cherished hypotheses against all comers.

One of the proofs that Creolists invoke in favor of their claim is that NNE is systematically different from other varieties of English. But this argument is flawed because *all* dialects are systematic, hence systematically different from each other. I think that the few definite traces of West African speech in NNE can be accounted for by the sorts of carryovers that occur whenever speakers of one language learn another. Would we say that Italian ethnic dialects of English are Creoles because they use originally Italian words like *pasta* or *manicotti* or because of the Italian intonations that occur in that ethnic dialect of English? No matter what its origins, NNE is far more like SE than it is like African languages. As Stewart (1967) notes, NNE has been progressively becoming more and more like "White" English over the centuries. This seems to me to indicate that Blacks in America are slowly assimilating. One hopes this means that they are feeling less and less like strangers in their own land. Finally, whether or not the features of NNE derive from Africa or English, they are what they are, and teachers must recognize them to teach its speakers effectively.

8.29   *Basil Bernstein and restricted codes*

The British sociologist Basil Bernstein investigated mother–child interaction in the middle and working classes. He found that middle-class mothers habitually appeal to reasons for doing or not doing things. If a middle-class child is noisy and the mother is on the phone, she says something like, "Please be quiet so that I can hear Granny." Or, if the child does not want to visit a sick grandparent, she might say, "I know you don't like to kiss Grandpa, but he's fond of you and it makes him happy." Working class children are just told how to behave. If they object, they are likely to be told, "I don't want none of your nonsense." If reasons are given, they are what Bernstein calls position oriented, such as "Boys don't do things like that."

Bernstein hypothesized that such practices have great repercussions for adult speaking abilities. Middle-class children, he says, develop elaborated codes geared to discussing the whys and wherefores of events. They are good at discussing alternatives and abstract concepts. Their sense of personal worth is great, but social identity is weak. The working class children develop restricted codes that are poor for analyzing and explaining. They become bewildered when faced with alternatives or abstract discussions. They are poor in analyzing personal emotion. Their feelings of self-worth are poor, but their social identity is strong. By social identity, Bernstein meant they perceive themselves primarily in terms of their roles in society.

Bernstein attempted to test these hypotheses by asking British working class boys attending state schools (equivalent to American public schools) and students of public schools (the equivalent of American private schools) to debate classmates about capital punishment. Predictably, the public school students were able to out-argue those from the state schools.

Bernstein also tested ability to form a verbal narrative from looking at pictures on a card. Middle-class children again excelled in that they told a story that anyone could understand without looking at the pictures. Working-class children kept referring to the objects with pronouns like *he, she,* or *it* without first elaborating on who was who and what was what. In other words, in order to follow the working class narrative, one had to see the picture.

As provocative as Bernstein's theory is, there are some problems with it, especially if we are to think in terms of elaborated and restricted codes. The tasks Bernstein used were geared to middle-class speech capabilities. Debating social issues like capital punishment is a usual public school activity in Great Britain. Boys well schooled in such debates naturally did better than those who were not. Had Bernstein tested the prowess of working class men in the pubs arguing about labor unions, he might have gotten elaborated codes from them as well.

Middle-class children are also usually read to a great deal. They are used to storytelling narratives. Since children's books are lavishly illustrated, middle-class children are adept at matching a story to a picture when they are very young. Those who had gone to nursery school had probably even done a task identical to the one presented them by Bernstein.

Moreover, there is no real proof that mother–child interaction is the final arbiter of adult speech competence. Even within the middle class, some are better at analyzing consequences and personal motives than others. Many highly educated people are inarticulate when confronted with the need to state a case, whereas many less educated people are highly adept at the same task.

Furthermore, it is only in relatively recent times that parents have started to give their children reasons why they should behave in a given way. Bernstein's description of working class rearing practices sounds suspiciously like the generally repressive pre-Freud, pre-Spock childrearing practices of the middle and upper classes, practices far from dead. Many of the greatest analytical minds were the products of both rigid parenting and rigid schooling. Also, if Bernstein's theory were correct, there would be no way to account for the many analytical, inquisitive scholars who come from working class backgrounds.

Finally, Bernstein does not give enough weight to peer interaction. Even if children do not learn to weigh consequences at home, they may do so on the streets. As has already been noted (Chapter 7), children of blue-collar and lower class parents often spend a good deal of time arguing about points of logic and reason.

These objections do not mean that Bernstein is wrong but that the evidence is not all in. Until it is we must always remember that someone's performance in a particular situation is affected by his or her socialization. If he or she has not been taught to speak up in a situation, performance will be poor. If he or she has, it will be better. The trick, then, is to find the situation that elicits good performance for any group tested. Above all, it must be remembered that people are not necessarily stamped in a mold forever by upbringing. They can and do learn to sharpen and change their speaking and reasoning skills throughout life.

EXERCISES

1. Can you think of a(ny) phonological variable(s) in your community? Is it (or are they) characteristic of an ethnic group or social class, or of men or women?

2. Make up one task that will test for at least one of the variables you mentioned in Exercise 1.

3. Devise one field method designed to elicit speech in a variety of styles: on college campus, where you work, or in your neighborhood.

4. If you know someone with a small child, observe the interaction between parent or babysitter and child for an hour (or more, if you can). What communicative strategies are taking place? What might the child be learning about communication? Do you find any strategies or patterns that do not seem to be used between adults?

chapter 9

VOCABULARY AS A MIRROR
OF SOCIAL REALITIES

All languages can say the same things, although many people imagine that their language can say things that others cannot. In order to compare vocabularies of different languages, it is important to consider semantic features of words. The vocabulary of a language reveals underlying attitudes of the society that produced it, as in euphemisms, taboo words and propaganda. The relationship between specific languages and thought must be considered in the light of what we know about vocabularies.

9.1   *All languages can say the same things*

So far as linguists know, all languages are mutually translatable. What can be said in one language can be said in any other—somehow. All languages are so constructed that new thoughts can be expressed in them. To be sure, it is easier to express some ideas in one language rather than another. This is because the vocabulary of each language develops partly according to the priorities of its culture. The objects, relationships, activities, and ideas important to the culture get coded into single words which are often highly specialized to express subtle nuances. Everyone's favorite example is the Eskimos, to whom snow is a central feature of life. For this reason, they have anywhere from eight to twelve distinct words for it: such as, one for the kind to make igloos with, and one for snow good for snowshoeing. European languages, having to deal with snow, but not so extensively as the Eskimos, typically have at least one word for it as opposed to rain. African languages, spoken where there is no snow, do not have a word for it. Still, they could describe it, as, for example, white, cold flowers from the sky that turn to water when they are touched.

People make their language say what they want it to, as we saw with jargons. If it were possible to say certain things in one language but not another, then we would have the problem that people who speak one language could know things that those in another could not. Bilinguals might have the problem of being able to know something in one language but not another. In fact, although it may be difficult to express a given idea in one language rather than another, there has never been any proof that it is impossible.

9.2   *Semantic features*

Words do not have holistic meaning. Rather, they are composed of features of meaning. For instance, *boy* is composed of features like [+human, +male, −power]. Features of one word can be transferred onto another, which is one important way we get meaning. Uriel Weinreich (1966) gave an apt example. *Pretty* has a feature of [+female]. If *pretty* is used with *boy,* the [+female] gets transferred so that *pretty boy* implies a feminine young male. In American culture, this often also implies a tinge of homosexuality. In the Eagles song "Hotel California," it is sufficient to say that a woman is surrounded by "pretty, pretty boys" to indicate their sexual persuasion. *Handsome,* which has the feature [+male], when used with *woman* implies an older woman, not a 'sex kitten' or 'sexpot.' Interestingly, this does not imply homosexuality.

Differences in meaning between two dialects or languages are often differences in the way features are attached to words. For example, in England, the features [+car, +top, +front] are attached to *bonnet,* but in America to *hood.* In the American South, the verb *favor* includes [+look like], but it does not in most of the North.

9.3   *Euphemism*

Words take on the semantic features [+good] or [+bad] according to how a particular culture feels about the item designated. If a word marked [+bad] denotes something that must be mentioned in the course of daily routine, other words are substituted. The substitutes, called **euphemisms**, are close in meaning, but do not quite mean the "bad" thing. Instead of having the feature [+bad], they are neutral or even pleasant.

One example is the attribute *fat.* The feature [+bad] is firmly attached to *fat* in America nowadays. It is no longer desirable on meat, much less on people. This poses a problem for clothing stores that wish to sell specially cut garments for the obese. These certainly cannot be called what they are: clothes for fat people. Rather, there are for girls: *chubbette, pretty plus*; for boys, *husky, husky plus*; for men, *portly, big*; and for women, *women's sizes* (as opposed to *misses* or *junior*), *full sizes, half-sizes,* and *hard-to-fit. Stout* used to be a euphemism, as in *stylish stouts,* but when it ceased being used in the general language in its original sense of 'healthy' and 'brave', it came too directly to mean 'fat'. One hardly sees the term in clothing departments any more. Similarly, the male *portly* is being replaced by *big* on labels.

Even in casual conversation, referring to a person's bulk, people skirt around the word *fat.* Instead, they say "Well, he certainly is big." or "It's hard for a big woman to find clothes." *Plump,* an older, favorable term for 'fat' is today pretty much reserved for chickens or pillows. Students in my classes, when asked to rate words for *fat,* typically consider *plump* archaic and humorous. The only word associated with obesity that can be positively evaluated is *jolly*. Even so, this is restricted to Santa Claus and babies, who are still allowed to be fat in our society.

Cultures that do not find fat repugnant treat it differently in their word stock. In both Italian and Yiddish, for instance, the same word can be used for both *fat* and *healthy*. Occasionally, in English, *fat* and *healthy* can be used synonymously, as in *fat profit* and *healthy profit*. The choice of one over the other depends on our feeling about the profit in question: *fat* if we disapprove of or are gloating over the profit, *healthy* if we approve.

Some of the euphemisms for *fat* used to be words meaning 'strong' and 'tough', such as *stout* and *husky*. *Portly* used to mean 'imposing, dignified'. The euphemistic character of *pretty plus* is obvious, as is reference to *half-sizes* instead of the true 'size and a half'.

Euphemisms usually occur in sets of several words, none meaning exactly the thing referred to. When one euphemism becomes too directly associated with the disvalued meaning, it is replaced by other euphemisms.

This is clearly seen in euphemisms for the places where Americans urinate and defecate. Even with the supposed lifting of taboos in modern times, American prudishness about voiding remains in full force. Taboos about swearing, sex, and nudity have all weakened, but the bathroom functions still disgust us. One consequence of this is the dearth of public restrooms in America. In England, as one enters a town, there is usually a welcome sign proclaiming *Toilets*, with an arrow pointing the way. When Sigmund Freud visited the United States, he was appalled at the lack of facilities. Anyone who has ever traveled across country with small children still is.

The discomfort Americans have in mentioning elimination is well illustrated in the preceding paragraph. Except for the erudite Latinate *defecate* and *urinate*, there is not one direct polite term for the process under discussion. Nor is there even one direct term for the room where the body functions are performed. *Bathroom* actually means 'the place where one takes a bath'. In England, it still means that, since, unlike Americans, the British do not keep the tub and the "hopper" in the same room. *Toilet* originally meant 'getting dressed' as in the archaic, *She made her toilet*, or the survival *toilet water*. It must have been assumed that part of the process of getting dressed was *'going'*. Of course, *restrooms*, another designation of the place to *go* are not for resting. Since we all know that the only place to rest when away from home is a hotel room, we hear *restroom* as a euphemism for the place in which we rest (stop) briefly for unmentionable purposes.

How unmentionable these purposes are is seen by general terms like *facilities* for the place and *going* for the acts. In many languages use of very general, virtually empty terms, indicates a taboo. In English the word *facilities* usually has to be followed by *for X*, as in *the facilities for cooking*. When it occurs alone, as in *I have to use the facilities*, it usually means the "loo," to use a British slang word for it. Similarly, *going* is normally followed by an adverb of place or manner, as in *going to New York* or *going by plane.* By itself, it means one is voiding. Compare this with the general *doing it* used without reference to a previously stated act, which means 'fornicating'.

The sheer number of euphemisms for voiding indicates the degree of discomfort Americans have about bodily waste: *powder room, comfort station, head, lavatory, basement, John, little girls' room, little boys' room, lavette, commode, half-bath, loo.* In a restaurant, one often has to guess if the right room has been found, especially if only a coy picture is used on the door. Usually, there are two signs indicating male and female gender: *buoys, gulls; knights, damsels; his, hers; signor, signorina.*

In contrast, there is only one word in English for the place where food is prepared: the kitchen. Clearly, that is not taboo which, when you think of it, is odd in a society that disvalues fat.

9.4   *Propaganda*

Propaganda depends upon euphemism, on calling unpleasantness by another name. As in use of stylistic variation, everyone knows what is being referred to, but the meaning is backgrounded, thus softened. Propaganda cannot use common euphemisms, for these would be too direct. A case in point is death, another phenomenon with which our culture is uneasy.

Again, we can tell that English speakers are uncomfortable with death by the number of euphemisms for it. People do not die, they *pass away, pass on, go to sleep, go to the other side, meet their maker, go to rest, go to their final reward, croak, kick the bucket, buy the farm, buy it,* and become *traffic fatalities,* or we *lose them* (as in *I recently lost my favorite aunt*). Our pets are *put to sleep, put away,* or *put down,* not killed (except by a cruel outside party). Gangsters *deep-six* or *waste* rather than murder.

Our uneasiness about mentioning death conflicts with the military's need to talk about it. The military is in an exceptionally difficult position, for if we cannot talk directly of natural death, how can we talk of unnatural death? Yet soldiers must deal both with killing and being killed. Death must be mentioned in their training, but if it were mentioned too directly, soldiers would be too often reminded of their mortality and of the true awfulness of what they are supposed to do.

Robert Sellman, a ROTC student, examined military euphemisms for death in a field manual *The Combat Training of the Individual Soldier and Patrolling.* He showed that the manual is written in a highly impersonal, distant style, which is "designed to negate the psychological impact of killing and destroying." One way this is done throughout is to use the modal auxiliary *may,* as in "A nuclear explosion *may* cause heavy casualties among your leaders" and "*may* even completely destroy your unit's chain of command." Nuclear explosions will, not may. By using *may,* the field manual makes it much less certain, much less frightening. Also, referring to "heavy casualties" as a cover term, rather than elucidating with direct words like *the dead, the burned, the wounded,* or *radiation sickness* glosses over the true horror. The stress on the leaders' being destroyed is especially interesting. Nuclear bombs are not selective. Anyone around gets it. By overtly citing "leaders" and "chain of command," but not actually mentioning enlisted persons or peers, the potential deaths of the ordinary soldiers are backgrounded. It is not so much that the manual lies. It just mentions part of the truth.

Sellman focused on two other terms: *fire for effect,* and *engage the enemy.* The first is the command to the artillery to destroy an area with its explosives. Sellman points out that the emptiness of *for effect* matches that in the euphemism *do it.* He feels that this emptiness minimizes the personal involvement of the artillery observer who has to give the command. The second term also does not mean what it says. It means 'fight, shoot, kill'. It says, 'take part in an activity with the enemy'. There is but one likely activity that one engages in with the enemy. The soldier has no difficulty extrapolating the meaning, but the meaning is never explicitly given. The reason is simple. If the field manuals were explicit, if they directly reminded soldiers what they were training for, to kill and to be killed, getting soldiers onto the battleground could become more difficult.

Both of these terms illustrate a common factor in euphemism: **circumlocution,** which means spreading meaning over several words rather than using a single one. This weakens meaning and is one way to avoid confronting an unpleasant issue head-on. *Kill* is not only more semantically direct than *fire for effect,* it is more powerful because meaning is concentrated on one word. In the same way, *engage the enemy* is weaker than *fight.* A beautiful example of the semantic weakening by circumlocuting is the U.S. Army's statement of intent: "the management and application of controlled violence." In other words, *war.*

Sellman also examined the slang terms that soldiers use for death. He notes that these allow soldiers to discuss the unpleasant aspects of their job while still keeping their courage and morale up so that they can function as soldiers. The euphemisms for death are unusually explicit, but they keep soldiers at a remove from the true horror by denying the humanity of the corpse. For instance, *die* is 'get iced', or 'get waxed'. Dead fish are usually put on ice, and mannequins are made of wax. Dog tags are really death tags, used to identify dead soldiers, but who would put them on if they were reminded of that? Sellman suggests that "Making the dead seem inhuman allows the individual to say it can't happen to himself. This is the attitude that the soldier must have in order to throw himself in front of bullets."

Euphemism is also accomplished by **understatement,** using words whose combined semantic features do not add up to the meaning intended. Saying that children are "nutritionally deficient" when you mean 'starving' is an example. Sellman also gives one from soldier slang: *zap* rather than *kill. Zap* can also mean 'strike a blow' that is not fatal.

9.5   *Multiple terms*

The preceding sections claim that things people are uncomfortable with have many euphemistic names and phrases. These all mean roughly the same thing, although typically they do not quite mean what they say. **Metaphors** and **idioms** are very common as euphemisms, perhaps because they are the very embodiment of circumlocution, of not calling a spade a spade.

A metaphor is a word used so that its central meaning cannot be taken. Rather, one must extend its meaning. For instance, *that old bag* in the right context means 'the old, unpleasant, unattractive woman'. The extension of *bag* to mean 'woman' is a metaphor.

Idioms are different from metaphors in that a mere extension of meaning of the words used will not give the intended meaning. The meaning of the idiom is not garnered by an examination of its parts. Rather, the entire group of words has a meaning as if it were one word (Chafe 1968). Frequently, idioms consist of whole parts of sentences (Fromkin and Rodman 1978, p. 177) such as predicate [verb + (object)]. The difference is that it is not the meaning of each word in conjunction with the others that counts in idioms. It is the meaning attached to the whole. For instance,

1. *Idiom*	*Literal Word*
put one's foot in one's mouth	verbally blunder
shake a leg	hurry
pull (someone's) leg	deceive teasingly
chew the fat	talk
shoot the breeze	talk
kick the bucket	die
roll in the hay	fornicate
shake the dew off the lily	urinate

Many although not all idioms are used as euphemisms for things we feel uncomfortable speaking of directly. Because the actual meaning of idioms is so removed from the meaning of the sum of their parts, idioms are the epitome of beautifully indirect reference. It follows, then, that one way to uncover the attitudes of a people is to examine their idioms and other euphemisms.

At the beginning of this chapter it was mentioned that a culture has multiple terms denoting items or activities that are important to it. There is a difference between these multiple terms and euphemism. In euphemism, all the terms mean the same thing. In contrast, multiple terms for culturally important referents all refer to slightly different aspects of the same activity, object, or concept. Consider synonyms of *talk:*

2. chatter, gab, prattle, gossip, jabber, nag, babble, clack, jaw, jibber-jabber, B.S., shoot the breeze, shoot the s--t, chew the fat

All of these refer to idle talk or ordinary sociable talking with no intellectual or business purpose. People who talk a lot are

> 3. talkative, gabby, wordy, glib, bigmouthed, fatmouthed, full of hot air

or are

> 4. gossips, nags, shrews, chatterboxes, windbags

Although there is no noun that specifically means 'a person who does not talk a great deal', there are a number of adjectives to describe such a person:

> 5. quiet, laconic, reticent, taciturn, reserved, closemouthed

Recall how many words exist for idle talk. Just about all have the connotation of 'not desirable' and 'stupid.' Some like *prattle, babble,* and *chatter* also carry the connotation of 'childish'—and 'feminine.' Besides the feminine *gossip,* and *nag* with their connotations of nastiness and triviality, the only phrases for idle talk that do not carry bad overtones are those that refer to the casual speech of men: *chew the fat* and *shoot the breeze.* Likewise, the adjectives in 3 denoting the quality or trait of talking a lot, and nouns denoting people who talk a lot are not only demeaning but feminine. From these words, it certainly seems that the speech of men is more valued in our society than that of women. Notice that there are few common words to describe someone who does not talk very much. Most of the adjectives in 5 are somewhat literary. In contrast with the words for talking too much, none of these is exclusively feminine.

Clearly, talking per se is not a highly valued activity in the general American culture. There is no term in English that is equivalent to the Yiddish *shmuesen,* 'social talking for the purpose of enjoying each other's company', a word applied equally to adults of both sexes.

Black English has a multiplicity of terms for talking, each carefully delimiting a somewhat different speech activity.

> 6. shucking, jiving, rapping to, marking, signifying, running it down/running it by, mounting, charging, talking smart, hipping, running a game

> *(Abrahams 1974)*

This terminology matches what we already have learned about speech in Afro-American culture, that all speech is a performance. It is not only what you say, but how you say it that is important—how cleverly, poetically, and artistically. Northern urban Blacks, especially those who are not middle class, constantly engage in oral competition with each other. Speaking itself is an event. Therefore, NNE's multiplicity of terms for talking, with each different speech event being accorded its own precise name, shows the importance of talk in that speech community as compared with the SE speech community.

A good example of this difference in attitude is the term **signifying**. Claudia Mitchell-Kernan (1972) wrote an important article about Black speakers' great interpretive skills enabling them to derive symbolic meaning from context rather than being dependent upon dictionary entries for words. This remarkable skill is not uniquely Black, however, for all speakers have it. She specifically cites the activity of "signifying" as evidence for this exceptional skill.

Signifying is the term that NNE speakers use for indirect criticism of the variety 'If the shoe fits, wear it'. Although speakers of other dialects engage in indirect criticism too, NNE speakers are distinct in being conscious of it as a specialized activity within the category of talking. Many of the kinds of talking that NNE speakers label occur in other cultures, albeit without special labels:

7a. *shucking* 'pretending to be humble' (as when one speaks to the police)

b. *hyping, running a game on someone* 'passing on information that is not valid'

c. *jiving* 'lying'

d. *marking* 'making fun of someone by parodying his or her speech'

e. *running it down* 'passing on valid information upon which another is to act'

f. *mounting* 'serious angry speech' used when *getting on someone's case*

g. *hipping* 'casually telling another what's happening'

(definitions based on Abrahams 1974)

List 7 is not complete and may not be current because terminology changes just like any other fashion. The point is that any group who so finely labels different kinds of speaking is one to whom speaking in and of itself is important. Predictably, we find that the same cultural group has a term for one who speaks normally, but without grace, wit, or style: a *lame*. In NNE communities poor speaking skills are tantamount to being physically crippled. This is not to say that these speakers disdain knowledge, or feel that the clever turn of phrase is all. We saw in Chapter 7 that displays of knowledge are important as well. The person who is *heavy in the head* ('knows a lot') is valued. There is even a special speaking style devoted to the display of heavy knowledge. As in middle class scholarly style, this involves using learned, Latinate words and avoiding contractions such as *haven't*. It also makes use of special intonation patterns and stress.

The importance of speech as an activity within traditional Afro-American communities that is revealed by NNE vocabulary is verified in actual social behavior. For example, talk often occurs on the streets where there is an audience. It is not likely to be wasted on two-person conversations, for what is the use of wit and skill if they cannot be displayed?

There is at least one psychological consequence for Blacks of their attitude toward talk. If an NNE speaker is asked to *run something by* a listener—that is, to repeat something that was said—he is likely to give a verbatim retelling, even of a lengthy conversation (Mitchell-Kernan 1972). Most SE speakers are more likely to repeat the semantic content of what was said but make little effort to repeat the exact words. Most of us have had the experience of having to recount a conversation, only to have our interlocuter insist, "But what exactly did he/she say?" Typically, we find ourselves answering, "I remember what he/she said, but I can't remember the exact words." Of course, if one's culture values speech in its own right, the exact words may well be remembered. There is experimental evidence confirming that subjects will remember content, not form, when asked to memorize, unless they are told to do otherwise. NNE speakers who remember exact words of lengthy conversations do it because their culture, says, in effect, that the form is as important as the content. Other speakers do not remember form because their culture says that talking is not important. And vocabulary confirms both attitudes.

9.6   Women's talk

Throughout this text in mentioning general human competence in speaking, I have been careful to say *he* or *she, his* or *her,* and *him* or *her.* The alternative that was for many years considered correct was to refer to all human beings as *he,* as if men alone constituted humanity, and women were only a part of men. Yet in all of the discussions of NNE, reference is almost always only to males: *he, his,* or *him.* Why? The reason is simple. Just as the middle class subsumes all women under the male pronoun, so have investigators, mostly middle class, primarily studied Black male speech, and then called it NNE. This, in itself, should tell us about the worth society places on women. The rest of this chapter will examine many aspects of language differences between men and women. The focus is not intended as feminist polemics. The topic has been chosen for three reasons: First, a good deal of research on the subject has been done. Second, it is something all of the readers know about. Third, speech about and by women provides us with a superb example of how language behavior mirrors social attitudes and facts.

Attitudes toward women are clearly revealed in English vocabulary and confirmed by differences in male/female speaking practices. It has already been noted that English vocabulary reflects a disvaluing of talk for its own sake. Moreover, it was shown that most words that mean 'idle talk' in SE also are marked to mean [+female], and/or [+young, +trivial]. A person who is gabby, talkative, and gossipy, a nag, a shrew, or a chatterbox, must be a woman. What are the male equivalents? There are none. A woman is a nag when she asks for something too often. What is a man? Persistent. A woman who complains or criticizes is a shrew or bitch. What are men called who do the same? There is no single word for it. Women gossip. But men? They "shoot the breeze," a far more pleasant and potent activity.

An important difference between words marked [+female] and those marked [+male] is, in fact, potency. All the words that refer to women's talk mean 'talk that is inconsequential'. It is not talk of important, valuable issues, or, indeed of issues at all. The equation between women's talk and baby talk is seen in words like *babbling, chattering,* and *gabbing,* all essentially mindless, aimless speech production. Furthermore, note who babbles: babies, women, the insane, and brooks.

Men may be glib, but this implies expertise in using language persuasively. Glibness does have a somewhat negative connotation, but it is still positive in that it denotes a speech trait leading to success and, unlike those ascribed to women, one applied to goals. I can refer to men as *bigmouthed* or *fatmouthed* although many of my students find even these refer to women. *Loudmouthed* can describe a man as well as a woman. Words like these that do refer at least sometimes to men are more potent than those reserved exclusively for women. Someone who 'is full of hot air' is not a quiet, retiring type; hence, men may also be so described.

The term *eloquent* is about the only one in SE for one who talks both well and at length. Ostensibly, both men and women can be eloquent, but the *Oxford English Dictionary* (OED) gives as examples of usage recorded over the centuries (hence the unusual spelling and capitalization):

> 8a. Eloquent speakers are enclined to Ambition.
> b. Her dark eyes—how eloquent.

And, the quality of being eloquent is illustrated by:

> 9a. His eloquence was irresistibly impressive.
> b. Her tears were her only eloquence.
> c. A Scantling of Jack's great eloquence. . .

When the female is specified, it is only tears and eyes that give eloquence, not her speech. Under the entry for *nagging* only feminine nouns and pronouns are given as examples.

To complete the picture, the words for male idle talk are all idioms with at least one word that indicates [+power, +activity]: *bulls--t, shoot the breeze, chew the fat.* Not one word for idle, trivial talk in English refers exclusively to men, although several refer exclusively to females—and babies, fools, or the insane. Words for idle talk that are masculine at all are marked for potency and activity. Those that are feminine exclusively have no sense of potency or activity, or even a modicum of intellect. Clearly, not only is the mainstream attitude toward talk revealed by vocabulary but very different cultural attitudes toward the talk of women and men. As we shall see, these attitudes are mirrored in speech activities.

9.7   Language change and what it shows

This disparity extends to words for other aspects of male/female behavior. A man is *aggressive*; he has *a lot of guts.* A woman has *a lot of nerve.* A man is *short-tempered.* A woman is *bitchy.* A man is *forceful.* A woman is *a tough broad* or *one tough cookie* or, worse, *pushy.* Again, the connotations on the words for women are all trivial, weak and unfavorable, but those for men are potent and positive. Powerful women are certainly not admired in our society.

This lopsidedness when referring to masculine versus feminine speaking pervades the entire vocabulary. Robin Lakoff (1973) pointed out that words that were once equivalent terms for males and females have often diverged in meaning over time. Consider the following, for instance.

Master/Mistress   These were once counterparts of each other as shown in the children's rhyme "Mistress Mary, quite contrary/ How does your garden grow?" The modern *Mrs.* was originally an abbreviation of *Mistress,* although today, they can rarely be interchanged. Rare survivals of the original meaning of *mistress* do occur, as in "The walls are full of pictures of famous people, all of them autographed to the mistress of the house, former movie star Shirley Temple Black" (Dubois and Crouch 1975). Note that this quotation expands on the word *mistress* so that the wrong meaning is not derived. Moreover, the mistress here is that paragon of sweetness and virtue, Shirley Temple. Therefore, the older, non-sexual meaning of *mistress* is forced. The first meaning of *mistress* today—that is the more common usage—is 'woman kept by a man for sexual purposes.' It is probably not without significance that the surviving pronunciation for the abbreviated spelling, *Mrs.,* hides the original derivation from *mistress.*

Sir/Madam   The same fate has befallen *madam:* It too has taken on a sexual meaning. Its older use as a form of address signifying respect does survive, at least in impersonal situations as when salesclerks address female customers. Even here, it is usually replaced by its short form: *ma'am.* Despite its survival as a politeness marker (*May I help you, Ma'am?*), its primary meaning is 'keeper and procurer of women for men to use for sexual purposes'. In other words, a madam is a mistress of a house of ill repute.

Some might object that, after all, *madam* and *ma'am* still do survive as polite forms beside *sir,* and ask what difference it makes that *madam* has also taken on another, sexual meaning. The difference is that, over time, terms for females in authority have taken on sexual meanings. Worse, these terms originally denoting high female position have been demeaned to refer to women with the least admirable feminine sexual behavior. The lofty *mistress* and *madam* have been lowered to provide elevated terms for those held in contempt: whores and procurers. A mistress is one better than the prostitute on the streets or in the "houses that are not homes," but, still she is a whore. The madam? Well, we do not call a pimp a *sir.* Elevated terms for men do not suffer such a fate.

King/Queen   This is also evident in the words for the highest ranking of all in the English-speaking world. A *king* is either a crowned head or a top dog. A woman may be the former and, in her home, the latter. Elsewhere if she acts like a queen she is likely to be considered a bitch rather than a top dog.

But, *queen* has two other meanings as well, both unfavorable, both sexual. The first, most common today, is 'male homosexual who acts like a woman.' A female homosexual who acts like a man is not called a king, however. Rather, she becomes *butch,* an older nickname for a tough, lower class boy. An outcast male who acts like a woman is called a queen, the highest ranking woman. A woman who acts like a man becomes a lower class boy, not even a man, much less a king.

The second use of *queen,* occasionally still found among older working class men in Eastern New England is for the woman other than his wife with whom a man has sexual relations. This may come from older *quean* (the *ea* used to be pronounced differently from *ee*), originally a word for a woman. The *Oxford English Dictionary's* definition of *quean* says it all:

> 10. a woman, a female, *hence,* in disparagement: a bold or ill-behaved woman; a jade; a harlot, strumpet (es. 16–17 c.) [This notation in parentheses means that this usage was most common in the sixteenth and seventeenth centuries.]

Note especially the logical connector *hence.* It follows for the writers of that venerable dictionary that a woman who is bold is sexually promiscuous. It also seemed to follow for them that a term for a woman would be demeaned as a matter of course.

The latter sense of *quean* eventually won out, so that when *quean* began to be pronounced just like *queen* (just as *meat* came to sound like *meet*) then *quean* pretty much died out. Some historians of the language think that this is probably because of its scurrilous meaning, which conflicted with the fact that England does have a queen. In context, *queen* as homosexual causes no confusion.

Gentleman/Lady   This pair shows a curious disparity. *Gentleman* seems to be dying out. It survives in the stock salutation: "Ladies and Gentlemen!" In a fancy restaurant or store one might hear "The gentleman wishes to order/see . . ." And, once in a while one sees it on restroom doors. It has been replaced for the most part by *Men's* as a designation for clothing departments, stores, and toilets. If not used as gender specification, its meaning seems limited today to 'very polite and honorable', as in "He's a real gentleman."

The feminine counterpart, "She's a real lady," also survives. But, beyond that, some strange things have happened to *lady*. Robin Lakoff (1975) pointed out that unlike the many terms for females that have taken on a sexual connotation, *lady* connotes sexlessness. She gives as examples

> 11a. She's my woman, so don't mess with her.
>   b. *She's my lady, so don't mess with her.

In linguistics, a star (*) before a phrase or sentence means it would not be likely to be said. Sentence 11b is starred because a man "messes with" a woman sexually. Since *lady* does not imply sexuality, a man would not tell another not to mess with her. Of course, he might say "don't mess with my ol' lady" now that *my old lady* means 'my woman'.

That Lakoff is correct in saying that *woman* in and of itself implies sexuality is shown by the song from the movie *Saturday Night Fever:* "She's More Than a Woman to Me". In contrast, the force of Bob Dylan's song "Lay, Lady Lay" ("upon my big brass bed") is that ladies are not usually seduced.

Lady seems to have become a desexed term for *woman*. This, in itself, is noteworthy. Why do we need a desexed word for women? There isn't one for men. If *gentleman* ever was a candidate, it certainly is not now, as its usage is becoming more and more restricted. *Lady,* on the other hand, seems to be as alive and well as ever. The expression *lady of the evening* shows that *lady* did start on the path of sexual derogation. However a need for a term for women that had no sexual implications apparently overrode that natural course.

Lady has had yet another fate. Lakoff points out that it is used in trivial contexts. It is *Women's Strike for Peace,* but *Ladies' Garden and Browning Society.* A great-uncle of mine, complimenting me on my sons admonished me, "Now don't go joining that ladies' lib." His choice of words gave me his opinion of it. Just as there is no counterpart for the desexed meaning of *lady* in terms for men, there is no counterpart for its meaning of [+trivial] in a general term for men.

A third thing has happened to *lady,* this not at all unexpected in the light of other once elevated female terms. Although *lady* is still elevated or at least genteel in some contexts, it is insulting if used as an address form without a name. *Lady* followed by either first or last name is still an honorable title in England, as in "Lady Margaret" or "Lady Grey." However, "Look, lady" is a rude putdown. In contrast, "look, sir . . . ", its counterpart, is very polite, even in anger. Its other possible counterpart, is not even said, "*Look, lord . . . " Note also that the rude, equalizing "hey" does not co-occur with *sir,* although it does with *lady,* as in "Hey, lady, you dropped your purse." There is no equivalent, "*Hey, sir, you dropped your wallet."

The unmistakable degradations over time of terms for women speaks most strongly of the position of women in our culture. This is especially true since there is no such degradation of terms for men.

9.8   *Words for men*

This does not mean that rude terms for men do not exist. They do, but they are composed of words completely different from the titles of address for men used to signify respect. Terms for degraded men are not subversions of elevated terms. Rather, they are separate: *tramp, bum, stud, thief, pimp, jerk, dope, drip.* Rude address forms for men also are not degradations of higher titles: *mac, bud, fellah,* and so on. Do *king, gentleman, lord,* or *sir* ever mean 'pimp' or 'stud' or 'cheat' or 'forger'? Yet, sirs, kings, lords, and supposed gentlemen can be all of those bad things as well.

What is at issue here is not so much meanings per se, but that meanings change in certain ways for terms for women, but not for equivalent terms for men. Faced with the prospect of a female judge, the United States Supreme Court quietly dropped the *Mr.* from their usual address: *Mr. Justice.* This was done to avoid the presumed awkwardness of having to say "Madam Justice." In itself, this sums up the preceding discussion. One gets the impression as one views the history of words for women that any feminine word that is elevated in meaning will eventually be degraded. It is as if women who achieve high status in our society must somehow be brought down.

This is clearly seen in terms derived from less elevated masculine ones, such as *majorette* from *major,* or *governess* from *governor.* In such words, the female term does not take on an immoral sexual connotation, but, rather, adding the diminutive feminine ending makes it applicable to a more trivial or low ranking function than its male counterpart. In these two examples the actual role denoted is different, but in some words denoting identical functions the feminine ending often carries the implication of less seriousness, as in *poetess, sculptress, authoress.* Apparently, for this reason, many of the older *-ess* words are rarely used today. Racial terms like *Jewess* or *Negress* sound archaic now. It is not without significance that in earlier times females of the despised minority groups were designated with the *-ess* endings, much like females of animal species (*lioness, tigress*). There was never, so far as I can tell, *Christianess, *Frenchess, *Italianess, or *Caucasianess.

Perhaps most revealing of sexual prejudice are words that mean different things when applied to each gender. Consider, for instance, *tramp, dog, beast, pig,* and *professional.* A male tramp has no job or home; a female tramp is a loose woman. A loose man is casual; a loose woman is a tramp. If a man is untrustworthy and adventurous, he is a dog; a woman who is a dog is sexually unattractive, unsuitable for dating. As women are modeling their behavior on men's more and more, they are beginning to call some men dogs in the sexual sense as well. However, liberated or not, a woman is never called a dog in the sense of 'rogue' or 'rascal' though a man may be. *Beast* shows a similar split in meaning. Of a woman, it means 'even less sexually attractive than a dog'. Of a man, it means 'sadistic', 'brutally strong'. Interestingly, many women attach a connotation of sexual attractiveness to *beast* when using it to denote a man.

Pig is a widely used epithet in our society, referring both to men and women. For older speakers, *pig* referring to a human male means 'dirty' or 'sloppy'. It can mean a policeman as well. College students also interpret it as referring to a male's sexual habits. A guy who is called a pig is one who will "do it with a dog, or even a beast," both animal terms referring to human females, that is. The same epithet referring to a woman means 'sexually promiscuous' to older as well as younger speakers, although 'dirty', 'sloppy', and 'fat' are also meanings.

For older speakers "She's a professional" implies that sex is her profession. Among younger speakers especially, the word *professional* seems to be getting a better connotation. For them, referring to a woman as a professional can mean that she has a career such as in law, medicine, business or academia. As society changes, so does its vocabulary.

9.9   Multiple terms for each sex

Earlier we saw that topics with which a society is uncomfortable are referred to with a multiplicity of terms. What are we to make, then, of the multiplicity of terms for females: *dame* (another originally elevated term), *broad, piece, dish, tomato, chick, filly, bird, fox, tiger, baby, poontang, better half, little woman, hag, shrew, bitch, old bag, prude, dried up prune*? Many of these have practically the same meaning, especially the numerous terms for sexually attractive females.

In contrast, most of the terms we have for men, good or bad, refer to somewhat different aspects of masculinity except, perhaps, those referring to male incompetence in dealing with life, such as: *jerk, drip, dope, nurd, turkey, wimp* or *shnook.* English speakers who are privileged to live near speakers of other languages may also have picked up such terms as Italian *gibroni* or *shtoonatz* or Yiddish *shlemiel,* or *shnook,* all of which refer to general incompetence. In contrast to the terms for women, there are far fewer favorable terms for sexually attractive men, and none specifically for sexually unattractive men.

The preceding lists of words for women and men are certainly not complete, nor could they be, since they are of active concern in society and hence constant additions and deletions can be expected. Still the lines are already clearly drawn, with women being defined by their sexuality, men by what they do or the kinds of persons they are.

There are, to be sure, terms for sexually attractive males—*hunk* and *stud*—although nowhere near the number of terms for females. What is missing are masculine parallels to words like *old bag, old maid, hag,* and *prude,* words that denote a person who does not care for sex or at least makes no attempt to be sexually attractive.

There are many terms to denote weak or effeminate men: *fag, queer, fairy, wimp, swish, sissy, gutless wonder,* even *girl.* These do not imply lack of sexuality, but sexual preferences not approved by society. Since physical bravery is valued as a masculine trait, words meaning 'coward' often come to be used for homosexuals as well. It is assumed that homosexuals, not being 'manly,' are also neither strong nor courageous. Our culture's unease with homosexuality is well-exemplified by our vocabulary.

Why are there so many more sexual or demeaning terms for females than for non-homosexual males? One possible answer is that men have the power in our society, hence the right to coin words. Or, it may be, as Robin Lakoff suggests, that men coin so many words because of their discomfort with women. She claims that this discomfort arises because women are viewed primarily in sexual terms, and sex, being taboo, leads to the same unease as bathroom functions. Yes, that sounds shocking, even disgusting, but the evidence from vocabulary is very strong. If women are not primarily sex objects in our culture, why do words for women take on sexual connotations over time? Why are elevated terms so regularly degraded? Why are there so many terms for sexually desirable women? Why are there words for women who do not put themselves forth sexually, all of them uncomplimentary?

As further proof that this analysis of our vocabulary is on target, consider the sentences,

> 12a. You know what SHE needs.
>   b. She needs a good you know what!

This last was once said to me by a Roman Catholic male college professor about a nun! Everybody knows by such omissions that what the female "needs" is sex from a male. Notice that these are empty sentences, equivalent to the empty phrases *do it* to refer to the sexual act, *go* for bathroom functions, or fire *for effect* for 'kill.' Both 12a and 12b are empty in that the she in both might actually need anything from the universe of needs, but the answer to both is always 'sex provided by a male'.

9.10   *Words and attitudes*

At least three conclusions should emerge from the foregoing discussion:

1. Covert attitudes can be uncovered by examining the vocabulary of a society, attitudes that its members might hotly deny holding. Since again and again we find that vocabulary is not accidental, that it correlates both with social situation and with attitudes, then we have to admit it can also uncover attitudes we are not proud of having. The alternative is to explain why in the instance of words for women there is so much pejorative skewing or negative bias in the coining of words and their meaning. The expression of covert attitudes in vocabulary parallels the expression of social stratification in dialect, stratification that speakers often deny as well.

2. The words themselves are not causing the attitudes. They reflect them. As with dialect, the linguistic situation mirrors the social situation and changes readily as the social situation changes. We saw ample proof in the way jargons developed new words in response to the social needs that had given birth to the jargons. Thus many younger people hear "she's a professional" as referring to a profession other than the so-called oldest profession, prostitution. The term *stud* is replacing older *wolf* for sexually attractive men. *Wolf* referred to a man who treated women as his prey. A *stud* also has connotations of animal magnetism, but women are willing partners or at least not victims of a stud. To be sure, however, *womanizer* still has no counterpart *manizer*.

3. It does no good, in my opinion, to try to legislate linguistic change. It will occur naturally as attitudes change. Until then, any attempts to change usage will do little good. A case in point is *Ms.* One clear expression of the female as sex object is that, as part of the system of address in the English speaking world, women are tagged as to their sexual availability. *Mrs.* equals married, hence not available. *Miss* equals unmarried, hence fair game unless of course the miss is an *old maid* or a *beast.* As cruel as that sounds, it is the way society codifies female status in language. It is the social attitude that gives rise to the vocabulary that is cruel. Early on, feminists objected to such marking of women. They pushed for one neutral form of address for both married and unmarried women, *Ms.* as a parallel to *Mr.* Since society is not yet ready for such a change, it has been treated with derision on TV, in the popular press, and by men and women alike. The last should come as no surprise. As we saw with dialect, people take on society's evaluations of themselves, and some women act and talk as society tells them to: like passive, trivial, sex objects. Of course, that behavior is slowly changing, and with it Ms. seems to be inching forward in acceptance.

9.11   *Corroborating Evidence*

How much does other language behavior fit with the social image of women portrayed in English vocabulary? Do other speech behaviors support the view of women as passive, essentially trivial sex objects? Robin Lakoff suggested that, in many ways, women themselves talk in weak, ineffectual ways that prevent them from being taken seriously. Unfortunately, she made no attempt to verify any of her intuitions by experimentation or careful, controlled observations. More recently, it has also become clear that the supposedly feminine patterns that she delineated are characteristic also of children and of men in subordinate positions (see Crosby and Nyquist, 1977). It seems that those of inferior status speak in certain ways, and that includes much speech by women, especially in male/female interactions.

However, Robin Lakoff certainly has pointed the way for subsequent research. While definitive answers are lacking and in an area of such fast change will be lacking for some time to come, certain trends suggest that Lakoff was not far off the mark.

Briefly, Lakoff claimed that women (and, as we now know, other subordinates):

- Use empty nonforceful adjectives and expletives, such as *charming, divine, darn* and *shoot.*
- Use more hedges in their speech, such as qualifying adjectives with *so* (*It's so nice*), *I guess,* and *maybe.*
- Use tag questions more, thus weakening their statements, as in "Tastes good, doesn't it?"
- Use more extreme intonation contours, allowing their voices to fluctuate in pitch more dramatically, the way young children do.
- End statements on a questioning, rising pitch. When asked, "What time is dinner?" a woman may answer "At eight?"

One obvious problem with such assertions is that they are tough to prove. They do not lend themselves to laboratory experiments, and they are likely to vary according to social situation and perhaps according to idiosyncracies of particular speakers. They can be investigated by observing interactions between males and females matched for age and status. Eakins and Eakins (1978) for instance, analyzed male and female speech during faculty meetings. Even more than with dialect investigation, there are so many relevant features in studies of natural interaction that it is very time consuming. Still, some, like Soskin and John (1963) and Pamela Fishman (1978), have braved such studies.

Lakoff is correct in her first assertion, that the more feminine words do not co-occur with important subjects. It certainly would sound unnatural for someone to say "Shoot! They vandalized my house!" or "The nation's economy has been divine all summer." The real problems with her assertion, however, are that no one seems to use the alleged feminine speech forms much anymore and that men as well as women do use them in some circumstances.

Cathy Kubaska, as part of a student project, tried to elicit empty "feminine" adjectives from both male and female college students by showing them pictures in the Neiman-Marcus Christmas catalogue. Males and females alike used terms like *pretty, great,* and *terrific. Charming* and *divine* were virtually nonexistent, as was another feminine adjective, *lovely.* In line with Lakoff's hypothesis, however, is that women use adjectives men also use, adjectives that can be used to refer to important as well as unimportant things. As with dialects, people copy those they admire, those in power, just so long as they have a chance of joining in.

The use of softened expletives, such as *shoot* or *fudge,* for their forceful and taboo counterparts may be characteristic of some women, but it also is of some men. In fact, the very last *fudge* I heard was from a young man who dropped a jar. He looked normally masculine and was surrounded by a wife and young children, which, combined with his being in a public place, may explain the "Fudge!"

Certainly, Lakoff was correct in considering the stronger words as specifically masculine, however. Men have always had more leeway in using such words, especially in masculine company. Today, in order to signal that they are liberated many women deliberately use taboo words, especially when first meeting other women. It seems to be a verbal badge of liberation. Often, this is done only once at the beginning of an acquaintance. The taboo word functions like an address form in that it makes a statement about the speaker that is to be remembered throughout interactions with her. In any event, there is not likely to be much problem collecting plenty of examples of younger women spicing their speech with strong language, especially when the company is not mixed.

Eakins and Eakins found that at academic meetings or conferences, there was a tendency for women to use more hedges or disclaimers than men, although they did not collect a significant number of such hedges in their sample. However, they were investigating academic women who are used to competing with men intellectually. Considering this, that they found even a trend may be significant. Even these women preceded statements by disclaimers like "I know this sounds silly, but . . . ," ". . . this may strike you as odd . . . ," "you're going to think this is stupid, but . . . ," "Well, I'm not the expert, . . . ," Such data cetainly support Lakoff's premise that women's speech habits weaken their assertions.

Tag questions like *isn't it, aren't you,* and *aren't they?* have many uses in English. Males and females alike use them in polite chitchat of the *Nice day isn't it?* variety. They are also used for genuine requests for information as in

13. "The factory grosses $150,000, doesn't it?"

They can also be used after statements, as in

14. "Tastes good, doesn't it?
15. It isn't right the way he's getting pushed around, is it?"

Dubois and Crouch (1975) roundly criticized Lakoff for her stance on tag questions. They taped a meeting in which all of the tag questions were posed by men. The problem is that Dubois and Crouch never specified which kinds of tags the men used. From the few they report, it seems as if they were like 13, legitimate information-seeking tags. Eakins and Eakins found other uses of tags almost exclusively from female faculty. My own students, as a regular assignment, have been asked to count all tags during a family meal or gathering, classifying them as to type. So far, the results have been overwhelming. If one can believe the evidence from tags, women do not trust their own sight, hearing, tastebuds, or judgment, for they continually attach tags to personal statements. Outside of greetings, men rarely do. Furthermore, in many families, there is a difference between the generations, with grandmothers using more tags than mothers and daughters using them the least. This also reflects an educational difference: typically the younger generations have more formal education than the older. The question of tags should highlight for the student how careful one must be in an investigation both to classify one's data properly and to gather sufficient amounts of it.

9.12   How do women talk?

In sum, our vocabulary treats women as passive, trivial, sex objects. It treats women's talk as trivial, carping, annoying, and as foolish as a baby's or mental incompetent's. Furthermore, so the myth and our language go, women talk a great deal, and their speech is irritating and unpleasant. Indeed, so the myth goes, women are at no disadvantage when talking to men. A man can hardly get a word in edgewise when the *old biddies* or *young chicks* start clucking at their *hen parties*. And certainly, the myth implies, women are as assertive as men—so much so that if men are not careful, women (being hens, I guess) will *henpeck* them or, worse, *pussywhip* them. (Significantly, our language has no equivalent terms for masculine domination of women). Does our vocabulary lie? Not at all. What women actually do and what they are perceived as doing are quite different things, but our vocabulary explains the perception.

Scholarly investigation shows that the blindness to the actual situation is reminiscent of people's blindness to the way they themselves speak. One of the most enduring myths of our society is that women talk more than men do. Given the tremendous differences in personality from individual to individual, one might reasonably expect that some men talk more than some women and vice versa. The amount of talking is an individual trait, but in male/female interactions evidence shows that males tend to dominate. Considering the sheer volume of such interactions, one would expect that a randomly observed few would show some male-dominated conversations and some female-dominated. One would also expect that tremendous numbers of interactions would have to be observed before any trends, if present at all, would emerge.

In most encounters, however, apparently males dominate females in interactions between the sexes. This is evinced in many ways. Men talk more than women. Men interrupt women with startling frequency, more than women interrupt men (Zimmerman and West 1975). The very way that our language describes women's speech suggests that men would encourage women to continue speaking less than women encourage men. That has also been borne out by objective studies. Men even choose the topics of conversation, deciding what will be talked about (Fishman 1978).

All of these assertions have been verified by taping conversations between men and women in a variety of naturalistic settings. Zimmerman and West did this in drugstores, coffee shops, and other public places by placing their tape recorder in a knapsack. Others have done the same by putting a recorder in a purse, a shopping bag, or, if using a microrecorder, even in a pocket. Unfortunately, although it violates people's right to privacy, covert taping is the best way to get natural data of frequency of speaking and the like unless one wishes to confine oneself to academic meetings and classrooms and other such limited arenas of talk.

In such a study, the sociolinguist counts both the number of turns each party takes and the length of each, as well as things such as the number of interruptions, who makes them, and how the interrupted party responds. This last does not have to include personal semantic information. It is sufficient to count how many times the interrupted party protests, ignores the interruption, falls silent, fidgets, or the like. This can be done with worksheets upon which an observer keeps a tally while pretending to do homework or write a letter.

Evidence from both male and female students, many of whom first insisted that women did indeed talk more than men and who professed annoyance at the entire topic of sexism in language, confirmed other investigators' findings. Women are likely to talk more than men only when explaining how to do tasks considered feminine in our culture, such as changing a baby's diaper or cooking. So far, in all other observed instances, males talk more frequently than females and talk for a longer time.

One major reason for men's talking more is that men feel free to interrupt women, but not vice versa. Zimmerman and West found this in California. My own students have found it in Rhode Island. Whether it is between husbands and wives, male and female faculty, and students of all ages, at home, on the street, at parties, at sports events, at concerts, and in restaurants, men interrupt women more than the reverse. In one sample observation, for instance, husband and wife were observed for three hours during a social gathering. The man outtalked his wife, five minutes to every one she spoke. Furthermore, in that period, he interrupted her ten times, whereas she did not interrupt him even once. All participants afterwards characterized the man as being very quiet, docile, and good natured. His wife was considered exceptionally talkative, forceful, and dominating.

Zimmerman and West found in mixed male/female interactions that 96 percent of all interruptions were by men. Moreover, women do not object when men butt in. Although women will say "One minute!"; "Please let me finish"; or "Wait until I'm done" if other women try to interrupt, they offer no objections to men. One is strongly reminded of the way adults interrupt children. Zimmerman and West comment that the right of females to speak "appears to be casually infringed upon by males." What this means is that both men and women subconsciously concede that men have the right to control conversation, and that women may speak only if men wish them to.

9.13   *The right to speak*

As startling as this conclusion may seem, it is reinforced by other findings. Pamela Fishman, for example, found that women raised as many as 62 percent of the topics in ordinary household conversations with their husbands. However, of these, only 17 out of 28 were responded to by their husbands. If husbands did not respond to a topic, it was dropped. By contrast, 28 out of 29 topics raised by the husbands in this study got discussed. Even the remaining one was not dropped outright. Fishman claims that the content of the women's topics were indistinguishable from their husbands' but that men have the right to control what is to be talked about. Fishman believes that women raise so many topics in an effort to increase their chance of success, because so much of what they say is ignored by men.

Many other female speech tactics can also be seen as ways of getting attention or getting some kind of control over conversation. Men do the same things as women when they want or need some attention and response. But what is significant is that in ordinary male/female conversations, women resort to such tactics far more frequently than men do. For instance, women ask three times as many questions as men. Questions force hearers to make a response and are therefore powerful controllers of interactions.

Women, like children, use "D'ya know what?" very frequently. The answer to this—"What?"—guarantees that the first speaker will be able to elaborate on his or her chosen topic. It is no surprise that those whose right to choose topics is curtailed—women and children—resort to this question far more frequently than do men unless men are talking to male superiors. Women also introduce topics with comments like "This is really interesting!" far more often than men do. Again, this seems to be a ploy to get attention. In some transcripts it has been found that women use pause fillers like "you know" as much as ten times more than their male co-conversationalists. Women do this the most when men are giving the least response (Fishman 1978).

Typically men give women very little feedback during conversations. As men talk, women give little murmurs of encouragement, such as "mmhmmm," "uh huh," "yeah," or "oh." Men do not reciprocate. It is very difficult to keep on talking if the other party does not make such sounds. Similarly, women look at men more when they are talking than men look at women. In effect, then, women encourage men to talk, but men do not encourage women to.

Furthermore, silences in conversations are not equally distributed between the sexes. Women are silent when men interrupt. And, they remain silent longer after a man's interruption than a man does if he is cut off. Women are also silent if men give them a delayed minimal response. This is the dampening pause, as in

16. *Woman:*   [joyfully] Oh boy! You'll never guess what happened to
  me today!
  Man: [long, long pause] . . . What?

The man's delayed response is calculated to convey complete lack of interest. The impression is that the man responded at all only because of the woman's "You'll never guess . . ." a powerful opener, equivalent to a question in eliciting the response "What?"

The entire picture that emerges is one of men controlling male/female interaction in every way and not being overly concerned with what females wish to talk about. Females can, by special strategies, force their topics into the conversation, but men may break in on the woman with impunity.

9.14   *The dating game*

Neither sex gets a completely fair shake in dating. Traditionally men have the unnerving task of having to initiate encounters with women, of having to ask for a date. Women have the right to refuse and not necessarily too kindly. If a woman accepts, however, it is her job to draw the male out, to discover what he wishes to talk about.

If a woman were as verbally unresponsive on a date as a man is allowed to be, she would be considered rude and sullen. Such is the fate of a female, that not only does a man have the right to choose topics, but he has the right to make a woman find the topic he wants, especially on their first date or two. It is as if a woman has to demonstrate her ability to please a man.

9.15   *A case in point*

A heartbreaking example of this social burden on women is unwittingly given in a report of experimental conversations with a schizophrenic female, Carrie (Seeman and Cole 1977). She was obligated to have conversations with a male medical student every week, as part of an experimental procedure. What actually happened is that she talked and he did not respond.

The psychiatrists analyzing these conversations claim that Carrie's conversation became more and more disjointed every week. From this, they concluded that schizophrenics deteriorate as interpersonal relations develop. Actually, Carrie's conversation is the typical female pursuit of a response from a male, flitting from topic to topic until he picks up on one. Since the medical student rarely seemed to respond, even with minimal polite comments, she finally complained:

> You know and you're talking about yourself personally yesterday and I didn't really have any feeling at all. It was kind of like a release. I like people to confide in me, but, like, where is it going? What? It must serve some purpose; I don't have any theories about it. All I know is that I do get involved with people and it usually ends the same way: I, I become very angry and you know something, well not always, but I always get taken, I get sucked in, you know, and I, I was just immobilized last night, I didn't accomplish anything and here again today I, I haven't accomplished anything and I think it's a hang-up I have got with you, but I, I don't think I'm alone. Maybe, maybe it's your hang-up, too. I, I really don't know. But I do get involved in, with and when someone tells me I want to help out, and I want also to give something of myself like I'm older than you like I would like to give you some of my own insights and I, I don't know if it's appropriate what we are talking about—what is it we're talking about? We're just talking about relationships and they're different—you're a man and I'm a woman and I guess I identified a bit with your girlfriend because I've done that with my boyfriend.
>
> *(Seeman and Cole 1977, p. 289)*

The disjointed sentences are typical in unplanned conversation, becoming more and more characterized by false starts and fragments, the more excited the person, or the more complex the topic. In this experiment, Carrie was put in the untenable position of being forced to talk to an unresponsive male, a position that even a woman with no history of mental illness might find disconcerting. Carrie says that she does not know where it is all going. She says she would like to give the student advice but does not know if that is appropriate. She even notices the parallels between their sessions and normal boy/girl relationships. Understandably, because they were not aware of recent research into the nature of normal conversations, Seeman and Cole, the investigators in charge of this experiment, thought that Carrie's speech proved that schizophrenics become more disorganized the more they become personally involved with someone. That may be true, but her conversation here actually illustrates how uncomfortable it is to have to converse when one's partner does not help carry the ball. One consequence of the lopsidedness in responsibility for conversation is that like Carrie, women do indeed often prattle when in the company of men.

9.16   *Requesting versus commanding*

Given what we already know about male/female speaking rights accorded by custom, one would expect that women give more indirect requests than do men. Eakins and Eakins (1978, p. 47) had students tell each other how to draw an arrangement of squares. Only verbal cues were allowed. They found a decided tendency for males to tell where the lines should be penciled in, but for females to request. They offer as examples:

17. Man: Next! put your pencil on the bottom left corner of the square . . . Draw your line at a 45 degree angle to the left side of the square . . . Now get this! This line is the top side of a second square . . . Don't get it off center or you'll blow the whole thing.

18. Woman: Then I'd like you to construct another box just below the first one, all right? Only this time, try to arrange it so the left point of the first box touches the top of the second box . . .

One problem with this task as proof that women are always more indirect than men is the very task involved. As with everything else, social situation may make a difference. For instance, the task here seems to be masculine, related to the drawing of blueprints or other mechanical—hence our society, masculine—pursuits. One wonders if a female would be more direct in explaining how to make a bed, change a diaper, or cook a meal. Also, females can be quite direct in ordering husbands to do domestic chores that some wives believe they have a right to expect, such as picking up food on the way home.

Although extended tapings of daily domestic conversations between husbands and wives would yield more definitive answers about the directness of women's requests, these are not only tough to get, but horrendous to analyze. Another solution might be to show audiences videotapes of scenes in which women and men order each other about both directly and indirectly as a consequence of the action portrayed. The audience would indicate on a card fitting adjectives for both sexes in the scenes. It would probably be important both to portray families of different social and ethnic groups and to have representatives of different ones do the judging.

So far, all indications are that men can be silent and unresponsive, placing on women the full burden of relieving the awful silence (Malinowski 1923).

Recall, women remain silent after being interrupted, but men do not. Men do not give up the floor so easily as women. Men are silent when it comes to encouraging women to talk. They may also be less cooperative in a conversation, unless the topic is to their liking. Given all this, it would not be at all surprising that women's speech is more tentative than men's, more loaded with hedges and qualifiers. So far at least, the evidence for vocabulary has been confirmed by speaking practices.

9.17   *Implications for studying social groups*

The vocabulary of a language, then, indicates what is important to its speakers. It also indicates how certain aspects of culture or society are valued: whether favorably or unfavorably. It tells us what makes speakers uncomfortable and what they feel about the rightful role and behavior of different members of society. In two instances, speech activities of Blacks and women, a strong corroboration was shown between the attitudes revealed in vocabulary and actual behavior. This does not mean that the vocabulary is shaping behavior or shaping thoughts. The fact that we can think things quite opposed to what our vocabulary encodes is in itself proof that although vocabulary mirrors, it does not shape. Despite what English has always said about women and their speech, with little encouragement from society, many feminists have been able to say that women are as bright as men and that they should not be defined in terms of their sexual relations to men. Further, they have set out to show that the vocabulary lies.

9.18   *The Whorfian (or Sapir-Whorf) hypothesis*

Although it bears his name, Benjamin Lee Whorf was not the originator of this hypothesis. Wilhelm Von Humboldt, in the nineteenth century, and later, Edward Sapir, argued that people who speak different languages perceive the world differently. That is, people are prisoners of their language. All that we have seen about the flexibility and creativity of language use denies such a proposition. Yet such notions, especially as promulgated by Whorf, persist.

Whorf, like his followers, cites two sorts of evidence for his view. The first is the evidence from translation, and the second is evidence from **lexical decomposition** (Lenneberg 1953). The translation evidence always involves an argument that someone has to behave in a certain way because his or her language says or does not say something. The famous Whorfian example is of the man who tossed a cigarette butt into a gas drum marked: empty. Whorf claimed that English forces the word *empty* even though fumes are still in the drum. He argued that the use of the word *empty* allowed the careless smoker to think of the drum as having nothing in it, thereby disregarding the vapors and behaving as if they were not there. One flaw in such reasoning is that Whorf did not show that the smoker realized that an empty drum could have vapors. In other words, the mistake could have been caused by sheer ignorance. Even if it were not, English certainly allows one to say that although marked empty of one substance, gas, a drum still can be full of flammable vapors.

Similarly, Edward Stewart (1979) claimed that the A-bomb was dropped on Japan because the Japanese had marked the Japanese equivalent of *ignore* on the U.S. communique informing them of what was going to happen if they did not surrender. Stewart argues that the Japanese, in line with their culture, needed time to deliberate, and that is what they meant by "Ignore." Our culture, supposedly being more hasty, puts another meaning on *ignore.* So, we dropped the bomb. This is a prize example of poor translation. Hasty and fast-acting culture or not, English is perfectly capable of expressing the idea of holding off on a decision. *Put aside, Delay decision,* or even *Ignore until deliberations are completed* all would have conveyed that idea. *Ignore* means 'do not pay attention.' Whoever chose that word for *delay decision* was not a proficient translator. Again and again, when Whorfians or others insist that something cannot be said in one language, it turns out to be just such a case of translation difficulty. Indeed people commonly say "You can't say X in English [or some other language]" and then proceed, by circumlocution, to tell the hearer exactly what they have just claimed you can't say in that language!

Translation is often extremely difficult, as no two languages cut up the semantic universe the same way. Meanings and connotations get attached to words differently. English, for instance, uses *eat* for what both people and animals do. German distinguishes between human beings, who *essen*, and animals, who *fressen*. It is not that English speakers do not perceive a difference between animal and human eating. They do, as witness the simile, *eat like a pig.* English just does not happen to codify that difference as German does, although it makes other distinctions that German does not. For example English distinguishes between *tall* and *long,* whereas German does not.

Sometimes these differences, as indicated above, do reflect cultural attitudes. If so, whole sets of words will be implicated. Sometimes these differences are accidental. No language can have a separate word for each and every concept a speaker might wish to convey. If it did, vocabularies would be horrendously long. Also, language would be static, with a one-to-one correspondence between word and meaning. Metaphor and other figurative language could not exist, as these are the product of the fact that in all natural languages any given word can mean many things. Because languages are constructed so as to have a great deal of *polysemy* (multiple meaning on a word), related words often take on different meanings in different languages or even different dialects. As an example, in Great Britain, the notion of a hike in pay is attached to *rise,* but in America, to *raise.* The time between acts of a play is called *interval* in Great Britain but *intermission* in the United States; either word, by extension from its basic meaning, could easily be extended to mean a recess from a performance. It seems to be quite accidental which one became usual in each dialect.

9.19   *What difference does a vocabulary make?*

Research has shown that people are somewhat quicker to name something for which their language has a specific name, but they are not hindered in their perceptions of things the language has no name for. It may take them longer to match up things for which they have no ready name, but their thinking appears otherwise unaffected.

Perhaps having a name for it focuses attention on an item or category. Or perhaps speakers use a testing strategy to get rid of the easy cases first, those for which they have a name and then turn to those for which they do not have a name. Some groups, such as the Kpelle in Liberia, have been found to flunk a supposed test of cognitive abilities. However, when observed in daily activities, they can be seen to use those abilities regularly (Scribner 1977). No one knows how to test unerringly for cognitive abilities. Therefore, we cannot claim that people do or do not have abilities on the basis of what we think we know about their language (Cole 1977).

Many Whorfians are not equally proficient in all the languages they are comparing. When they state that one cannot say something in a given language, perhaps they really mean that *they* do not know how to say it.

9.20   *Comparing language data*

One other serious problem underlies much Whorfian commentary. Its proponents frequently do not seem to be comparing on the same level. For instance, Whorf (1956, p. 241) waxed poetic about the marvelous ability of American Indians to perceive the world as processes, as opposed to the static, compartmentalized perceptions of those who speak what he termed SAE (Standard Average European). As an example, he presented the Apache way of saying "It is a dripping spring."

> Apache erects the statement on *ga:* 'be white . . . With the prefix *no-,* the meaning downward motion enters: 'Whiteness moves downward.' . . . The result corresponds to our 'dripping spring', but synthetically it is: 'as water, or springs, whiteness moves downward.' How utterly unlike our way of thinking!

In like manner, Whorf showed that the English *it is* would be rendered in Apache by *golgha* 'the place is white, clear; a clearing, a plain.' According to Whorf, English *It is a dripping spring* is in Apache the equivalent of 'the place is white, clear; a clearing, a plain, as water, or springs, whiteness moves downward.' Whorf concluded that some languages use a means of expression in which terms flow together into plastic synthetic creations rather than being separate as they are in English.

It should be noted that Whorf derived the supposed Apache meaning from only two Apache words, which he broke down into their component semantic features. Had he done the same for the English sentence, he would have come up with an equally flowing, plastic, synthetic creation (Lenneberg 1953, p. 159–160). In English, the phrase *It is* is a dummy with no real meaning beyond marking off positions in a sentence. The *a* means 'one out of many such'. *Dripping* means 'slow, regular falling of water or other liquid in drops'. *Spring* means 'active, not static; leap into the air; constant arching of water, so that upward leap is followed by downward movement, with continuous bubbling and white frothing'. Translating the English as Whorf did the Apache one could get, then, 'slow, regular falling of water after actively leaping into the air, constantly arching so that upward leap is followed by downward movement with water frothing and bubbling continuously'. The English, as I translate it, is, if anything, more flowing than the Apache, at least as Whorf translated it. If one is comparing two languages, one must be most careful to compare the same levels of meaning and not, as Whorf did, compare whole words (in English) to semantic features of words (in Apache.)

Comparing semantic features at all is a risky business. For one thing, what about synonyms, other ways of saying the "same things"? Before one can say a language does nor does not express a notion in a certain way, one must consider all possible ways of expressing that notion. Whorfians typically do not do this.

Another problem with semantic features is that speakers are not bound by them. We have already seen that people can understand things figuratively as well as literally. Also, morphemes and words can lose some of their meaning in certain contexts or come to mean something quite different from their literal meaning. For instance, how often do you consider breakfast as an actual breaking of a fast? A dogfight takes place in the air between two planes, not on the ground where dogs fight. Did you ever notice the *-th* in words like *health, wealth, stealth, truth, length,* or *width?* Do you perceive these are *-th* added onto *heal, weal, steal, true, long,* or *wide?* The *-th* once meant 'state of', but most speakers today perceive these as whole words (not consisting of two morphemes). An outsider might nonetheless assume that English speakers break *health* down into *heal + th* in deriving meaning. Whorf's breakdown of the Apache words is as improbable.

Examination of a vocabulary can reveal a good deal about a culture. The lexicon of a language is, to a degree but not wholly, a mirror of its speakers' attitudes and ideas. A mirror reflects. It does not determine; it does not hold prisoners.

EXERCISES

1. Compare male-female interactions on a television show: a soap opera, an adventure show, a sitcom, talkshow, or newscast. Log all

instances of one of the following: males and females interrupting each other; tag questions, carefully noting the kinds used, by each sex; hedges and other statements that weaken assertions (for example *I guess; It's so-o-o nice).* Do your observations confirm or invalidate the contentions of this chapter?

2. Examine five TV and radio commercials and/or newspaper and magazine advertisements. Carefully chart the role of females and males in these commercials and/or ads. Relate this to the products being sold. What differences, if any, do you find in male/female roles? What does this show about society today? Do the same for race and/or region of the country. What does this tell you about stereotypes?

3. Find two examples of culturally loaded words, words that state an attitude as part of their meaning (for example, *fat profit* vs. *healthy profit*). Give the full linguistic and social context in which you find the words being used, and explain the attitudes that they reveal.

4. Check a store catalog and/or advertisements in order to show how language is manipulated there to make you want to buy. List words with favorable cultural biases. What words could be substituted that would make you not want to buy? Alternatively, find an example of propaganda or reporting that glosses over the truth. Show how words are avoided or utilized to achieve these goals.

5. Look up the word *incident* in a dictionary such as the Oxford English Dictionary or Random House Dictionary. What was its original meaning? Compare it to contemporary political and newscasting use as in "incident at My Lai" referring to a massacre. How is such usage manipulative?

chapter 10

BILINGUALISM:
LANGUAGES IN CONTACT

Bilingualism is the study of those who speak two or more languages, when and where they speak each, and the effect of one language on the other. We can tell a good deal about cultural attitudes and relative social status of two neighboring cultures by observing word borrowings and which language is used for which purposes. In order to teach speakers of other languages effectively, one must know where their languages differ from that of the teacher and in what ways. It is also important to know the conditons under which a language will be retained and those under which it will not.

10.1   *Languages in contact*

Pidgins, with their eventual transformation into Creoles, are not the only outcomes when two languages come into contact. More usually, if adult speakers have to learn another language, they learn it in its entirety (or try to at least). Very commonly a second language learned in adulthood is acquired as if through a filter, the filter being the first language. Some speakers retain strong accents, making grammar errors based on their first language, and misuse words in accordance with their first language even if they have spoken the second language for more years than the first. Moreover, they retain the accents even if they have spoken the second language more frequently than the first during those years. Immigrants who came to America in their twenties may still speak with an extremely thick accent when they are in their seventies. Others will learn the second language with no trace of an accent. The amount of formal education the speaker has received does not seem to be a determining factor in whether or not an accent is retained, although the amount of formal instruction in the new language may be (Krashen 1973). Some immigrants may never learn the language of their new country at all. Others learn just enough to get by at work.

Once a new language is learned, it becomes available as part of a speaker's stylistic repertoire. As with dialects and styles, whether a particular language is selected in a given situation depends upon the topic, the social scene, the relative status of speakers, their aspirations, and feelings of identity.

10.2   *The first language filter*

Many linguists believe that some time after the onset of puberty a person's ability to discriminate new sounds becomes impaired. *New* here is used in the sense 'different from those in any language(s) already learned by the speaker'. Whether this impairment is purely developmental or whether it is at least partially social is not certain. There is a bit of folk wisdom that claims that adults lose their ability to learn new languages without an accent. It may be, however, that adults do not have the same motivation as children do to learn a new language rapidly without an accent (Lambert and Gardner 1972; Lambert 1969). Perhaps, too, the adult retains an accent as a way of signaling that he or she identifies with the people of his or her original homeland. Certainly, individual differences exist in learning a new language with or without an accent.

One famous and important statesman in the 1970's, Henry Kissinger, could not manage accent-free English although he came to the United States at age fifteen, but many immigrants who arrived here in their teens speak with no trace of an accent. So far as linguists know today, retaining an accent or not has little if anything to do with intelligence or special aptitudes.

Second languages do not appear to be learned by mimicking any more than first languages are. People who have learned at least two languages in their childhood seem to learn third or fourth languages more easily than a monolingual adult can learn a second. Even so, most such bilinguals but not all still have an accent in the language learned as an adult. Perhaps once we know more about second language learning, especially by adults, we may find that many factors determine how accent-free the learner of a new language becomes.

10.3   *Interference: phonological*

Accents seem to be caused partially by an inability to perceive. The speaker actually does not hear the precise sounds used in the target language, the one being learned. The language learner seems to be in the same position as the young child who does not hear the difference between /f/ and /θ/. When confronted with a new language, at first a speaker converts strange sounds into the closest ones that are already in his or her language repertoire. This is not done consciously. We do not know all of the factors that may lead a given speaker to abandon or overcome these first errors. Many speakers, if not most, obviously never do, which is why they are said to have a foreign accent. Do not forget, however, that what is foreign depends upon who is speaking. English speakers are the foreign ones when they attempt Italian, German, Chinese, or whatever.

The process of converting sounds into those of one's native system was thought to be so regular that linguists believed that if they knew what a language learner's first language was they could predict what errors the speaker would make in the new, second language (Weinreich 1968). Recently some doubt has been cast on this premise (Nickel 1971). It is true, nonetheless, that speakers of a language all tend to make much the same errors in learning certain sounds foreign to that language. For example, French speakers learning English usually hear /θ/ in *thing* as /s/ and /ð/ in *this* as /z/. Russian speakers seem to hear them as /t/ and /d/, respectively, as do Swedish speakers. However, these are only likely errors. It may not be wholly inevitable that all speakers of Language A always hear a sound in Language B in exactly the same way or for all time.

Some inroads into misperception can be made by good teaching, by focusing the learners' attention on certain sounds and how they should be made. The attitude of the learner may play a role as well. For instance, German speakers, like the French, seem to hear the English *th* sounds as /z/ and /s/. Many Germans who resettled in America during the 1930s and 1940s still say "zis" for *this* and "sing" for *thing*. However, younger Germans born since the end of the Second World War, who live and have always lived in Germany, often pronounce those sounds exactly as native born English speakers do, apparently because some teachers of English in Germany concentrate on the sounds. Also, many of these younger Germans are extremely proud of their accent-free English. Younger German scholars tell with pride of academic conferences held in Germany, by Germans, entirely in English, with the proceedings written and published in English. Such a desire to learn a second language without an accent may make the difference in breaking through perceptual barriers.

Anyone who has taken an introductory linguistics or phonetics course has probably had the experience of learning to discriminate new sounds. At first, one simply does not hear what the instructor says are different sounds. But since one's grade depends upon learning to discriminate between many closely related sounds, somehow one learns many brand new ones. Nowadays, many people take their first phonetics courses well after puberty, when they are in their thirties, forties, even fifties. Still, they learn to hear different sounds. Interestingly, many linguists find that their ability to discriminate new sounds actually improves with age, not diminishes. Since they are attuned to listening for new sounds, they are not so likely to convert them into their old systems. The fact that older people can learn to discriminate new sounds in phonetics classes argues against the proposition that human beings lose their ability to perceive new language forms after puberty. I believe that most of the apparent loss of language learning ability after puberty is caused by social factors as much as developmental ones.

10.4   *Interference: grammatical*

Grammatical interference may also arise from misperception, or, perhaps, failure to perceive at all. The kinds of grammatical errors that bilingual speakers make usually can be traced to the grammar of their native language (Burt and Kiparsky 1972; DiPietro 1971; Weinreich 1968). Apparently, speakers often do not notice that the rules of the new language differ from those in their old, or, if they have, they have not gotten the new rules down pat yet. They may not be wholly sure how and under what conditions all of the grammar rules of their new language apply. Alternatively, even if they do know, in the heat of encoding ideas in the new language, they fall back on the grammar they have most thoroughly internalized. Probably both factors are at work in grammatical error or, for that matter, in any kind of bilingual interference. Whereas children seem to be able to figure out grammars of new languages on their own, adults seem to need formal instruction to do so (Krashen 1973).

Speakers learning a new language do have to learn some of its grammar rules, but many never seem to grasp the finer points. As Uriel Weinreich pointed out in his landmark study *Languages in Contact,* the errors made usually can be explained on the basis of the facts of the first language. For instance, most Europeans and Arabs learning English do learn the progressive verb forms, as in *I am going to the store, He was fighting,* and *They will be doing that by now.* What they do not always learn is the exact conditions that call for the progressive. Thus, one hears bilingual errors like *I am studying in my room every night,* or *I was walking all the time in the old country.* Lest native speakers of English snicker, they might be reminded that unless they have studied Modern English grammar, they themselves might be hard put to explain exactly how and why the progressive is normally used. And, of course, they would make errors when speaking languages that they had not learned in childhood.

Often, the foreign speaker's error is a direct transfer of a rule in his or her native language. Take something as simple to speakers of English as *the* and *a.* Often, native speakers of Russian use them sporadically, if at all, as their language has no analogs to them. The celebrated ballet dancer Mikhail Baryshnikov, on a TV salute to Broadway with Liza Minelli, said to her that they could "go through mirror" (to Wonderland). When she asked, "Do you know who he is?", pointing to the character from *Cabaret,* he answered "Master of Ceremonies," rather than "The Master ..."

Many European speakers simply transfer their own rules for articles to English, saying things like "I broke the hand," because, in their languages the equivalent of *my* would not be used. My grandmother always washed her "hairs" rather than her "hair" because in her native language *hair* took a plural ending.

Germans whose English is otherwise impeccable may still say, "I appreciate to keep in touch." Because the rules of infinitives and gerunds (English *to*+verb and verb+*ing*) differ so from one European language to the next, this often is an area of bilingual error. Americans learning Portuguese, for instance, mistakenly say "Ele tem de *falando*" for 'He is afraid of speaking', rather than the correct "Ele tem de *falar.*" The problem is that the form *falar* is roughly equivalent to the English 'to speak', and the form *falando* is roughly equivalent to the English 'speaking'. As it happens, Portuguese uses *falar* after *medo de* and English uses *speaking* after *afraid of.* Since *medo de* is the translation of English *afraid of,*

English speakers substitute *falando* for *falar* even after they have been repeatedly corrected.

This interference of rules across languages is reminiscent of the baby who persists in saying 'goed' or 'nother one spoon.' The rules the child has figured out for himself or herself seem to act as interference much as the rules of an older speaker's first language interfere with learning a second language. Another factor may also come into play in such interference. Recall that unless there is some social reason for so doing, speakers often do not remember the exact words and phrases used in a conversation. They remember semantic content or actual lexical choices, not syntactic form. The parallel to this phenomenon is that people do not always notice the syntax that another speaker is using to encode an idea. Much of the so-called bilingual interference perhaps proceeds from the same cause. That is, the speaker simply does not always notice the grammar actually used by native speakers, much less all of the particulars of where it differs from his or her own first language. This explains why people can live in a country that is not their native land for most of their lives and never get the grammar rules of the newer language down pat. They can get their ideas across well enough without knowing all the fine points, so they do not necessarily notice them. It is even an economy not to get hung up on all the fine points of a second language. One can communicate without them. Furthermore, some grammatical errors are acceptable when uttered by persons who are patently not native speakers. If speakers were not willing—or able—to communicate in a new language without native speaker competence, it would hinder them greatly in social interaction. Imagine if one had to stop to notice every single grammatical form one wanted to use, comparing it to one's native language to notice under what conditions one would use it in both the old and the new! Perhaps bilingual interference results more from the wish to hurry up and speak the new language than from any loss of ability to learn new grammars after a certain age.

10.5   *Interference: lexical*

There are far more words in any language than there are sounds or grammar rules. Learning new words must continue throughout a person's lifetime, especially in societies where there are always new objects being invented, new ideas requiring new labels, even new words for old things. For instance, who today speaks of a *piazza* rather than a *porch* or *deck*? Do you drive a *machine* instead of a *car*? If you do, you would be marked as an out-of-date person. Your grandparents probably do not speak of *behaviorism* as a theory in childrearing. But, younger educated speakers may prefer that word, which makes the time-honored system that grandparents used, that of rewarding good behavior and punishing bad, sound more modern and scientific.

Recall that even if two languages both have a word for the same thing, other meanings of that word will not necessarily be the same. In no language does a word have just one meaning. That would be most uneconomical, requiring that speakers have separate words for each and every concept. Also, it would prevent language from being flexible. Only if a word can mean many things is flexibility ensured, so that old words can be used in new ways. Each word has attached to it a constellation of meanings. During former President Carter's visit to Poland, a U.S. government translator embarrassed the government by mistranslating the verb *desire,* accidentally choosing a completely inappropriate Polish word translatable by one meaning of English *desire.* Unfortunately for the dignity of the United States, it was the Polish word for 'sexual desire, lust'. The Polish have a completely separate word for English *desire* in the sense of 'would like to', as in "We desire (would like) to be friends." English happens to attach both meanings as well as others to that one word, but Polish happens not to.

Similarly, Americans are unfamiliar with the older Germanic meaning of *corn,* meaning 'grain'. They think that the Bette Davis movie *The Corn Is Green* refers to American ears of corn, missing the metaphor of the title completely, since corn on the cob is, of course, green on the outside. In some American cities there are Jewish bakeries that sell corn bread. Americans, even those who are Jewish, often assume that such bread is made from corn meal, but it is not. It is made from rye, one of the grains called *korn* in Yiddish. In older English *corn* also meant 'rye' as well as other grains. I have seen people leave a bakery emptyhanded when told there is no corn bread, only rye.

Often general words, words without very specific semantic features, are transferred from one language to another. For instance, the Pennsylvania Dutch say "It gives rain" under the influence of "Es gebt rejje." Native speakers of Yiddish can be identified by "Give a look" on the model of Yiddish "Gib a kijk!"

If the bilingual's original language has a word that sounds like one in the target language but has a different meaning, frequently that word will change to the meaning of the new language. This has been the fate of the Italian *fattoria*, which in America now means 'factory' but in Italy meant 'farm'. Greek *karro,* now 'car', originally meant 'wagon'. American Portuguese *pinchar* now means 'pinch' as well as its original 'jump' (Weinreich 1968).

English words have crept into virtually all of the immigrant languages. Florida Spanish has *pelota de fly* for 'fly ball' (Sawyer 1964). American German has *fleysch pie* for 'meat pie'. Italian restaurants now offer *zuppa di clam* rather than *zuppa di vongole,* a dish of clams in tomato sauce. Mexican American boys can be very *tufo* (tough) as they race cars with tires that are *eslica* 'slick'. A car has a *breca* 'brake', *bomper* 'bumper' and *guipa* 'wiper.' 'To be out of control' is *esta fuera de control* (Ayer 1969). A great number of such examples could be supplied from every language spoken in the United States and Canada. Even where immigrant languages have survived, often they become Americanized.

10.6   *Borrowing*

This is not a true creolization process, however. What happens is that people borrow into their own language words from cultures that are their points of reference. This is a counterpart of dialect copying. Janda (1975) shows that Hungarians in Chicago who are bent upon not becoming Americanized and refuse to learn English still borrow English words. Similarly, despite the railings of purists, people in one country will borrow words from another language if they admire its speakers or consider them the trendsetters. In France, for example, to the horror of some academicians, words like *drugstore, weekend,* and *interview* have been adopted into French. In Israel, English words have been adopted wholesale into Hebrew, such as *bebi siter* 'baby sitter', *agresii* 'aggressive', and *obyektiviut* 'objective' (Davis 1979). In the United States, many immigrants borrowed Americanisms because they were anxious to become American as soon as possible. They did not want to be considered "greenhorns." Even those who were less anxious to assimilate had to borrow some aspects of U.S. culture and inevitably some vocabulary.

English itself has a long history of such borrowings. Even common words like *veal, pork, beef, chair, table,* and *very* derive from the days after the Norman Conquest when the conquered English borrowed French culture. A major part of our educated and scientific vocabulary was borrowed from Greek and Latin, long the languages of all scholarly writing. Among these borrowings are *physician, mathematics, logic, ambulatory, pontificate,* even the word *educate* itself. Words for art and music have been borrowed from Italian, such as *arpeggio, opera, tempo, chiaroscuro,* and *concerto.* The words borrowed from another language give an indication of what that culture is admired for: sports, food, music, clothing, science, academics, art, fighting, or whatever.

If a speaker loses his or her native language but retains some words, typically those words will relate to certain spheres—home, religion, and ethnic culture. A survey of first and second generation Portuguese, Jewish, Italian, Polish, and French Canadian college students revealed that all pretty much knew words and phrases for the same things in their grandparents' native languages: 'understand', 'eat', 'go to sleep', 'go away', 'a rag', words for food, and curses like "Go to Hell."

10.7   *Bilingualism across generations*

During the great waves of immigration to the United States in the nineteenth and early twentieth centuries most who came learned English. Their children learned it, often with no trace of accent of the native language. Usually immigrants' children born in this country learned their parents' language at home, though not always very well. The grandchildren, however, frequently did not learn it at all, except for a few words here and there. Some groups, worried about deculturization, instituted after-school instruction or parochial schools in which at least half-days were done in a foreign language. Greeks, Armenians, French, Chinese, Poles, Germans, Ukrainians, Italians, and Jews are among those who have tried, or are trying, such schooling.

This is quite different from public bilingual schooling for children who come to school already speaking a foreign language which might or might not be their only language. The special after-school or Saturday schools usually are a salvaging attempt. Most have been for children who do not know their grandparents' language or do not know much of it. These have become popular with the increased interest in searching for "roots." Robert DiPietro tells me that there are 250 pupils enrolled in an Italian cultural school in Washington, D.C. There are also foreign language parochial schools that often have both bilingual and monolingual English-speaking pupils; which language predominates depends upon the particular locale of the school.

Both the after-school instruction and day schools run by Jews illustrate especially well the general factors in keeping second languages alive. Rarely if ever are the Jewish schools devoted to keeping Yiddish alive. Their mission is Hebrew, the language of Jewish prayer, of the Bible (Old Testament), and most Jewish explication of the Bible.

Most of the Jews in America today are of Eastern European origin. Their ancestors brought Eastern European pronunciations of Hebrew to their praying and Bible reading. Many American Hebrew schools ignored these traditions, teaching instead the pronunciation of Hebrew used in Israel. This is based upon the Arabic traditions of Hebrew pronunciation, not the European. American Jews largely rejected their Eastern European origins, a fact reflected in the dramatic loss of Yiddish within only two or three generations, as well as the changes in Hebrew pronunciation. Over 1000 years of degrading and humiliating persecution is associated with Yiddish and Eastern European Hebrew. The Israeli Hebrew is associated with bravery, independence, and victory— hence, that is the language taught.

Two small groups of Jews have retained Yiddish: the Chasids and the ultra-Orthodox. The Chasids live in close-knit communities. They and the Orthodox send their children to parochial schools, many of which in New York City are conducted in Yiddish. For these groups, Yiddish is a symbol of their religious commitment, as is education. Because they see Americanization as leading to a loss of religion, they retain Yiddish, although both first and second generations also speak accent-free English. It can be seen that complex factors determine which variety of a language will be retained or dropped, and whether a language will be retained at all.

10.8   *Other groups*

Just as Jews have largely abandoned one variety of Hebrew, many immigrant groups have formally taught their children a standard form of the language, not the dialects they actually brought with them. Many spoke dialects associated with poverty and ignorance, dialects scorned in their native countries. They naturally preferred English, the language of upward mobility and, if it was taught in the public schools, the standard dialect of their native speech.

The larger the community of speakers of a given language, the longer the language is likely to be retained. In earlier decades in areas with large populations of non-English speakers, business, social, and church matters often were not conducted in English. Foreign language newspapers, societies, and radio shows flourished for speakers of Polish, German, Portuguese, Italian, Swedish, Norwegian, Chinese, French, Hungarian, Serbian, Yiddish, Japanese, Greek, Ukrainian, and other languages. With time there has been a steady erosion of non-English languages in the United States (Fishman 1966).

The Lutheran churches traditionally have held services in Norwegian, Swedish, Danish, and German in this country (Hofman 1968). Gradually, however, their services are being switched to English. Similarly, many of the older Italian, Polish, Portuguese, and French Catholic parishes now have most of their masses in English, rather than in the language of the grandparents. (Although masses used to be conducted in Latin, the homilies were often in the language that the immigrants brought with them.)

Foreign language newspaper circulation has been steadily declining for years (Fishman 1966) for most originally non-English-speaking ethnic groups. Robert DiPietro (personal communication) counters that "While some attrition is noted among older newspapers, several new ones have been founded recently. The Italian-English bilingual newspaper called *L'Agenda* is an example."

This points up an interesting development in ethnic newspapers. In recent years the older papers, which were not written in English at all, have declined. They have been replaced by papers that use both English and another language or are printed solely in English. To me, this is another indication that English is winning out at the expense of other languages. It need not be so. In many areas of the world, bilingualism, even multilingualism, is the norm, and everyone is expected to command two or more languages. In Europe, for instance, knowing many languages is a sign of culture and education. In the Philippines it is not unusual for people to speak four or five languages. Social attitudes determine how many languages and which one(s) will be learned.

Before enlarging on this, however, a little digression is in order. Science is not just a matter of gathering data. The same data can be interpreted quite differently by different investigators, with reason and justness on all sides. The issue of ethnic languages in the United States is a case in point. How we evaluate the future of foreign language speaking in America depends partially on our natural optimism or pessimism, as much as on the data. To me, the very fact that ethnic papers must resort to English at all is a reflection of the decline of the languages in question. To Professor DiPietro, the publication of new papers proves that foreign language speaking will survive in this country. Similarly with statistics, Professor DiPietro very conservatively estimates that even if only 5 percent of the Italo-Americans in this country retained their native speech, there would be 1,100,000 Italian speakers. He looks at those who still speak; I look sorrowfully at the 95 percent who do not. Admittedly my own pessimism colors my own conclusions as to the fate of foreign languages in the United States. The readers must beware, however, for others do not share that pessimism. Furthermore, my views are colored by the social situation in the United States to date, but changes in attitude may occur, altering that situation. It must be strongly emphasized that the issues that determine linguistic pluralism are sociological. The United States is used as an example of which factors lead to linguistic pluralism and which do not. It should be pointed out that the following remarks do not apply to Canada, which has a stronger tradition of linguistic pluralism. That country officially is both French- and English-speaking, and, in large cities, such as Toronto, there are sizable enclaves of speakers of other languages as well.

10.9   *Isolation*

It has already been noted that foreign languages survive best where there are large enough populations so that daily social activities can be carried on in that language. The corollary to that is that languages survive where their speakers live together in the same neighborhoods or communities. A further corollary is that the languages survive where people are somewhat isolated, physically or psychologically, from the mainstream.

The Chasidic and Orthodox Jews who manage to retain Yiddish live together in their own neighborhoods. One is reminded also of the retention of Chinese on the streets of the Chinatowns of large cities like New York and San Francisco. The isolation of Puerto-Ricans and Mexican-Americans has led to their retaining their dialects of Spanish.

As each originally foreign group has produced college graduates and other upwardly mobile young, their old neighborhoods have started to disperse. The population of the German neighborhoods of Chicago, for instance, decreased from 161,567 to 99,413 in the ten years from 1960 to 1970. Despite the existence of German shops, churches, radio programs, children's singing groups, soccer teams, choruses, clubs, and Saturday schools to teach German, the language is less and less spoken (Taylor 1970). Many of those who spoke languages other than English have joined the rest of the middle-class in flight to the suburbs. With this often comes weakening of ethnicity and second language speaking. It is only natural that creatures as social as human beings wish to be as much like their neighbors as possible.

This occurs even in tight-knit groups most determined not to lose their identity. For example, many Ukrainians sought refuge from Communism in America after World War II. Hoping to return to their homeland, they made very sure that their children learned to speak Ukrainian with native speaker competency, to cook Ukrainian foods, to dance all the traditional dances, and to do all the traditional crafts, including the intricate art of dying Easter eggs in exquisite patterns. Above all, they tried to instill in their children a love for their ancestral homeland. To Americans, these Ukrainians seem to have done a marvelous job of keeping their language and traditions alive. However, Olenka Hanushevsky, an American-born Ukrainian, informed me that the older generation exclaim at "how American the young are becoming." Similarly, Hungarian refugees from the Russian invasion in the 1950s who have never become acclimated to their new homes have children who are proficient in English and are becoming increasingly American (Janda 1975).

The tendency for other languages to be abandoned in favor of English has traditionally been powerful among immigrants to the United States. Where this has not happened, certain sociological factors have usually prevented the absorption of a particular community into the mainstream culture. Frequently such factors have been imposed on the community from the outside. No matter how much national ethnic pride a given group has, experience in this country has shown that its language will give way to English. This is not to say that all languages other than English are doomed to extinction. A new pride in their original languages seems to be manifested by many groups. Perhaps this will help the survival of these languages in at least some social contexts in future years.

10.10   *Resisting English*

The original languages of some groups have remained dominant for two, three, and four generations. This includes those, such as Mexican-Americans, whose ancestors spoke those languages on this continent before English became the rule. In spite of the fact that Spanish was spoken in the American Southwest long before English, for instance, it is surprising that English is not the dominant language for everyone there today. Nor is it for many Puerto Ricans in the Northeast.

This has not been the case with other non-English speakers on this continent. The Louisiana and French Canadian speakers have as much historical justification for their languages as do English speakers. In the United States, nowadays, those who speak French usually also speak English and, as with other language groups, there has been a falling off of younger bilingual speakers. Even the American Indians have, by and large, become speakers of English. The trend usually is toward the language of those who wield the power.

On another continent with a parallel situation, the Irish, despite centuries of brutal treatment by the British, largely abandoned Gaelic as their first language. By 1850 only about 5 percent of the Irish were monolingual Gaelic speakers. Macnamara (1971) claims that this is because English is the language one must know in order to get and hold a job.

This is not a plea for Spanish speakers to give up Spanish. Far from it! It is just that in the normal course of things most Americans, even those with a tremendous pride in their national origins, have begun to favor English. Why, then, has a large population remained primarily Spanish-speaking, especially when the language needed for advancement in jobs and education is usually English?

10.11   *Isolation as a factor in language retention*

The reader may recall that dialect investigations show that the lowest classes make virtually no attempt to adopt features of prestige speech. Having no hope of entering the middle classes, these speakers do not bother with middle-class prestige norms. There seems little sense in talking like people one has no hope of joining. Members of the lower middle class, who are more likely to move upward, have been found to use prestige features in formal situations even more than the middle class itself (Labov 1966). This was a clear sign of their upward mobility.

Donald Lance (1972) offers a neat example of generational differences in speaking Spanish. In one family he found that the grandparents, although born in Texas, were both illiterate. The grandmother did not speak English at all, although she appeared to understand it. The grandfather, a gardener, spoke English only if the hearer did not know Spanish. The daughter and her husband seemed equally proficient in both Spanish and English, although when speaking Spanish they would throw in a few English words. When speaking English they did not seem to interject Spanish words. In the presence of an "Anglo," they relied on English. Their children were also bilingual but were inhibited about using Spanish and could not talk into a tape recorder at all in Spanish. Although they admitted they could talk Spanish with a Hispanic person, they found it almost impossible to do so with an Anglo. This could indicate that they had been socialized to speak Spanish only with Spanish speakers and to do so with others would be as impossible as arguing with a priest's sermon during a mass at St. Patrick's Cathedral. The words just would not come out! One is reminded of schoolchildren who do poorly in testing situations that do not conform to the conditions for verbal performance for their culture.

Janet Sawyer (1964) found that in the Southwest Spanish speakers avoided using Spanish terms whenever they could, even terms that Anglos typically use like *corral, lariat, frijoles,* and *chaps*. If they must utter a Spanish word, even their own names, they anglicize it.

Such behavior is typical of other originally foreign-speaking groups as well. Jews anglicized the names of their foods, so that, in New York City, *kishke,* a kind of sausage, became *stuffed derma* on many a menu. *Kneydlach*, little dumplings, became *matzoh balls*. People with Yiddish names Americanized them, so that *Bayla* became *Bella,* and *Tible* became *Toby*. Not always knowing that some names were really nicknames in English, they erroneously adopted them, like *Jack* for *Yankel,* or *Ted* for *Tunnie*. The Italian *Roberto*s, *Vincenzo*s, and *Pasco*s of my high school years have all turned into *Robert*s,

*Vincent*s, and *Pat*s. Like the Spanish, the Italians have anglicized Italian words borrowed into English, including names. In last names like *Miglaccio,* the *g* would not be pronounced in Italy, but in America it is, and names like *Cedrone,* which has an Italian pronunciation of "Chedrone" are Americanized to /sɪdron/. Such anglicizing has generally characterized those who eventually gave up their native languages. Whether this will happen with the Southwest Spanish, too, remains to be seen.

10.12   *Who retains Spanish?*

Those who cannot join it do not bother trying to talk like the mainstream. In dialect investigations, recall, it was found that the lower classes prefer features associated with that class. It is solidarity, not status, that those speech features signify. The analog to this situation is seen in Spanish speakers in the United States. Since they have been effectively barred from upward mobility, many Spanish speakers have not bothered much with English, the language of mobility. Why bother if it gets you nowhere? Unfortunately, much of the retention of Spanish by the North American Hispanic population attests to their degree of social isolation. There may well be mitigating factors, however, that will enable Spanish speaking to remain alive in the United States even as the Hispanic population loses its isolation.

It must not be supposed that the only Hispanics who have retained Spanish are the lower class poor. Far from it! The very numbers of Spanish speakers in the United States are a big factor in that language's not dying out. Those who moved upward still have families and many friends who speak Spanish. The need for Spanish bilingual professionals is very great; Spanish-speaking teachers, doctors, lawyers, nurses, and social workers are in demand. This helps the middle class to keep the language. Having had the opportunity to see how other languages have fared once their speakers moved upward may make middle-class Hispanics more careful to ensure that their children do learn Spanish. Finally, unlike many of the languages brought to these shores, Spanish, like English, is very widely spoken throughout the world. In terms of business, politics, and education, it is an extremely valuable international language. This too may help ensure its survival alongside English in the United States.

10.13   *Language shift as a bonding device*

Fishman (1970) gives a long dialogue between a Hispanic employer and secretary. He shows that the man used English to dictate a business letter and the woman responded in English. As soon as the dictation was done, however, conversation moved to the topic of a coming Puerto Rican parade.

Concurrent with the topic shift came a shift in language. The switch into a second, shared language symbolizes the values associated with a cultural activity, such as the Puerto Rican parade, itself an affirmation of group loyalty.

Gumperz and Hernández-Chávez (1972) show similar language switching between Mexican-Americans:

> *Woman:*   Well, I'm glad that I met you, okay?
> *Man:*   Andale, pues and do come again, mmm? . . . Con ellos dos. With each other. La señora trabaja en la canería orita, you know? She was . . . con Francine jugaba . . . with my little girl.

Gumperz and Hernández-Chávez point out that this kind of switching is not related to differences in topics or setting, factors that often determine style shifting within a language. Rather, lapsing into Spanish signifies more warmth. It is akin to using a more casual, intimate style within a language.

Sometimes a language switch is used for emphasis, as in "I say, Lupe, no hombre, don't believe that." A Yiddish parallel is "I'll give you nothing, gar nisht!" An Italian one is effected kinesically by flicking the forefinger under the chin, which is jutted out belligerently. In areas where Italians and Jews are in frequent contact, it is not uncommon to see the "gar nisht" accompanied by the Italian gesture.

The change from one language to another, in itself, has meaning. No matter what else such a switch means, it reinforces bonds between speakers. Such switching can obviously only be done between those who speak the same languages. It may be done in the presence of non-speakers as a way of excluding them, just as jargons may.

Sometimes a foreign language phrase will be thrown out to see if a stranger really belongs. Italians, for instance, often interject a "Kabeesh?" 'understand?', or Jews ask "Verstehst?" The NNE *dig* for 'understand' has been traced to West African *dega,* apparently having once been used the same way. This can be done by people who have no real knowledge of their ancestral tongue, commanding only a few words or phrases. Paradoxically, it can also be used by those of other ethnic backgrounds as a way of saying 'Even though I am not of the same group as you, I still feel warmth for it.' or even 'Just because I'm not one of you don't think you can put one over on me.' All of these messages can be made across dialects as well, with someone deliberately throwing out a word or pronunciation in another's dialect. It is also heard stylistically, as when someone raises or lowers style either to achieve more intimacy or to sound tougher or more in the know.

Switching to a second language when talking about cultural or home affairs is also a way of reinforcing that the cultural heritage is not that of the first language. Susan Ervin-Tripp (1967) found that Japanese war brides had to slip into Japanese when talking about domestic concerns. It may also be that the person is used to discussing certain matters in one language rather than another, and the grammar and vocabulary in the more familiar language are therefore more accessible than in a second language.

A bilingual speaker's use of two languages, then, is strongly motivated by social situation and topic of conversation, as well as by the very real need to identify with compatriots. Language switching is the counterpart of dialect and style switching, with the difference that bilinguals have the resources of another language in their repertoire.

10.14   *The future of bilingualism in the United States*

Until recently, Spanish has been retained largely because of the real alienation of a large proportion of Hispanics and their inability to enter the mainstream. Fortunately this isolation seems to be changing, so that more Spanish speakers may achieve upward mobility as other groups have. This does not mean that Spanish speaking is going to die out in the United States. There is reason to believe that Spanish may not suffer the same fate as so many other non-English languages. One factor in the survival of Spanish certainly is the continuing immigration of Hispanics into the country, as well as the ready contact with relatives and friends from Spanish-speaking countries. Continued influx of speakers helps in the maintenance of a language.

Southeastern Massachusetts and Rhode Island have seen this dramatically with Portuguese speakers. Once liberalized immigration laws were effected, newly arrived Portuguese speakers encouraged previously settled Portuguese to retain or even learn the language. A demand grew for bilingual teachers and other professionals, so that interest in the formal study of Portuguese grew. Americans of Portuguese ancestry who were foremen in factories, shop stewards, and builders and who had not learned Portuguese as children soon saw a need to learn it in adulthood. Others who had, now had good reason not to forget it.

Another factor that may help keep bilingualism alive is that nowadays even people of ordinary means can travel. The advent of the airplane and charge cards means that people can visit their homeland or that of their parents. This is another powerful influence in retaining an ancestral language. Members of many ethnic groups—Ukrainians, Finns, and Greeks, for instance—have all told me that their children learned those languages so that they could speak with their relatives in the Old Country during visits.

10.15   *American Indians*

One reason that earlier immigrants gave up their native languages was that one had to speak English to be American. The only groups to which this did not apply were the Spanish and the French. Large parts of North America were

Spanish speaking and Mexico and Puerto Rico still are. Louisiana was originally French speaking and, of course, Quebec still is.

Ironically, the original inhabitants of America, the Indians, were never allowed to claim their languages as American. Many people naively think of American Indians as being a monolithic group. Actually, different tribes with very different cultures and languages extend from Maine to Florida, Alaska to California, and all points in between. There were at least thirteen large and extensive Indian language families. Each family had or has several separate languages and dialects. (A language family is a group of languages that can be shown to have sprung from one common language. Most of the languages of Europe and some of India, for instance, have all descended from one now dead language called Proto Indo-European. English, Russian, German, French, Italian, Swedish, and Rumanian are all members of this family, for example. Chinese belongs to a completely different family, as does Finnish.) Imagine thirteen language families among the American Indians! The languages within each could be as different as Sicilian is from Prussian, and from one language family to the next, as different as Japanese is from Gaelic.

Yet so unimportant have American Indians been to their usurpers that Ohanessian in 1972 could complain that we did not know how many Indians of any type were monolingual Indian speakers, how many were bilingual, what sorts of English were spoken by different Indian groups, how many did not speak tribal languages at all, in what social settings Indian languages were used and in what settings English was used, what sorts of differences there were between the generations in language use, or what attitudes the Indians had toward English and toward their tribal languages.

These are crucial questions if Indian children are to be educated effectively. For instance, it is well known that non-standard-speaking children stand a far greater chance of learning to read if teachers understand how their dialects differ from SE. Then, teachers can translate from the children's dialects into SE. They know in advance what will require special attention. In order to teach speakers of other languages, it is best to know where the two language systems conflict.

Ohanessian points out that different tribal attitudes and beliefs may have strong implications for whether or not Indian children learn English at all. The Mojave Indians think that the Indians know their language at birth. Some Indian groups believe that there is a relationship between race and language and that Indian blood is a prerequisite for learning Indian speech, an idea that no doubt was reinforced by the failure of Anglos to learn Indian tongues. The implication of such a belief is that Indians cannot learn to speak English.

Such a belief can be a definite hindrance in learning a new language. In fact, the reason that many Americans give for being monolingual is that they "don't have an ear for languages." Yet in many cases, their ancestors were bilingual or even multilingual. We know that people will speak more than one language if their society expects it. Language learning is not a matter of individual heredity, but of cultural attitudes and social necessity.

This is not to say that most American Indians do not speak English. Many have almost completely lost tribal languages, but some of these speak dialects of American Indian English that differ considerably from SE. It has long been established that such differences can be a prime cause of school failure if the teacher is not aware of them. Considering the grinding poverty on the reservations, this is not a slight problem.

Sociolinguistics has a great deal to contribute to Indian education. Studies of differences in discourse practices between Indian and Anglo, such as those by Susan Philips for the Warm Springs Indians (1970, 1976), would make schoolteaching far more effective. Contrastive analysis of American Indian English versus Anglo speech would make instruction in reading and writing far more effective (Labov 1967; Baratz and Shuy 1969, DiPietro 1971). Where an Indian population is bilingual, contrastive analysis between their language and English would enhance teaching in English.

10.16   *Diglossia*

Some countries normally have what Ferguson (1971) labeled a **diglossia** situation. This means that one language is normally used for high matters such as government, religion, and education and another for everyday concerns. Diglossia can occur with dialects as well, as when a speaker always uses one dialect in some situations and another dialect in other situations. The typical examples in the English-speaking world are American Blacks and British regional speakers. Many Blacks command both NNE and SE, switching from one to the other as the occasion demands. Some speakers of British regional dialects also command RP, switching according to social situation. Typically, with diglossia each language or dialect is used only in specified situations. Diglossia is actually an extreme case of style switching, one in which an entire dialect or language is used as the marker of style. Whether one switches styles or dialects or languages depends upon the individual's repertoire of language. Each person has a repertoire from which to draw for different social purposes.

Diglossia can occur in many situations. It is evident in the Southwest Spanish speakers who feel inhibited about speaking Spanish in Anglo situations. In Paraguay the Indians use Guarani for intimacy and other matters relating to social solidarity, but Spanish for education, religion, government, and high culture. Pre-revolutionary Russians of noble birth spoke French on social occasions, as did many of the high-born throughout Europe, but spoke Russian elsewhere.

Religion is a common sphere for diglossia. Roman Catholics used to say their prayers in Latin, and their theologians discussed religion in Latin, but other conversation was in the national languages. The high-flown, archaic English of the King James Bible is a dialectal diglossia limited to religion. Religions typically depend upon dead languages and archaic dialects, a form of speech no longer used for daily business, for their scriptures and prayers. Sanskrit, Hebrew, and Latin are examples of dead languages so used. The dead language separates religion from mundane activity and, since it is ancient, it has an aura of purity about it that spoken languages lack. Religions that do not have dead languages often use archaic forms for the same purpose, such as English *thou art* and *he leadeth.*

It should not be supposed that situation alone determines switching from one language to another. It is just that in a book devoted to the social aspects of language use, situation of language choice is naturally emphasized. The interested reader will want to delve more deeply into the linguistics and psycholinguistics of bilingualism.

10.17 *Language planning*

In as monolingual a country as the United States, it is hard to realize how important the issue of language choice is in much of the world. The issues have always been clear for our own foreign speakers. English is the official language of the land for all purposes, and if one wishes to enter into mainstream society, one must learn English. This is not necessarily a bad thing. A unified country requires that one language be understood and usable by virtually everyone.

We have already seen that a common language forges social bonds. The corollary is that different languages reinforce separation, even hostility. For example, recently the New England Telephone company has started printing its bills in Spanish and Portuguese as well as English. As harmless as this may seem, it has excited irritation and hostility from some Americans who apparently feel that if immigrants are going to come here, they can jolly well learn English. Interestingly, much of this hostility comes from first and second generation Americans who say that their forebears had to learn English and these immigrants should have to as well.

All modern nations require an official language. This creates and has created some tremendous problems in countries in which the choice has not been so clear as in the United States. In Canada, for instance, the French have an equivalent, actually a prior, claim to official status for their language. They bitterly resented the concept of English as the official language for everything, wanting French to have equal status in education and law. Accordingly, recent laws have instituted bilingual education, so that younger speakers can converse with each other and even read the same books. Now many English speakers bitterly resent having to learn French!

Teaching in French legitimizes that language. Children taught French as a medium of education are more likely to feel that it is as "good" as English than they do if French remains only the language of the home and the streets. It must be emphasized that in Canada bilingualism extends through the university levels. French is equivalent to English at all ranks of education.

Various ethnic groups in the United States want similar bilingual education. When the United States government funds bilingual programs typically they cover the elementary grades, and most have the aim of turning foreign speakers into English speakers. This is frequently deplored. However, there are some arguments in favor of such an aim. English has become the language of scholarship throughout the world. Many textbooks are written solely in English. As noted previously, academic conferences, including those in other countries, are often held in English. As students go further up the educational ladder, English becomes more and more important, even in countries in which English is not an official language.

There is some question about teaching basic skills in one language when the higher studies based on those skills have to be done in another language. This is a consideration especially in mathematics. It is not known to what degree, if any, learning basic mathematics in one language can hamper a person in complex mathematical formulations in advanced studies. Paradoxically, it is advantageous to teach reading to future English users in languages like Italian and Spanish rather than English. Whatever skills are involved in reading alphabetic systems are apparently similar from one to the other. Once someone learns to read one alphabetic system, it is not difficult to transfer those skills to another, especially to one that uses pretty much the same letters. Since both Italian and Spanish spelling have a good fit with the actual pronunciation of both languages, it is relatively easy for their speakers to learn to read them. English spelling shows a very poor fit to even the standard varieties of the language. Furthermore, it is often chaotic. Consider, for instance, that the letters *ea* are pronounced differently in *head, great, heart* and *meat.* It is far more difficult to learn to read English than languages like Spanish and Italian. Because of this, children who learn to read in those languages learn more quickly and are thus able to get a jump start on subject matter. It has been found that if Spanish-speaking children are first taught to read in their own language, they accelerate more rapidly than children who have to learn to read in English. Once children have cracked the code, that is, figured out what is going on in reading, it is easy for them to transfer their reading skills to English.

As tough as it may be for speakers of other languages living in the United States, for reasons of personal advancement they really have to learn English. In contrast, English-speaking Americans often see no reason to learn other languages. The situation is compounded by the fact that so many American speakers of other languages prefer not to speak them with outsiders, reserving those languages for purposes of solidarity.

So long as English is the language of higher education, business, and government in the United States, it will be the language everyone has to learn to advance. To put it another way, if we do not make a strong effort to teach it to children who speak other languages, then we are ensuring that those children will have little chance for advancement later. This does not mean that other languages must be obliterated, only that English must be taught for some educational and social purposes.

10.18   *Other countries*

Things are not so clear in other countries. Many modern nations have been forged from disparate groups or tribes, all speaking radically different languages, all having a stronger commitment to those languages than to their governments or other peoples in the new nation. Yet official languages are needed both for government and for education.

In most instances, a colonial power bequeathed its language: French, Dutch, Spanish, Portuguese, or English. This is retained for government and higher education. As already noted, to be able to read advanced textbooks, students going on to college must know a European language, with English increasingly taking the edge. The colonial languages might seem to be good choices as national languages for the new countries that inherited them. But language is a very personal, very emotional issue. Former colonies often hated their old rulers. European languages are anathema to many in the Third World. Even those who see the need for French, English, or Spanish in international affairs or at university level education deplore such languages for primary school children or even for local government. They do not want four-year-olds to have to learn them as the sole languages of school. Nor do they want businesses conducted in them, or radio or TV shows. In regions where as many as ten or even twenty separate languages are spoken, this is no trifling matter.

The problem is compounded by the lack of writing systems for many native languages. Phonetic transcriptions can be devised by linguists, but, even if they are, what will become the official orthography for the country? What script will newspapers use? What will be used in business? All of these problems are further complicated by the intense emotional commitment of people to their own language. Recall that after generations of terrible oppression the Blacks in South Africa finally rioted over the issue of what language would be used in the schools for Blacks in Soweto. Language riots have occurred in other countries, as in India after the British withdrew.

Because of the problems caused by multilingualism in new nations, some linguists and sociolinguists have become involved in language planning. Before a language is made official, a careful study is needed to determine the attitudes toward it. Planners must decide what language(s) will be used in elementary schools. It must be one that will not repulse natives, one that natives feel comfortable using in the social situations: school, business, movies, etc.

Planners must acknowledge that such decisions have far-reaching social and political effects. If one language is not used for schooling, business, or government, it is likely to lose prestige socially. Judging by the experiences of the United States, if enough speakers get an opportunity to learn another official tongue, their children will make less and less of an effort to learn their family's original language(s). This can lead to weakening of family and social bonds. The old grandmother or grandfather who cannot speak the new language, or cannot speak it well, cannot converse readily with the younger generation.

Worse, perhaps, grandparental authority is weakened. If the language becomes outdated, then the traditional wisdom of the old is also considered outmoded. Many an immigrant grandmother in twentieth century America found herself denied traditional grandparenting with her children's children, who literally could not speak her language. It has long seemed to me that this has been one cause of the "old age problem" in America today. Choosing of official languages must take this into account. What is the role of the elderly in a culture, and what language(s) are those roles encoded into? How can these languages be preserved as worthy means of communication even if another must be made official for other reasons? Such questions and their solutions must be a part of any language planning. Perhaps the solution should be the same as one that has been used effectively for teaching SE to NSE speakers: set up sociodramatic situations in the school in which different languages would be switched into and out of according to the drama being enacted. In other words, schools in multilingual countries should teach and encourage language switching as part of their regular curriculum. This should be done in American bilingual programs as well.

Language planners, in their selection of one language over the other, must also be very aware of political consequences. Natives who already speak the language chosen have an advantage over those who do not. In terms of carving out sinecures and of getting advantageous connections, this edge can last for generations. The fact that one language is chosen also makes its speakers seem more important than those of languages not chosen. If Western experience is any guide, usually the language not chosen is doomed unless its speakers are isolated. The reverse may also become true as those who do not speak the official languages are likely to become isolated.

There is no way to consider language use without considering its impact on the very fabric of society and government. There is no way to consider any human group without considering its language use. There is no way to consider language fully without considering its social uses, nor to consider any society without considering its language use.

EXERCISES

1. Survey foreign language newspapers or radio or TV shows in your locality. How many for each language can you find? Select one for in-depth reporting. Is it monolingual or bilingual? If the latter, what percentage of time is English used? (For shows, take an average hour, or morning, etc.)

2. From any of your sources above, note what languages advertisements are in and for what items. What gets advertised in the foreign language medium? What conclusions do you draw from this about the prestige of English and the other language, how each is viewed, and for what purposes?

3. Take five words pertaining to religion, science, or foods. Using a dictionary like the Oxford English Dictionary or Random House, check on the derivation of these words. Make a chart of those that were originally borrowed from other languages. What does this chart tell you about points of reference for each of your categories?

REFERENCES

Abbott, E. A. 1870. *A Shakespearian Grammar.* New York: Dover Publications. Reprinted 1966.

Abercrombie, D. 1967. *Elements of General Phonetics.* Chicago: Aldine.

Abrahams, R. D. 1972. The training of the man of words in talking sweet. *Language in Society* *1*:15–30.

Abrahams, R. D. 1974. Black talking in the streets. In R. Bauman and J. Sherzer, eds., pp. 240–262.

Adams, P. ed. 1972 *Language in Thinking.* Baltimore: Penguin.

Alatis, J., ed. 1970. Monograph series on Languages and Linguistics. Bilingualism and Language Contact: Anthropological, Linguistic, Psychological and Sociological Aspects. Washington, D.C.: Georgetown University Press.

Allen, H. B. and G. N. Underwood. 1971. *Readings in American Dialectology.* New York: Appleton–Century–Crofts.

Allport, G. W. and H. Cantril. 1934. Judging personality from voice. In J. Laver and S. Hutcheson, eds., pp. 155–171.

Andreasen, N. 1973. James Joyce, a portrait of the artist as a schizoid. *Journal of the American Medical Association. 224:*67–71.

Anshen, F. 1978. *Statistics for Linguists.* Rowley, Mass.: Newbury House.

Argyle M., and J. Dean. 1965. Eye contact, distance, and affiliation. In J. Laver and S. Hutcheson, eds. pp. 301–316.

Austin, J. L. 1962. *How to Do Things with Words,* 2nd ed. J. Urmson and M. Sbisa, eds. Cambridge, Mass.: Harvard University Press.

Ayer, G. 1969. Language and attitudes of the Spanish-speaking youth of the Southwestern United States. In G. Perren and J. Trim, eds. pp. 115–120.

Bailey, C. J. N. 1973. *Variation and Linguistic Theory.* Arlington, Va.: Center for Applied Linguistics.

Bales, R. F. 1955.How people interact in conferences. *Scientific American.* March pp. 3–7.

Baratz, J. and R. Shuy, eds. 1969. *Teaching Black Children to Read.* Washington, D.C.: Center for Applied Linguistics.

Barker, R. G. M., ed. 1963. *The Stream of Behavior.* New York: Appleton–Century–Crofts.

Baron, N. 1977. The acquisition of indirect reference: functional motivations for continued language learning in children. *Lingua 42:*349–364.

Baumann, R., and J. Sherzer, eds. 1974. *Explorations in the Ethnography of Speaking.* New York: Cambridge University Press.

Bazell, C. E., J. C. Catford, M. A. K. Halliday, and R. M. Robins, eds. 1966. *In Memory of J. P. Firth.* London: Longman.

Befu, H. 1975. Konnichiwa, an essay read at the Japan Society luncheon, San Francisco, April 28, quoted by E. Goody in E. Goody, ed. p. 9.

Bellugi, U., and S. Fischer 1972. A comparison of sign language and spoken language. *Cognition 1:* 173–200.

Berko, J. 1958. The child's learning of English morphology. *Word 14:* 150–177.

Bereiter, C. and S. Engelmann. 1966. *Teaching Disadvantaged Children in the Pre-School.* Englewood Cliffs, N.J.: Prentice–Hall.

Bernstein, B. 1971. *Class, Codes, and Control,* vol. 1. London: Routledge & Kegan–Paul.

Birdwhistell, R. L. 1970.*Kinesics and Context.* Philadelphia: University of Pennsylvania Press.

Bloom, L. 1970. *Language Development: Form and Function in Emerging Grammars.* Cambridge, Mass.: MIT Press.

Bloomfield, L. 1965. *Language History from Language.* H. Hoijer, ed. New York: Holt, Rinehart, and Winston.

Blount, B. and M. Sanches, eds. 1977. *Sociocultural Dimensions of Language Change.* New York: Academic.

Boggs, S. 1972. The meaning of questions and narratives to Hawaiian children. In C. Cazden, V. John, and D. Hymes, eds., pp. 299–327.

Bolinger, D. 1975. *Aspects of Language.* New York: Harcourt, Brace, and Jovanovich.

Bowen, J. D. and J. Ornstein, eds. 1976. *Studies in Southwest Spanish.* Rowley, Mass.: Newbury House.

Brown, P., and S. Levinson, 1978. Universals in language usage: politeness phenomena. In E. Goody, ed., pp. 66–69.

Brown, R. 1973.*A First Language: the Early Stages.* Cambridge, Mass: Harvard University Press.

Brown, R., and A. Gilman. 1960. The pronouns of power and solidarity. In T. Sebeok, ed., pp. 253–76.

Burt, M., and C. Kiparsky. 1972. *The Gooficon: a Repair Manual for English.* Rowley, Mass.: Newbury House.

Butturff, D. and E. Epstein, eds. 1978. *Women's Language and Style.* Akron, Ohio: University of Akron Press.

Carranza, M. A. and E. B. Ryan. 1975. Evaluative reactions of bilingual Anglo and Mexican American adolescents towards speakers of English and Spanish. *International Journal of the Sociology of Language 6:* 83–104.

Carswell, E. A. and R. Rommetveit. 1971. *Social Contexts of Messages.* New York: Academic Press.

Cazden, D., V. P. John, and D. Hymes, eds. 1972. *Functions of Language in the Classroom.* New York: Teacher's College Press.

Chafe, W. 1968. Idiomaticity as an anomaly in the Chomskyan paradigm. *Foundations of Language 4:* 109–127.

Chaika, E. 1973. Hi! How Are You? Paper delivered at Linguistic Society of America 48th annual meeting, San Diego, Calif. ERIC documents.

Chaika, E. 1974. A linguist looks at "schizophrenic" language. *Brain and Language 1:* 257–276.

Chaika, E. 1976. The possibility principle in semantics. *Interfaces 6:* 9–12.

Chaika, E. 1977. Schizophrenic speech, slips of the tongue, and jargonaphasia: a reply to Fromkin and to Lecours and Vaniers-Clement. *Brain and Language 4:* 464–475.

Chaika, E. 1978. Grammars and teaching. *College English. 39:*770–783.

Chomsky, N. 1959. Review of Skinner. *Language 35:*26–58.

Chomsky, N. 1965. *Aspects of the Theory of Syntax.* Cambridge, Mass.: MIT Press.

Chomsky, N. 1972. *Language and Mind.* New York: Harcourt, Brace, and Jovanovich.

Clark, H. and P. Lucy. 1975. Understanding what is meant from what is said: a study of conversationally conveyed requests. *Journal of Verbal Learning and Verbal Behavior 14:* 56–72.

Cohen, B. D. 1968.Referent communication disturbances in schizophrenia. In S. Schwartz, ed., pp. 1–34.

Cole, M. 1977. An ethnographic psychology of cognition. In P. N. Johnson Laird and P. C. Wason, eds. pp. 468–482.

Cole, P. and J. Morgan, eds. 1975. *Syntax and Semantics,* vol. 3, *Speech Acts.* New York: Academic Press.

Crosby, F. and L. Nyquist. 1977. The female register: an empirical study of Lakoff's hypotheses. *Language in Society 6:*163–189.

Dalby, D. 1971. Black through white: patterns of communication in Africa and the new world. In W. Wolfram and N. H. Clarke, eds., pp. 99–138.

Darwin, C. 1965. *The Expression of Emotions in Man and Animals.* Chicago: University of Chicago Press.

Davis, L. M. 1979.The perils of purism: the anti-English purists in Israel. *American Speech 54:*175–184.

Deutsch, M., and Associates. 1967. *The Disadvantaged Child.* New York: Basic Books.

Dil, A., ed. 1971a. *Language Acquisition and Communicative Choice: Essays by Susan Ervin-Tripp.* Stanford, Calif.: Stanford University Press.

Dil, A., ed. 1971b. *Language Structure and Language Use: Essays by Charles Ferguson.* Stanford, Calif.: Stanford University Press.

Dil, A., ed. 1971c. *Language in Social Groups: Essays by John Gumperz.* Stanford, Calif.: Stanford University Press.

Dil, A., ed. 1972a. *Language, Psychology, and Culture: Essays by Wallace Lambert.* Stanford, Calif.: Stanford University Press.

Dil, A., ed. 1972b. *The Ecology of Language: Essays by Einar Haugen.* Stanford, Calif.: Stanford University Press.

Dillard, J. 1973. *Black English: Its History and Usage ın the United States.* New York: Random House.

Dillard, J. 1979. Joinder and rejoinder. *American Speech 54:*113–114.

DiPietro, R. 1971. *Language Structures in Contrast.* Rowley, Mass.: Newbury House.

DiPietro, R. 1977. Got your ears on? *Interfaces 7:*1–3.

DiPietro, R., and J. Blansett, eds. 1976. *Third LACUS Forum.* Columbia, S.C.: Hornbeam Press.

DuBois, B., and I. Crouch. 1975. The question of tag questions in women's speech: They don't really use more of them, do they? *Language in Society 4:*289–294.

Dundes, A., J. Leach and B. Ozkok. 1972. The strategy of Turkish boy's dueling rhymes. In J. Gumperz and D. Hymes, eds., pp. 180–209.

Eakins, B. W., and R. G. Eakins. 1978. *Sex Differences in Human Communication.* Boston: Houghton–Mifflin.

Efron, D. 1972.*Gesture, Race, and Culture.* The Hague: Mouton.

Eibl-Eiblesfeldt. 1972.Similarities and differences between cultures in expressive movements. In S. Weitz, ed., pp. 37–48.

Ekman, O., and W. Frisen. 1976. Measuring facial movement. In S. Weitz, ed., pp. 64–76.

Ellis, J. 1966. On contextual meaning. In C. E. Bazell et al., eds., pp. 79–95.

Ervin, S. Imitation and structural change in children's language. In E. Lenneberg, ed., pp. 163–189.

Ervin-Tripp, S. 1961. Learning and recall in bilinguals. Reprinted in A. Dil, ed., 1971a.

Ervin-Tripp, S. 1967. An Issei learns English. Reprinted in A. Dil, ed., 1971a.

Ervin-Tripp, S. 1972. On sociolinguistic rules: alternation and co-occurrence. In J. Gumperz and D. Hymes, eds., pp. 213–250.

Escholz, P., A. LaRosa, and V. Clark. 1978. *Language Awareness,* 2nd. ed. New York: St. Martin's Press.

Fantini, A. 1977. Language choice and social variables: case studies of two infant bilinguals. Paper delivered at second annual Boston University Conference on Language Development. October 1.

Fensch, T. 1978. CB radio: the electronic 'toy.' In Escholz et al., eds., pp. 157–167.

Ferguson, C. 1959. Diglossia. Reprinted in A. Dil, ed., 1971b, pp. 1–27.

Fischer, J. L. 1958. Social influences on the choice of a linguistic variant. *Word 14:*47–56.

Fishman, J. 1966. *Language Loyalty in the United States.* The Hague: Mouton.

Fishman, J., ed. 1968.*Readings in the Sociology of Language.* The Hague: Mouton.

Fishman, J. 1970. *Sociolinguistics: a Brief Introduction.* Rowley, Mass.: Newbury House.

Fishman, J., R. Cooper, and A. Cooper, eds. 1977. *The Spread of English.* Rowley, Mass.: Newbury House.

Fishman, J., C. Ferguson, and J. DasGuptas, eds. 1968.*Language Problems in Developing Nations.* New York: John Wiley.

Fishman, P. 1978. What do couples talk about when they're alone? In D. Butturff and E. Epstein, eds., pp. 11–22.

Frake, C. O. 1961. The diagnosis of disease among the Subanum of Mindinao. *American Anthropologist 62,* 1:113–32.

Frake, C. O. 1964.How to ask for a drink in Subanum. *American Anthropologist 66:*127–32.

Francis, W. N. 1958. *The Structure of American English.* New York: The Ronald Press.

Frazier, A., ed. 1967.*New Directions in Elementary English.* Champaign, Ill.:National Council of Teachers of English.

Freedle, R. O. 1979. *New Directions in Discourse Processing,* vol. 2. Norwood, N.J.: Ablex.

Fromkin, V., and R. Rodman. 1978. *An Introduction to Language.* New York: Holt, Rinehart, and Winston.

Gaertner, S. L., and L. Bickman. 1971. Effects of race on the elicitation of helping behaviour: the wrong number technique. *Journal of Personality and Social Psychology 20:*218–222.

Garfinkel, H. 1967.*Studies in Ethnomethodology.* Englewood Cliffs, N.J.: Prentice–Hall.

Giles, H., S. Baker, and G. Fielding. 1975. Communication length as a behavioural index of accent prejudice. *International Journal of the Sociology of Language 6:*73–81.

Giles, H., and P. Powesland. 1975. *Speech Style and Social Evaluation.* New York: Academic Press.

Giles, H., D. Taylor and R. Bourhis. 1973. Towards a theory of interpersonal accommodation through language: some Canadian data. *Language in Society 2:*177–223.

Givon, T., ed. 1979. *Syntax and Semantics,* vol. 12, *Discourse and Syntax.* New York: Academic Press.

Gleason, H. A. 1961.*An Introduction to Descriptive Linguistics.* New York: Holt, Rinehart, and Winston.

Gleitman, L., H. Gleitman, and E. Shipley. 1972. The emergence of child as grammarian. *Cognition 1,* 2/3:137–164.

Godard, D. 1977. Same setting, different norms: phone call beginnings in France and the United States. *Language in Society 6:*209–220

Goffman, E. 1955. On facework. *Psychiatry 18:*213–231.

Goody, E. N. ed. 1978. *Questions and Politeness.* New York: Cambridge University Press.

Gordon, D. and G. Lakoff. 1975. Conversational postulates. In P. Cole and J. Morgan, eds., pp. 83–106.

Grice, H. P. 1975. Logic and conversation. In P. Cole and J. Morgan, eds., pp. 41–58.

Gumperz, J. 1958. Dialect differences and social stratification in a North Indian village. Reprinted in A. Dil, ed., 1971c.

Gumperz, J. 1964. Linguistic and social interaction in two communities. *American Anthropologist 66:*137–153.

Gumperz, J. 1971.Social meaning in linguistic structures. In A. Dil, ed., 1971c, pp. 247–310.

Gumperz, J., and E. Hernández-Chávez. 1972. Bilingualism, bidialectism, and classroom interaction. In C. Cazden et al., eds., pp. 83–108.

Gumperz, J., and D. Hymes, eds. 1972. *Directions in Sociolinguistics.* New York: Holt, Rinehart, and Winston.

Hall, E. 1959. *The Silent Language.* Garden City, N.Y.: Doubleday.

Hancock, I. 1977. Lexical expansion within a closed system. In B. Blount and M. Sanches, eds.

Haugen, E. 1972. The ecology of language. Reprinted in A. Dil, ed., 1972b.

Herman, S. 1968. Explorations in the social psychology of language choice. In J. Fishman, ed., 1968, pp. 492–511.

Herndobler, R., and A. Sledd. 1976. Black English—notes on the auxiliary. *American Speech 51:*185–200.

Hofman, J. E. 1968. The language transition in some Lutheran denominations. In J. Fishman, ed., 1968.

Hymes, D. 1974. Ways of speaking. In R. Baumann and J. Sherzer, eds.

Janda, I. H. 1975. English Hungarian and Hungarian English interference in Chicago. In P. Reich, ed.

Johnson-Laird, P. N., and P. C. Wason. 1977. *Thinking: Readings in Cognitive Science.* New York: Cambridge University Press.

Keyser, S. J. 1976. Wallace Stevens: form and meaning in four poems. *College English. 37:*578–598.

Kokeritz, H. 1953. *Shakespeare's Pronunciation.* New Haven, Conn.: Yale University Press.

Kramer, E. 1963. Judgement of personal characteristics and emotions from non-verbal properties of speech. *Psychological Bulletin 60:*408–420.

Krashen, S. 1973. Two studies in adult second language learning. Paper delivered at the Linguistic Society of America 48th annual meeting, San Diego, Calif.

LaBarre, W. 1947. The cultural basis of emotions and gestures. *Journal of Personality 16:*49–68.

Labov, W. 1963. The social motivation of a sound change. *Word 19:*273–309.

Labov, W. 1964. Stages in the acquistion of standard English. In H. B. Allen and G. N. Underwood, eds., pp. 491–93.

Labov, W. 1966. *The Social Stratification of English in New York City.* Washington, D.C.: Center for Applied Linguistics.

Labov, W. 1967. Some sources of reading problems for Negro speakers of nonstandard English. In A. Frazier, ed., pp. 140–167.

Labov, W. 1969. The logic of nonstandard English. In J. Alatis, ed.

Labov, W. 1972a. The linguistic consequences of being a lame. In *Language in the Inner City.* Philadelphia: University of Pennsylvania Press, pp. 255–292.

Labov, W. 1972b. Rules for ritual insults. In *Language in the Inner City.* Philadelphia: University of Pennsylvania Press, pp. 297–353.

Labov, W., and D. Fanshel. 1977. *Therapeutic Discourse.* New York: Academic Press.

Labov, W., C. Robins, J. Lewis, and P. Cohen. 1968. *A Study of the English of Negro and Puerto Rican Speakers in New York City,* vol 2. Philadelphia: U.S. Regional Survey.

Lakoff, R. 1975. *Language and Women's Place.* New York: Harper & Row.

Lambert, W. 1969. Psychological aspects of motivation in language learning. In A. Dil, ed. 1972a, pp. 290–299.

Lambert, W., and R. Gardner. 1972. *Attitudes and Motivation in Second Language Learning.* Rowley, Mass.: Newbury House.

Lambert, W., H. Giles, and D. Picard. 1975. Language attitudes in a French American community. *International Journal of the Sociology of Language 4:*127–152.

Lance, D. 1972. The codes of the Spanish–English bilingual. In B. Spolsky, ed., pp. 25–36.

Laver, J. 1968. Voice quality and indexical information. *British Journal of Disorders of Communication 3:* 43–54.

Laver, J. and S. Hutcheson. 1972. *Communication in Face to Face Interaction.* Baltimore: Penguin Books.

Lenneberg, E. 1953. Cognition in ethnolinguistics. In P. Adams, ed., pp. 157–169.

Lenneberg, E., ed., 1964. *New Directions in the Study of Language.* Cambridge, Mass.: MIT Press.

Lenneberg, E., 1967. *Biological Foundations of Language.* New York: John Wiley and Sons.

Leslie-Melville, B. 1973. *There's a Rhino in the Rosebed, Mother.* New York: Doubleday.

Lyons, J. 1966. Firth's theory of meaning. In C. E. Bazell et al., eds., pp. 288–302.

Malinowski, B. 1923. Phatic communication. Supplement to C. K. Ogden and I. A. Richards, *The Meaning of Meaning.* London: Routledge and Kegan Paul.

Maher, B., K. McKeon, and B. McLaughlin. 1966. Studies in psychotic language. In P. Stone, D. Dunphy, M. Smith, and D. Ogilvie, eds., pp. 469–501.

McDavid, R. I., Jr. 1958. The dialects of American English. In W. N. Francis, pp. 480–543.

McDavid, R. I., Jr. 1979. Review of *Language in the Inner City and Sociolinguistic Patterns* by William Labov. *American Speech,* Winter:291–304.

McIntosh, A. 1952. An introduction to a survey of Scottish dialects. University of Edinburgh: T. Nelson.

Mcnamara, J. 1971. Successes and failures in the movement for the restoration of Irish. In J. Rubin and B. Jernudd, eds. pp. 65–94.

Menyuk, P. 1971. *The Acquisition and Development of Language.* Englewood Cliffs, N.J.: Prentice–Hall.

Millward, C. 1975. Language of colonial Rhode Island. *Rhode Island History 34:*35–42.

Mitchell-Kernan, C. 1972. Signifying and marking: two Afro-American speech acts. In J. Gumperz and D. Hymes, eds., pp. 161–179.

Muscovici, S., ed. 1972. *The Psychosociology of Language.* Chicago: Markham.

Nickel, G., ed. 1971. *Papers in Contrastive Linguistics.* Cambridge: Cambridge University Press.

Nilsen, A. 1977. Sexism as shown through the English vocabulary. In A. Nilsen et al., eds.

Nilsen, A., H. Bosmajian, H. L. Gershuny, and J. Stanley, eds. *Sexism and Language.* Urbana, Ill.: National Council of Teachers of English.

O'Cain, R. 1979.Linguistic Atlas of New England. *American Speech 54:*243–78.

Ohanessian, S. 1972. The language problems of American Indian children. In B. Spolsky, ed.

Parker, F. 1975. A comment on *anymore. American Speech 3–4:*305–310.

Perren, G. E., and J. L. M. Trim, eds. 1971. *Applications of Linguistics.* New York: Cambridge University Press.

Philips, S. U. 1970. Acquisition of rules for appropriate speech usage. In J. Alatis, ed., pp. 77–102.

Philips, S. U. 1976. Some sources of cultural variability in the regulation of talk. *Language in Society 5:*81–95.

Pyles, T. 1972. English usage: the views of the literati. In Shores, ed., pp. 160–69.

Reich, P., ed. 1975. The second LACUS Forum. Columbia, S.C.: Hornbeam Press.

Riecken, H. 1958. The effect of talkativeness on ability to influence group solutions of problems. In S. Muscovici, ed., pp. 308–321.

Robinson, W. P., and C. D. Creed. Perceptual and verbal discriminations of "elaborated" and "restricted" code users. In S. Muscovici, ed., pp. 191–205.

Rochester, S., J. Martin, and S. Thurston. 1977. Thought process disorder in schizophrenia: the listener's task. *Brain and Language. 4:*95–114.

Rommetveit, R. 1971. Words, contexts and verbal message transmission. In E. A. Carswell and R. Rommetveit, eds., pp. 13–26.

Rubin, J., and B. Jernudd. 1971. *Can Language be Planned?* Hawaii: University Press of Hawaii.

Sacks, H. 1964–72. Lecture notes. Mimeo.

Sacks, H. 1972. An initial investigation of the usability of conversational data for doing sociology. In D. Sudnow, ed., pp. 31–74.

Sacks, H. 1970. Discourse analysis. untitled mss. mimeo.

Sacks, H., E. Schegloff, and G. Jefferson, 1974. A simplest systematics for the organization of turn-taking for conversation. *Language 50:*696–735.

Sapir, E. 1927. Speech as a personality trait. *American Journal of Sociology 32:*892–905.

Sawyer, J. 1964. Social aspects of bilingualism in San Antonio, Texas. In H. B. Allen and G. Underwood, eds., pp. 375–381.

Schatzman, L., and A. Strauss. 1972. Social class and modes of communication. In S. Muscovici, ed., pp. 206–221.

Scheflen, A. E. 1964. The significance of posture in communication system. *Psychiatry 27:*316–31.

Schegloff, E. A. 1968. Sequencing in conversational openings. *American Anthropologist 70:*1075–1095.

Schegloff, E. A. 1971. Notes on a conversational practice: formulating place. In D. Sudnow, ed., pp. 75–119.

Schegloff, E. A., G. Jefferson, and H. Sacks. 1977. The preference for self-correction in the organization of repair in conversation. *Language 53,* 361–382.

Schenkein, J., ed. 1978. *Studies in the Organization of Conversation.* New York: Academic Press.

Scherer, K. 1973. Acoustic concomitants of emotional dimensions: judging affect from synthesized tone sequences. In S. Weitz, ed., pp. 249–53.

Scherer, K., and H. Giles. 1979. *Social Markers in Speech.* New York: Cambridge University Press.

Schlauch, M. 1959. *The English Language in Modern Times, since 1400.* Warsaw, Panstowe Wydaawnictwo Naukowe.

Schwartz, S., ed. 1978. *Language and Cognition in Schizophrenia.* Hillsdale, N.J.: Lawrence Erlbaum.

Scribner, S. 1977. Modes of thinking and ways of speaking: culture and logic reconsidered. In P. N. Johnson-Laird and P. C. Wason, eds. pp. 483–500.

Searle, J. 1975. Indirect speech acts. In P. Cole and J. Morgan, eds., pp. 59–82.

Sebeok, T., ed. 1960. *Style in Language.* Cambridge, Mass.: MIT Press.

Sebeok, T., ed. 1966. *Current Trends in Linguistics,* vol. 3. The Hague: Mouton.

Seeman, M. and H. Cole. 1977. The effect of increasing personal contact in schizophrenia. *Comprehensive Psychiatry 18:*283–92.

Sherzer, J. 1973. Nonverbal and verbal deixis: The pointed lip gesture among the San Blas Cuna. *Language in Society 2:*117–132.

Shores, D., ed. 1972. *Contemporary English: Change and Variation.* New York: J. B. Lippincott.

Shuy, R. ed. *Social Dialects and Language Learning: Proceedings of the Bloomington, Indiana Conference.* Champaign: NCTE.

Shuy, R. 1967. *Discovering American Dialects.* Champaign, Ill.: National Council of Teachers of English.

Shuy, R., W. Wolfram, and W. Riley. 1967. *Linguistic Correlates of Social Stratification in Detroit Speech.* Washington, D.C.: HEW.

Singer, J. 1977. *How to Curse in Yiddish.* New York: Ballantine Books.

Slobin, D. 1979. *Psycholinguistics,* 2nd. ed. Oakland, N.J.: Scott Foresman.

Sommer, R. 1965. Further studies of small-group ecology. *Sociometry 28:*337–48.

Soskin, W.F. and V. John. 1963. The study of spontaneous talk. In R. G. Barker, ed., pp. 228–281.

Spolsky, B., ed. 1972. *The Language Education of Minority Children.* Rowley, Mass.: Newbury House.

Stewart, E. 1979. Talking culture: language in the function of communication. First Delaware Symposium of Language Studies. October 19.

Stewart, W. 1965. Urban Negro speech: sociolinguistic factors affecting English teaching. In R. Shuy, ed., pp. 10–18.

Stewart, W. 1967. Sociolinguistic factors in the history of American Negro dialects. In H. B. Allen and G. Underwood, eds., pp.444–453.

Stewart, W. 1968. Continuity and change in American Negro dialects. In H. B. Allen and G. Underwood, eds., pp. 454–467.

Stewart, W. 1972. Language and communication problems in southern Appalachia. In D. Shores, ed., pp. 107–122.

Sudnow, D. ed. 1971. *Studies in Social Interaction.* New York: The Free Press.

Stone, P., D. Dunphy, M. Smith, and D. Ogilvie, eds. 1966. *General Inquirer.* Cambridge, Mass.: MIT Press.

Tannen, Deborah. 1979. When is an overlap an interruption? First Delaware Symposium of Language Studies. October 19.

Taylor, D. 1976. Linguistic change and challenge: preserving a native language in a foreign environment. German language in Bethlehem, Pennsylvania in the mid-1700's and Chicago, Illinois in the mid-1900's. In R. DiPietro and E. Blansett, eds.

Thorne, B., and N. Henley, eds. 1975. *Language and Sex: Difference and Dominance.* Rowley, Mass.: Newbury House.

Trudgill, P. 1972. Sex, covert prestige, and linguistic change in the urban British English of Norwich. *Language in Society 1:*179–195.

Turner, L. D. 1971. Problems confronting the investigator of Gullah. In W. Wolfram and N. H. Clarke, eds., pp. 1–15.

Underwood, G. 1974. How you sound to an Arkansawyer. *American Speech 49:*208–215.

Van Dijk, T. 1977. *Text and Context: Explorations in the Semantics and Pragmatics of Discourse.* New York: Longman.

Weinreich, U. 1966. Explorations in semantic theory. In T. Sebeok, ed., pp. 395–477.

Weinreich, U. 1968. *Languages in Contact.* The Hague: Mouton.

Weir, R. 1962. *Language in the Crib.* The Hague: Mouton.

Weitz, S., ed. 1979. *Nonverbal Communication,* 2nd. ed. New York: Oxford University Press.

Whorf, B. E. 1956. *Language, Thought, and Reality.* Cambridge, Mass.: MIT Press.

Williams, J. 1975. *Origins of the English Language.* New York: The Free Press.

Wolfram, W., and D. Christian. 1976. *Appalachian Speech.* Arlington, Va.: Center for Applied Linguistics.

Wolfram, W., and N. Clarke, eds. 1971. *Black-White Relationships.* Washington, D. C.: Center for Applied Linguistics.

Wolfram, W., and R. Fasold. 1974. *The Study of Social Dialects in American English.* Englewood, N.J.: Prentice-Hall.

Wooton, A. 1975. *Dilemmas of Discourse: Controversies about the Sociological Interpretation of Language.* London: Allen and Unwin.

Wyld, H. C. K. 1927. *A Short History of English.* New York: E. P. Dutton.

Zimmerman, D. H., and C. West. 1975. Sex roles, interruptions, and silences in conversation. In B. Thorne and N. Henley, eds., pp. 105–129.

SUBJECT INDEX

NAME INDEX